A NEW STOICISM

A NEW STOICISM

Lawrence C. Becker

PRINCETON UNIVERSITY PRESS   PRINCETON, NEW JERSEY

Published by Princeton University Press, 41 William Street,
Princeton, New Jersey 08540
In the United Kingdom: Princeton University Press,
Chichester, West Sussex

Library of Congress Cataloging-in-Publication Data

Becker, Lawrence C.
A new stoicism / Lawrence C. Becker.
p.   cm.
Includes bibliographical references and index.
ISBN 0-691-01660-7 (cl : alk. paper)
1. Ethics.   2. Stoics.   3. Virtue.   4. Happiness.   I. Title.
BJ1031.B439   1998
171'.2—dc21   97-15847   CIP

This book has been composed in Sabon

Princeton University Press books are printed
on acid-free paper and meet the guidelines
for permanence and durability of the Committee
on Production Guidelines for Book Longevity
of the Council on Library Resources

http://pup.princeton.cdu

Printed in the United States of America

10   9   8   7   6   5   4   3   2   1

To Charlotte _____

BEST FRIEND, BEST COLLABORATOR,

LOVE OF MY LIFE

Contents

Acknowledgments   ix

PART ONE: THE WAY THINGS STAND   1

1. The Conceit   3

2. A New Agenda for Stoic Ethics   5

3. The Ruins of Doctrine   8

Science, Logic, and Ethics   8
Norms and Moral Training   14
Virtue and Happiness   20
Commentary   22
Acknowledgments   30

PART TWO: THE WAY THINGS MIGHT GO   33

4. Normative Logic   35

Norms and Normative Propositions   36
Normative Constructs   39
Axioms of Stoic Normative Logic   42

5. Following the Facts   43

Impossibilities   44
A Posteriori Normative Propositions   46
Motivated Norms   52
Heteronomous Endeavors, Autonomous Agency, and Freedom   59
Commentary   69
Acknowledgments   80

6. Virtue   81

The Development of Virtue as the Perfection of Agency   81
   THE STRUCTURE OF AGENCY   82
   AGENCY CONSTRUCTED AND PERFECTED   103
   VIRTUE AS IDEAL AGENCY   112
The Argument for Virtue as the Perfection of Agency   114
Exalted Virtue   119
Commentary   123
Acknowledgments   137

7. Happiness 138

A Complete Life 138
A Controlled Life 142
Life on the Rack 146
Joy 148
Commentary 150
Acknowledgments 158

Appendix
A Calculus for Normative Logic 159

Notation and Interpretation 159
Basic Definitions, Rules, and Axioms 163
Normative Constructs 167
Axioms of Stoic Normative Logic 181
Immediate Inferences 182
Commentary 185
Acknowledgments 191

Bibliography 193

Index 201

Acknowledgments _____

REFERENCES to individuals who have commented helpfully on portions of the manuscript appear at the end of the relevant commentaries—to Chapters 3, 5, 6, 7, and to the Appendix. An early draft of some chapters was completed with the help of a fellowship from the National Endowment for the Humanities (1993–94), and a draft of the remainder was finished during a Faculty Research Assignment from the College of William & Mary (Fall 1995). I thank both institutions for their support. Portions of my article "Good Lives: Prolegomena," from *Social Philosophy and Policy* 9 (1992): 15–37, appear in Chapters 3 and 5, by permission of the publisher. And I acknowledge with gratitude the publishers, authors, and translators involved for permission to quote material identified more fully in the text of the commentaries in which they appear: Material from Cicero, *De Finibus* (translated by H. Rackham) *De Officiis* (translated by Walter Miller), and *Tusculan Disputations* (translated by J. E. King) is reprinted by permission of Harvard University Press and the Loeb Classical Library. Poem #249 from *The Poems of Emily Dickinson*, edited by Thomas H. Johnson, is reprinted by permission of Harvard University Press and the Trustees of Amherst College. Selections from *The Hellenistic Philosophers*, edited and translated by A. A. Long and D. N. Sedley are reprinted by permission of Cambridge University Press. A fragment from Hierocles, translated by Julia Annas in her book *The Morality of Happiness*, is reprinted by permission of the author and Oxford University Press. A passage from Sophie Botros, "Freedom, Causality, Fatalism and Early Stoic Philosophy," in *Phronesis*, is reprinted by permission of E. J. Brill (Leiden, The Netherlands), the current publishers of that journal. I thank also Akademie-Verlag, for permission to reprint material from Galen's *On the Doctrines of Hippocrates and Plato* (translated by Phillip De Lacey); the *Journal of the History of Philosophy*, for a passage from Amélie Rorty, "The Two Faces of Stoicism"; and the *Monist*, for a passage from Nicholas P. White, "Stoic Values." And this is the place to express my sincere gratitude to the many people who kept the project on the right path from disheveled manuscript to book. Ann Wald, editor-in-chief at Princeton University Press, saw the possibilities at an early stage and gave me persistent and effective support. Molan Chun Goldstein and Joan Hunter, respectively the production editor and copyeditor for the book, were outstanding. Maria I. Salazkina helped me read proof; she and Charlotte Becker helped me prepare the index.

Part One

THE WAY THINGS STAND

1

The Conceit

AFTER FIVE hundred years of prominence in Greek and Roman antiquity, stoic ethics was pillaged by theology and effaced by evangelical and imperial Christianity. A few stoic philosophers survived, most of them by providing analgesics for use in pastoral counseling, the military, and what then passed for medicine and psychotherapy. Only those shards of our doctrines were widely seen during the Middle Ages, and the term stoic came to be applied merely to people who used our remedies. This confusion persists.

In the Italian Renaissance there was a brief effusion of interest in our historical roots, and some of us were emboldened to publish the work we were then doing. A living philosophical tradition changes, and Renaissance neostoicism, as it is now called, quite naturally bore only a strong family resemblance to that of Zeno and Chrysippus. This wider interest in our views soon dwindled, however, and in still smaller numbers we again went back to private practice. A few major figures in modern philosophy continued to use our doctrines in their ethical theories, typically without attribution, and just as typically denounced us for good measure.

Modern science presented significant challenges to our metaphysical views, and during the seventeenth and eighteenth centuries we gradually abandoned our doctrine that the universe should be understood as a purposive, rational being. With that, we lost contact with theology of all sorts. Moreover, we continued to organize ethical theory along eudaimonistic lines, and thus lost contact with the secular side of moral philosophy as well, mobbed as it was (and is) by people clamoring for *a priori* principles, sentiment, commonsense virtues, utility, rights, duties, and justice in contractual arrangements. Our obliteration began in this period, with the emergence of claims for the autonomy of ethics.

Even our analgesics were discarded in the nineteenth century, largely due to the rise of romanticism. This Barmecidal substitute for religious fervor was (and in its current decadence still is) contemptuous of stoic moral training. But it was philosophy in the late nineteenth and twentieth centuries that finally laid waste to our project—not in direct attacks on stoicism's intellectual merit, but in a blizzard of fads that undermined commitments to reason and nature. The social sciences bought the fact-value distinction, and philosophy peddled it to them. Nonnaturalism arose, collapsed into noncognitivism, and rose again as intuitionism and constructivism. Moral truth was given a coherentist interpretation. Pluralism, relativism, and irony abounded, alongside various forms of dogmatism about natural duties and the intrinsic moral worth of human beings.

Only three small groups will now say anything in our favor. Some soldiers, actual or spiritual, still prefer our psychotherapy to morphine and mood enhancers. Logicians appreciate our early work on the propositional calculus. Hellenists admire the stoics of antiquity and argue that their ethical doctrines were not (for their time) foolish.

It is a complete disaster. Only a few are escaped to tell you.

2

A New Agenda for Stoic Ethics

IN ACADEMIC philosophy, stoicism has long been identified with a discredited form of naturalistic ethics—one in which the supreme principle is "follow nature." The ancient stoics apparently believed that nature was a teleological system—a vast goal-oriented entity. They apparently believed that within this vast entity, and with respect to its goal or end, humans had a discoverable role, both as a species and as individuals. And they apparently believed that following out one's natural role, immunized so as to be able to live contentedly whatever one's circumstances, was demonstrably the right way to conduct one's life.

These beliefs are now widely thought to be flagrant and uninteresting errors—errors that make stoic ethics wholly insupportable. Thus philosophers generally relegate serious work on stoicism to experts on Hellenistic philosophy, regard the medicinal properties of stoic training as mere placebo effects, and reject the ideal of the stoic sage (contentedly accepting her assigned role, immune from most suffering and able to endure the remainder) in the same gesture that dismisses tranquilizers and prefrontal lobotomies as means to a good life.

But suppose there were a book about virtue, happiness, and the good life that identified them all with living well—that is, with excelling or flourishing in terms of the available resources. Suppose this book were to argue that living well in that sense was the product of following the final, all-things-considered normative propositions of practical reason, and that those normative propositions could not be constructed *a priori* but rather depended crucially upon the fullest available knowledge of the natural world. Suppose the construction of those propositions always began in the particular—with what is possible for a particular agent with a particular history, character, and range of choices; that such particulars were generalized only to the extent that agents had a common history, nature, and situation. Suppose those propositions were rarely egoistic, in the sense of ratifying the agent's narrow self-interest, but rather that in typical cases following them meant realigning or overriding many of one's dearest wishes. Suppose the book described a character-building regime for this purpose, emphasizing control of one's mental states as a means of overcoming obstacles to living well. And suppose the book made clear how natural endowments and circumstances determined whether living well was compatible with intense longing, passionate commitments, grand gestures, reckless adventure—or whether it always required the colorless, cautious existence described in contemptuous essays on stoicism.

That book would be in the stoic tradition, in the sense that it put forward a cluster of doctrines traceable to central elements of classical stoic ethics. It would be eudaimonistic, in identifying the good life or happiness with flourishing—with being excellent-of-one's-kind. It would be intellectualistic, in identifying virtue with rationality—with carrying out the normative propositions of practical reason. It would be naturalistic, in its insistence that facts about the natural world were the substance of practical deliberation. And because the book would argue that virtuous conduct was always the same one thing (namely, conformity to practical reason), the book, like the stoics, would propound the formal unity of the virtues. Moreover, the book's focus on the full particularity of each agent could be seen as a remnant of the stoic notion of a role for each of us in the grand system of nature. The emphasis on self-mastery would also be familiar.

Many ancient stoic ideas would be missing, of course, and a major one would be cosmic *telos*—the notion that the natural world is a purposive system with an end or goal that practical reason directs us to follow. How could a book be a work of stoic ethics without such a doctrine? How could it solve the is/ought problem without it, or give plausibility to the "follow nature" motto? It seems that the book cannot be a work of *stoic* ethics without the cosmic teleology, but that it cannot be a credible work of ethics *with* such a cosmology. Yet it is interesting to try to imagine what might have happened if stoicism had had a continuous twenty-three-hundred-year history; if stoics had had to confront Bacon and Descartes, Newton and Locke, Hobbes and Bentham, Hume and Kant, Darwin and Marx, and the vicissitudes of ethics in the twentieth century. It is reasonable to suppose that stoics would have found a way to reject teleological physics and biology when scientific consensus did; that they would have found ways to hold their own against the attacks on naturalism launched in the modern era. And it is reasonable to suppose that the sheer variety of self-identified stoics over the centuries would have prevented, as it did in antiquity, the view that a stoic life is typically a bleak one.

The book that follows is less ambitious than the one we have just imagined, but it is in the same line of work. It outlines a contemporary version of stoic ethics, not a reconstruction of the ancient one. It does this in three steps: The first is a swift, largely declarative survey of the possibilities that remain open for stoicism (Chapter 3). The second is a compressed but detailed presentation of the logic and general character of a stoic form of naturalism (Chapters 4 and 5). The third step is a schematic account of virtue and a good life, designed to address persistent prejudices about stoic doctrine (Chapters 6 and 7). The book is thus neither a comprehensive ethical theory nor a practical handbook. It is rather an investigation of neglected possibilities, written by a stoic who is merely trying to show a skeptical audience that his ethical theory is philosophically viable.

A final warning label: This book is not an exposition or defense of ancient stoic texts. It does, however, aim to explain itself to loyal readers of those texts (readers not themselves stoics, which makes them all the more loyal to the texts). Such readers will want to know in detail how this work can justify calling itself stoic, and they will find such detail in commentaries appended to subsequent chapters. Hostile readers of the ancient texts—readers who find little in them worth admiring—will want to know why a revival of stoic ethics should even be attempted, and readers who are skeptical of brand-name ethics altogether will want to know whether a work on *stoic* ethics advances the enterprise of ethics, period. The remainder of Part One (like any introduction, meant to encourage people to read further) will be addressed to these dubious readers. It will not offer an overview of the book, but rather assemble some preliminary remarks designed to show that a philosophically respectable version of stoic ethics is both possible and interesting.

3

The Ruins of Doctrine

To MANY OF our critics, it seems that what is defensible in stoic ethics is not unique to it, but merely a reprise of various ideas drawn from other ancient sources. What is uniquely stoic, they say, is only a collection of very peculiar and ultimately indefensible doctrines. We continue to hold most of those peculiar doctrines. We hold, for example, that the final end of all rational activity is virtue, not happiness; that virtue does not admit of degrees, and among people who fall short of it, none is any more virtuous than another; that sages are happy just because they are virtuous, and can be happy even on the rack; that they must be able to say of everything other than their virtue (friends, loves, emotions, reputation, wealth, pleasant mental states, suffering, disease, death, and so on) that it is nothing to them. All of this and more we will recast and argue for in due course. We will also assume, and support more obliquely, some things that are not unique to stoic ethics but are nonetheless central to its project. Here, more in the form of announcement than argument, are some of those assumptions, mixed with other preparations.

Science, Logic, and Ethics

Natural science no longer gives grand teleological explanations. Thus we cannot plausibly propose to "follow" nature, as the ancient motto had it. Yet for stoics, ethics remains subordinate to science and logic in a way that separates us from most other contemporary ethical theorists. Non-stoics now typically want to maintain a sharp distinction between science and ethics. In fact, it is commonplace in modern philosophy to hold some version of the thesis that ethics is an autonomous enterprise. There is wide agreement that ethics is independent of religion. (And we certainly concur.) Moreover, ethics is meant to be about what ought to be the case, not about what is the case, so it cannot simply *be* a science, as we now use that term, and many philosophers reject the notion that ethical truths can even be derived from facts about the world at all. Some follow (or perhaps misinterpret) Hume in holding that "ought" cannot be derived from "is." Others follow Kant in rejecting the relevance of empirical knowledge altogether, at least for the foundations of ethics, by insisting that fundamental ethical truths are discoverable *a priori*. Intuitionists reject all inference at the foundational level, insisting that the right (or the good) can be known immediately. And noncognitivists of various sorts insist that ethical judgments are linked to empirical truths only psychologically, not logically. Even those nonstoics who want to endorse the importance of empirical knowledge are not typically prepared to say more than (roughly) this:

> Ethics is not a science; it is not descriptive, explanatory, predictive; not pursued by the experimental method. But beliefs about the natural world, human nature, social institutions, and psychological processes have an impact at the very foundations of ethics. Among such beliefs as might be held, it is scientific ones (rather than religious, cultural, or idiosyncratic ones) that ethics should use.
>
> Ethics is not mathematics. There is no moral geometry that proceeds with deductive certainty from one necessary truth to another. Ethics is based on facts about the world, and proceeds from one contingent truth to another. But among the ways we might proceed from truth to truth, it is those defined by the canons of logic that ethics should use.

This is something consequentialists, contractarians, pragmatists, evolutionary theorists, and perhaps many others can accept. But it will not do for a stoic.

We say that ethics is the last, and least, of the branches of human inquiry. It is last because it cannot begin until all relevant description, representation, and prediction are in hand, all relevant possibilities are imagined, all relevant lessons from experience, history, practice are learned—until, let us say, the empirical work is done. It is least because it has no unique subject matter or methods, and in practice often adds nothing but a unique purpose to the empirical work. We also hold, in no way paradoxically, that ethics is the first, final, and foremost human enterprise.

The general line of argument we offer in support of this is as follows: (a) The subject matter of ethics is human character, conduct, and associated mental and social phenomena. It shares this domain with narrative art, history, and social and behavioral science. (b) The methods of ethics are those of logic and reasoned argument, in the broad sense in which the elements of various systems of assertoric and normative logic can themselves be subject to reasoned inquiry. These methods it shares with all the liberal arts and sciences, and (in an informal way) with all literate, intellectual inquiry. (c) The general purpose of ethics is normative—to say what people ought to do and be, rather than to imagine, describe, explain, or predict their lives. This general purpose it shares with all practical advice-giving endeavors (e.g., etiquette, coaching, medicine, psychotherapy, and so on). (d) The unique purpose of ethics is its attempt to construct an account of the norms that are overriding—the norms that take priority over all others. (e) In practice, ethics often has little work to do beyond organizing fact-finding expeditions and sifting the results through a logical sieve. Careful empirical work and a thoroughgoing, reasoned attempt to discover the overriding norm for a given agent or group in a given case often reveal that the agents involved have no room for maneuver, and thus that further ethical inquiry is superfluous, or that the choice between available options is a matter of indifference.

We identify ethical reasoning with the most inclusive sort of practical reasoning anyone can do: ethics is the attempt to say what we ought to do or be, all-things-considered. Ethical judgment is thus overriding because it subsumes all other relevant practical considerations (self-interest, altruism, prudence, etiquette . . .) into one final judgment. By contrast, many contemporary philosophers adopt a special or narrow conception of ethics, identifying it with practical reasoning about a special domain, or from a special point of view, or from a special set of commitments, usually labeled "moral." The special moral domain, for instance, might be defined as consisting exclusively of universalizable prescriptions about matters that have a substantial bearing on human well-being; the moral point of view might be defined as that of an omniscient, impartial spectator, or that of a rational contractor disposed to cooperate; the special set of moral commitments may be defined in terms of ends such as maximal happiness, principles such as *prima facie* duties to keep promises, or traits such as beneficence.

Advocates of the special or narrow conception of ethics confront difficult priority problems: Why should these special moral judgments override other kinds of practical advice? Why should we be moral rather than egoistic, for example, when the two conflict? One strategy for answering is to argue that such conflicts are illusory—that self-interest, properly understood, will always (usually?) dictate doing the moral thing. More generally, one might try to argue that moral judgments just (usually?) turn out to be the ones that can be justified all-things-considered. Or one might argue that the moral sphere is dominant by definition, or by convention. To go beyond that—to assert, for example, that the moral point of view has no special priority—is to give up the unique purpose of ethics.

We are not interested in battling for the rhetorical high ground on this issue. Those who insist on the narrow conception of ethics or morality may, if they wish, say that stoics do not have an ethical theory or morality; that stoics address themselves only to what practical reasoning ultimately prescribes. To this we merely point out that ethical inquiry (in the narrow sense) does not settle anything philosophically without an account of whether moral norms override other ones—whether they define what we ought to do or be all-things-considered. It is this all-things-considered question that we, like all philosophers, are ultimately concerned with, and which we continue to call ethics.

When we say ethics is subordinate to science we mean, among other things, that changes in our empirical knowledge are likely to generate changes in ethics. When the best science postulates a cosmic *telos*, as it sometimes did in antiquity, so does stoic ethics. When the best science rejects the view that the universe operates teleologically, in terms of something like human purposes, and suspends judgment about whether cosmic processes have a *de facto* end, convergence point, or destination, so does stoic ethics.

Thus, on the basis of contemporary cosmic science, we reject anthropocentric views of the cosmos. We take it as settled that the universe is unimaginably large and old, and in constant, tumultuous, evolutionary change; that human history occupies a tiny temporal slice of universal history, and is confined to a small planet of an unremarkable star on the inner edge of one arm of what is in all probability an unremarkable spiral galaxy. There is no evidence that our galaxy, planet, or species is central to any cosmic process; no evidence that there is anything extraordinary about our origins; no evidence that the natural history of life on this planet is of any cosmic significance whatsoever. Our ignorance in these matters is abysmal. They and related metaphysical issues about the universe as a whole (and about consciousness; our subjectivity) may remain permanently beyond our reach. Cosmology does not tell us why there is something rather than nothing, and whether a god produced it. Metaphysics does not thoroughly reconcile human freedom with determinism, or with indeterminism, or with combinations of the two; it does not fully reconcile the description of human consciousness as an object with the nature of subjective experience; it does not fully resolve problems about the nature of time, identity through time, and causality. The scale of the universe precludes, for the foreseeable future, effective exploration of all but a very small portion of our galaxy—unless by chance we happen upon a cosmic version of the Internet. When we face the universe we confront its indifference to us and our own insignificance to it. It takes no apparent notice of us, has no role other than Extra for us to play, no aim for us to follow. The relevance of contemporary cosmic science for ethics lies in those humbling facts about our place in the grand (non) scheme of things, in the aesthetic and quasi-religious awe that the scale and complexity of the universe can arouse, and in what science can teach us about physical necessity and impossibility.

Necessities, impossibilities, and possibilities are either facts of logic (circles cannot be rectangles), of scientific theory (no object can travel faster than the speed of light), of the powers of agents or technology in some reference class (no one now competing in field events can pole-vault twenty-five feet), or of facts about particular agents in particular situations (he's too timid to pole-vault at all). Such necessity or impossibility may conflict with every other sort of fact relevant to practical reasoning: with what agents value, prefer, are committed to, are expected or directed to do, or are trying to do. It may also conflict with norms.

We construct normative propositions from facts about existing values, preferences, projects, commitments, and conventions. The logic for such construction is outlined in Chapter 4 and the Appendix, but the general idea is that goal- and requirement-defining facts may be restated as non-ethical judgments about what agents ought to do, or are required or forbidden to do. The task of ethical reasoning is then to find or construct the ethical, all-things-considered, overriding normative proposition.

Projects, commitments, and conventions may conflict with each other, raising questions of logical possibility, and may conflict with what is physically or technologically possible as well. In such cases it is not possible for agents to satisfy jointly all of the sound nonethical normative propositions constructed from the facts. It is then the task of stoic practical reasoning to resolve every conflict into a nonarbitrary, overriding, all-things-considered normative proposition.

Our appeals to human nature are schematic and probabilistic. Modern biological, behavioral, and social sciences do not license more than generalities like these: Huge percentages of normally formed human beings are purposive, socially interactive, reciprocally benevolent language users; they have complex emotional-response dispositions, and profound attachments or bonds to other people or things; they deliberate and make choices; they typically have some limits or boundaries that they will try to protect categorically. The full list of "normal" human traits is very long, but it defines tendencies, propensities, and probabilities in specified circumstances; it does not define essential characteristics. It is "natural" to find these traits in human character and conduct, but it is equally natural to find a significant number of exceptions. As a result, none of these characteristics fits into the most familiar forms of ethical argument from human nature, e.g., (a) that humans are by nature X, and that Y is contrary to X, hence, that Y is contrary to human nature; or (b) that X is what defines the unique function (the essence) of a human being, thus to flourish as a human being is to excel at X. Moreover, the traits we can identify as typically human are extremely schematic. People are purposive, but what purposes do they share? Science cautions us to take the diversity of human character and conduct seriously; to mistrust reductivism.

Even so, the biological, behavioral, and social sciences contribute to ethics in three important ways: they offer a wealth of material that can be used in the naturalistic arguments described in Chapters 5 and 6; they offer explanatory theories (e.g., from evolutionary biology) that help separate relatively fixed traits from transient or malleable ones; and they offer powerful, elaborate analyses of learning, rationality, and rational choice. Stoics use those results, but only in ways compatible with the available evidence about human diversity. For example, stoic moral training depends upon the defensibility of these schematic propositions: (a) Rational deliberative power (rational agency) is a defining feature of mature human consciousness. (b) Every agent's rational powers, whenever exercised, operate in a particular and intricate deliberative field, in Barbara Herman's felicitous phrase,[1] that is laden with projects, preferences, affects, and attachments. (c) Each person's deliberative field evolves continuously. Its initial information gathering and deliberative routines are givens (as if programmed) and, together with the initial situation, yield explicable beliefs. Initial sensibilities, sensitivities, values, aims, commitments, and preferences are also givens and, together with beliefs and deliberative routines, yield normative propositions for conduct. The circumstances in which such normative propositions are acted out or abandoned (that is, the relative strength or weakness of the will) are given, and actions follow. Each process from information gathering to action then becomes information for the next process. (d) The agent's awareness of and reflection upon these iterated processes varies. But when awareness is high, it is fair to say rational agency is a self-transformative power: over time, its reflexive, recursive operations can transform its own powers, deliberative field, and operations—hence its norms and actions. (e) Agents can thus remake their characters over time. Note, however, that no uniform, essentially human content is specified for the deliberative field. When questions of content arise with regard to schematic generalizations about human nature (when, for example, we want to add premises about self-interest or benevolence), we are careful not to claim more uniformity than the empirical work shows.

Ethics is ultimately about particulars—about how particular people in their particular circumstances ought to live. Modern behavioral and social sciences show the futility of trying to derive such particular judgments from universal propositions about human nature: The generalizations we know to be true are either not genuine universals, and thus do not allow inferences about arbitrarily selected individuals, or are merely schematic and thus are not determinate for particular cases. Moreover,

[1] Barbara Herman, "Agency, Attachment, and Difference," *Ethics* 101 (1991): 775–97.

the universal-to-particular approach, in the absence of a universal *telos*, raises the is-ought problem in an intractable form. But stoic ethical theory begins with the particular—with fully situated individuals—and works carefully out to more general matters. The idea is to incorporate into ethics the richest and most accurate descriptions of the way we live, drawn from the human sciences, law, history, medicine, languages and literatures, religion, philosophy, music, theater, the graphic arts, biography, and journalism.

In the particular—in the intricate web of desire, belief, commitment, aspiration, imagination, communication, cooperation, conflict, patterns of social practice, expectation, and opportunity within which we live— we have goals in abundance. Most of them are emergent—generated by the interplay of circumstance and need, our actions and the reactions of others. From such mundane goals (e.g., eliminating a toothache), in the middle of the activities they steer (going to the dentist), first-order norms come tumbling out (Don't make me wait. Don't make it worse with that pick. Novocaine *now*). Practical reason assesses the soundness of normative propositions for various purposes. Ethics tells us which ones are sound all-things-considered.

Norms and Moral Training

Values are facts of various sorts that sentences of the form 'X is good' conflate and obscure. *Affects*. Sometimes agents are the (understood) subjects of the sentence, and it asserts that they approve of X, or like it, or desire it, as an end. Valuing X in this way has its own internal motive force: from the affect, the agent is disposed to act to achieve X. This internal motive force may conflict with preferences, with judgments about what is possible, necessary, or impossible, or with norms about what ought to be done, all-things-considered. Stoic training aims to negate the internal motive force of affective valuations in such conflicts. *Effects*. Sometimes "X is good" asserts that X is an effective means for achieving some end. Valuing X as a means has no built-in motive force; it is not, by itself, a reason for action. (To say that a thumbscrew is good for inflicting pain is not to imply anything about one's intentions.) Nor does the means to an end always reflect the motive power of the end. Even if the agent desires the end (e.g., physical fitness), she may loathe or be indifferent to the means for achieving it. Even if she rejects the end (lung cancer), she may regret giving up cigarettes. Stoic training aims to inculcate internal, *categorical* motive force for all-things-considered norms, and to make the motive force of other sorts of norms yield in conflicts with all-things-considered ones. *Exemplars*. Sometimes "X is good" asserts that X is exemplary—good-of-its-kind. (As tribal rugs go, that is a good one.) Again this is not by itself a reason for action. Agents may believe such statements while despising the "kind." *Appropriateness.* Sometimes "X is good" asserts that X is suitable, appropriate, a good fit with other elements of its surroundings, given certain conventions or necessities. (Given the genre you're working in, that's a good name for the main character.) *Valuables.* Sometimes "X is good" asserts a dispositional fact about X, analogous to saying that it is magnetic: X is valu*able* in the sense that, under certain conditions, X will be valued (e.g., in one of the ways explicated above).

Summation. Sometimes "X is good" summarizes values, either within a type or across types. ("X has many uses. It's a good thing to have." "Considering what you like, as well as decorum, usefulness, and so on, X is a pretty good choice.") The empirical status of across-type summations is problematic. The values involved are only roughly commensurable, and thus subject only to fuzzy quantitative methods. Great effective value for a fundamental project no doubt cancels a weak, negative affective value. (The good of drug therapy that cures, without unpleasant side effects, a life-threatening disease cancels the fleeting unpleasantness of its administration.) But in many cases the comparisons will be more difficult, resulting at best in a less than fully explicable consensus. "X is good" may, of course, make a combination of assertions of the sorts just outlined. Sentences of the form 'X is better than Y' or 'X is best' assert, as matters of fact, ordinal relations either within one type of value judgment or across types. Within types, better and best refer respectively to the strength of agents' approval, the degree of X's efficacy, or excellence, or fittingness, or dispositional potency, or summative value. Across types, better and best assert fuzzy, summative comparisons.

Preferences are psychological facts: they are the beliefs or dispositions about ordinal relations, among things of value, that have internal motive force for an agent. If an agent prefers Y to X, the agent thereby has a motive for resolving conflicts between them in favor of Y. An agent's preferences do not necessarily track the way she values the objects involved. She can acknowledge the superiority of X over Y along every scale of value she can imagine, including her own affective approval of it, yet still prefer good old Y, in the sense that when faced with the choice, she nonetheless ranks Y > X every time. (Such preferences have saved many marriages.) Stoics hold that this is a form of *akrasia*, and thus a lemma of stoic practical reasoning is that preferences ought to track the facts about values. If X is of greater value than Y, it ought to be preferred to Y. Stoic training aims to negate the internal motive force of a preference when it conflicts with what is possible, or when it does not track the facts about values.

Categorical commitments[2] are another class of psychological facts with internal motive force. Such commitments are characterized by the unconditional way in which the agent experiences them, at least initially. Matters of dignity, integrity, honor, privacy, or legality are often experienced in this way—not as things to protect or uphold *if* certain conditions occur, or as means to some end, but rather as things one is bound to seek, or protect, or uphold, period. Like commitments generally, categorical ones may have neither affective value nor the motive force of a project. Rather, they are experienced as attachments, constraints, necessities, requirements, boundaries. Agents are often highly volatile when their commitments are ignored or overridden—more so, perhaps, than when their projects are frustrated. They typically employ metaphors of brokenness, violation, degradation, and disintegration to describe the harm experienced—for example, by invasions of privacy, breaches of trust, deliberate attempts to break one's resistance. If other agents are responsible for the harm, this may evoke long-lasting resentment, anger, rage, desire for revenge. If the agent himself is responsible for the harm, he may have disabling guilt or shame. These responses have valuable cathartic and motivational effects, but they are also frequently the cause of additional damage. (Embittered victims who cannot recognize sunk costs; aggressors freshly provoked by each retaliation.) Stoic training aims to make emotional response dispositions into homeostatic devices, set to eliminate damaging effects that do not have countervailing productive ones. It aims to keep volatile responses strategically sound—in deterring violators and strengthening victims—even if this means breaking the link between the degree of response and the degree of harm done to the victim. Residual unrequited harm is treated as a matter of (emotional) indifference.

The strength of categorical commitments is a contingent matter that by definition does not necessarily track preferences, or values, or ethical norms. It is a rule of inference in stoic practical reasoning that first-order normative propositions of the form "It is required (forbidden) that p, nothing-else-considered" may be constructed from categorical commitments. However, it is an axiom of stoic normative logic that normative propositions of the form "All-things-considered, A ought to do X" override conflicting categorical commitments and the normative propositions drawn from them. Stoic training aims to negate the internal motive force of a categorical commitment when it conflicts with what is possible, or with what ought to be done, all-things-considered.

---

[2] I am indebted to George Harris for the felicitous term, but he defines it differently. See his book *Dignity and Vulnerability* (Berkeley: University of California Press, 1997), chap. 1.

Projects are constitutive facts about agents: to be an agent is to be purposive or goal-oriented—that is, motivated (at least dispositionally) to act toward some end(s). The motive force is internal, built into the project, and typically experienced as coming from within—as pressing or pushing one to act. Agents may pursue a project of which they thoroughly disapprove—a project whose means and ends are repugnant, for example, but to which there are no alternatives. A project may include, exclude, or be concomitant with another. And such relations may be necessary or contingent, permanent or temporary, symmetrical or asymmetrical in surprising ways. The fact that project A (abandoning a medical career to become a poet) includes project B (moving to an isolated farm in Nova Scotia), for example, does not mean that it could not be the other way around. Let us say that a project is indelible to the degree that its pursuit or completion makes a permanent, perceptible difference in any agent's character or conduct; that it is enabling to the degree that it opens opportunities for any agent; disabling to the degree that it closes them; inescapable to the degree to which undertaking it (or continuing it) is necessary; comprehensive to the extent that it includes and dominates another project. At the level of general normative principles, there is little that is useful to say about these matters. Erasable, enabling, escapable projects, for example, are not even *prima facie* preferable to indelible, disabling, inescapable ones. (Think of the ways we want moral education to disable murderous impulses, and to be indelible.) Everything hangs on the details of particular cases. The dominance of more comprehensive projects over less comprehensive ones, however, is represented prominently in the rules and axioms of stoic normative logic.

Standards are conditional commitments that define the manner in which agents ought to conduct themselves in pursuing their projects. They are conditional in the sense that they are applicable if a given antecedent project is undertaken; they are commitments in that their internal motive force is experienced as constraint, necessity, requirement, or boundary. Such hypothetical commitments are sometimes used as criteria for deciding which projects to pursue. ("If I can't do it properly, then I won't do it at all.") Standards are legion. They range over all matters of degree relevant to performance of the given project (efficacy, efficiency, difficulty, elements of style . . .). They define points along a continuum of targets (from perfection to mere adequacy) in terms of an indefinite number of reference classes—from purely formal or logical possibilities (a perfect circle), through possibilities for world-class performers, through what it is reasonable to expect of a local expert, all the way to purely personal abilities. Some standards apply to outcomes only; others to the process; still others to both.

Failed projects and unmet standards can be a source of misery—misery that can be eliminated if one chooses fail-safe projects and meetable standards. It does not follow from this, however, that one ought always to make fail-safe choices. For example, unfulfilled aspirations and failures may contribute indirectly to a good life by motivating extraordinary achievement, which may in turn bring extraordinary satisfaction. It is an axiom of stoic ethics that an agent ought not to set unmeetable-for-the-agent standards (or undertake impossible-for-the-agent projects), but this is understood to allow attempts to turn impossibilities into possibilities, and to use unachievable ideals instrumentally. Stoic moral training cultivates the power of retrospective detachment (that is, the power to neutralize the psychological damage of losses) partly in order to reduce the harm of failure, and thus to *increase* the range of allowable projects and standards that risk failure. Stoic training does not aim to neutralize the harm of productive losses—that is, of harms that play a necessary causal role in producing countervailing goods.

Social roles, conventions, and institutions are facts about the expectations people have of each other, and their common dispositions to act, in various definable regions of social life—regions in which cooperative social activity is organized for some ends, or autonomous individual activities are coordinated, or disputes are settled. Such roles, conventions, and institutions may be as informal as being "it" in a game of hide-and-seek, as localized as a nuclear family's traditional Labor Day activities, as slight as tic-tac-toe; they may be as formal as being a party to a contract under seal, as widely shared as norms of reciprocity, as elaborate and important as a mature legal system. A full description of any such role, convention, or institution will include rules defining participants, and their aims and tasks as participants.

It is useful to think about roles, conventions, and institutions (hereafter abbreviated as institutions) as defined by these sorts of rules: *participation rules*, describing who can or must be subject to or a part of the institution, and what level of participation is appropriate for each; *teleological factors*, describing the institution's reason for being, and its ultimate or constitutive goals; *deontological rules*, describing conduct that is required and forbidden for each sort of participant, including entitlements, fixed standards, priorities, and aims; *valuational commitments*, describing the sorts of aims, interests, acts, products, traits, achievements, and abilities that are valuable for the institution, given its *telos*, and the weights assigned to them; *generative and transformative rules*, describing the institution's legislative processes, if any; *administrative rules*, describing the institution's executive and police powers, and adjudicative processes, if any; *regulative policies*, practices, and rules, describing the institution's modus operandi in implementing its rules; *legitimation as-*

sumptions, describing the grounds for recognizing a given commitment, policy, practice, rule, or assumption as one of the institution's own; *connectedness*, describing the extent and nature of the relations between each participant and all the others; *closure*, describing the extent to which participants in the institution are related only to other participants in it and not to individuals outside it; *mutuality levels*, describing the extent to which participants recognize themselves and each other as participants, make and recognize reciprocal contributions to each others' lives, have a common understanding of the nature of the group, and have univalent responses to it and to each other.

Institutional normative propositions are those constructed from an institution's rules, as applied to the agents at hand, nothing-else-considered. Think of a game. From its rules we can derive normative propositions about who can play, what the goal is, what moves are allowed, and what moves are best for particular players in particular situations. The same is true of social roles, customs, organizations, and fundamental legal, economic, political, and ideational systems. Such normative propositions may take the form of simple ought-judgments, or various forms of prohibitions, requirements, and unrestricted options (e.g., duties, rights), and they apply to or have force for an agent as a matter of fact about how others (and the agent) will conduct themselves. Thus if an institution, by its own rules, can conscript unwilling participants, agents can acquire institutional rights and duties against their will, or without their consent (or knowledge). Thus slaves have institutional obligations to obey their masters, if and only if such obligations follow from operative rules that permit slave holding. Of course these are first-order, nothing-else-considered obligations that typically conflict with the slaves' categorical commitments and preferences. Practical reason must address such conflicts, and may (or may not) prescribe resistance or rebellion, all-things-considered.

It is a lemma of stoic practical reasoning that agents ought to prefer having control of their own situations, experience, actions, and outcomes to lacking such control. It does not follow from this lemma that agents ought to prefer having control of others' lives to lacking it, nor that they ought always to exercise the control they have, even over their own lives. Nor does it follow, nothing-else-considered, that agents ought to seek the control over their lives that they lack, even if they do not expect to exercise it. (A folk singer says, about a flashy banjo player noted for his accuracy and speed: "I wish I could do that. And then not.") However, stoic moral training aims to develop in each agent the disposition to seek social roles, conventions, and institutions in which she has more rather than less control of her own life, unless having less can be shown to make a countervailing contribution toward a good life for her.

Virtue and Happiness

Stoic ethics is a species of eudaimonism. Its central, organizing concern is about what we ought to do or be to live well—to flourish. That is, we make it a lemma that all people ought to pursue a good life for themselves as a categorical commitment second to none. It does not follow from this that they ought to pursue any one particular version of the good life, or to cling tenaciously to the one they are pursuing. On the contrary, stoic training aims to make it possible for us to salvage some form of a good life under adversity, and to be able to handle sudden, massive changes in our circumstances. However, it does follow from the eudaimonistic lemma that stoic ethics will never prescribe sacrificing all possibility of a good life. In every case where the pursuit of a good life conflicts with other normative propositions of practical reason, stoic ethics will find either that agents ought to salvage some form of a good life for them-selves, or that the conflict is unresolvable by reason and that the choice is a matter of indifference. Thus in such conflicts it is always at least per-missible for agents to opt to salvage a good life. Notice here, however, the controlling role of reason—or as we shall say in later chapters, the exercise of our agency powers, in which practical reasoning all-things-considered has a dominant role. We hold that virtue is the perfection of such agency, and is in fact the only plausible candidate for an overarch-ing, final end.

Living virtuously is the process of creating a single, spatiotemporal object—a life. A life has a value as an object, as a whole. It is not always the case that its value as an object will be a function of the value of its spatiotemporal parts considered separately. But it is always the case that an evaluation of the parts will be incomplete until they are understood in the context of the whole life. What seems so clearly valuable (or required or excellent) when we focus on a thin temporal slice of a life (or a single, long strand of a life) may turn out to be awful or optional or vicious when we take a larger view. And it is the life as a whole that we consider when we think about its value in relation to other things, or its value as a part of the cosmos.

Stoic ethics retains the whole-life frame of reference for ethics that was prominent in antiquity. In our view, a focus on the parts of a life, or on the sum of its parts, obscures some important features of ethical inquiry. One such feature is the extent to which an agent's own estimate of the value of his life is necessarily inconclusive: others will have to judge his life as a whole, because its character as a whole is not likely to be predict-able while he is around to judge it, and because many important holistic considerations, such as its beauty, excellence, justice, and net effect, are things that he is either not well situated to judge or at least not in a privileged position to judge. Another feature obscured is the range of ways in which a single event or characteristic, without wide causal connections to other elements of one's life, can nonetheless ruin it; for example, the possibility that a monstrously unjust act can indelibly stain a whole life. A third, related obscurity introduced by ignoring a whole-life frame of reference is the extent to which both aesthetic criteria and the notion of excellence have clear roles in the evaluation of a life. The whole-life frame of reference, together with a plausible account of the variety of ways in which a life can be a good one, keeps stoicism sharply distinct from Epicurean doctrines, or their modern "welfarist" offshoots. How well my life is going from the inside, so to speak, *in terms of the quality of my experience*, is only one of the things that enters into a stoic evaluation of it.

We hold that there is a single unifying aim in the life of every rational agent, and that aim, guided by the notion of a good life (happiness, *eudaimonia*), is virtue, understood as the perfection of agency. The argument for that doctrine and its corollaries will occupy us throughout Part Two. It is important here, however, to quash the thought that the good life we have in mind is in some disappointing way uniform; that it is, for example, always going to turn out to be a contemplative life suspiciously like a philosopher's. Not so. The stoics of antiquity were as diverse as plebeians and aristocrats, rhetoricians and physicians, career soldiers and career poets, apolitical logicians and political advisers, slaves and emperors. And while modernity has narrowed that range (and postmodernity, for all its flash and fury, has done nothing to reverse the trend), such narrowing is a local phenomenon. In principle, the diversity of possible stoic lives—and the lives of stoic sages—is very great. The argument for that assertion is also a task addressed in Part Two.

Commentary

Ruined texts. Ancient stoics were prolific. Chrysippus alone is said to have written seven hundred "books"—which Diogenes Laertius undertakes to list by name in *Lives of the Eminent Philosophers*, VII. But not a single one of those books survives. In fact, no stoic texts from the Early and Middle Stoas survive intact. What we have from those periods are fragments, often in the form of quotations in books about the stoics (and other "professors"), often as not in books by authors hostile to stoicism. Galen, for example, who was no friend to us, nonetheless quoted extensively from Chrysippus, and preserved crucial passages from Posidonius (in Galen, *On the Doctrines of Hippocrates and Plato*). A great deal of such fragmentary material from the Hellenistic period has been collected, translated, and given a topical arrangement with philosophically acute commentaries in Long and Sedley, eds., *The Hellenistic Philosophers*. Volume I (translations and commentary) is particularly valuable for directing readers to complete texts such as Galen's, where we can then read an important fragment in an illuminating, if vexing, context.

From the Late Stoa, we do have some more or less intact texts: fragmentary sections of Hierocles' *Elements of Ethics*; four of the original eight volumes of *Discourses* from Epictetus, as well as a *Handbook* drawn from them, in the form of notes transcribed by Arrian, one of Epictetus' pupils; Marcus Aurelius' *Meditations* (most of which was probably not intended for publication, at least not in the form we have it); and a great deal of work from Seneca in essays, letters, and plays. Unfortunately, the most widely available texts from the Roman period—those of Epictetus and Marcus Aurelius—are quite misleading when read in isolation from earlier material. They are not systematic; they are preoccupied with moral training and the therapeutic aspects of stoic ethics; and they give great weight (some would argue undue weight) to the notion that everyone has a "role" in a cosmic plan. (In the case of Epictetus, it is unclear to us how much of this should be attributed to his lack of interest in systematic theory and how much of it should be attributed to Arrian's lack of interest in transcribing that sort of thing. Arrian's notes may well be a word-for-word transcription, as he claims; the question is how much he chose to transcribe. This thought is tantalizing in part because internal evidence from the *Discourses* suggests that Epictetus typically began class sessions by asking a student to read out and comment upon a text, after which Epictetus himself would make prepared comments on the same text. What were these texts? Arrian does not say, but it hardly seems likely that they were all of a therapeutic or theological sort.) Seneca is a better source in many respects, though less accessible in every way. Especially helpful discussions that make liberal use of his works include Nussbaum, *The Therapy of Desire*, and Rorty, "The Two Faces of Stoicism: Rousseau and Freud." Scholars who want to explore the notion that stoic ethics is universalistic and impartial sometimes take a Hierocles fragment as one of their texts. See Annas, *The Morality of Happiness*, 265–75.

Summarizing stoic ethical doctrines from the meager materials that remain is a challenging task in imaginative reconstruction. Such work has to rely in a substantial way on the classic (and probably quite fair-minded, if often cryptic) summaries by Cicero and Diogenes Laertius, together with the material (possibly from Arius Didymus, a Roman philosopher and confidant of Augustus in the first century B.C.E.) quoted without attribution in Ioannes Stobaeus' *Eclogae* or *Anthology*. The authorship and the merit of the material in Stobaeus is disputed, however. Long, in "Arius Didymus and the Exposition of Stoic Ethics," says it is "the longest and most detailed surviving account of Stoic ethics" (41), and argues that contrary to appearances, it is a more or less coherent presentation of it. White, in "Comments on Long's 'Arius Didymus and the Exposition of Stoic Ethics,'" cannot find a useful organizational principle in it, and suggests that it obscures rather than illumines the pivotal argument about developmental psychology that the stoics employed. (For discussion of that "cradle argument" and the psychological process that the stoics called *oikeiosis*, see Chapters 5 and 6, and the commentaries to them.)

Readers will notice that Epictetus and Marcus Aurelius do not figure significantly in the account of stoic ethics we present. That is because the therapeutic and quasi-theological aspects of stoic doctrine that are so prominent in those writers' works have been sources of great misunderstanding. This is not the fault of those stoics, whom we revere and read with pleasure and profit. It is the fault of those who read them (or write about them) in the abstract—in isolation from the larger theoretical enterprise of which they were a part. We think that, in the current climate, books that emphasize the meditative and pedagogical elements of our tradition are destined to refresh the caricatures we deplore. So, perversely perhaps, we will here leave aside all work in the Epictetan vein, such as Kimpel, *Stoic Moral Philosophies: Their Counsel for Today*. Moreover, we will even welcome trenchant criticism of our old therapies such as those to be found in Nussbaum, *The Therapy of Desire*, if it will help to turn readers back to our theories (as Nussbaum's book surely does).

In his biography of Zeno of Citium, the founder of stoicism, Diogenes Laertius gives thumbnail sketches of the views of many stoics. Much more valuable accounts are to be found in Cicero, *De Finibus*; *Tusculan Disputations*; *De Natura Deorum*; *De Fato*; and *De Officiis*. But Diogenes at least gives us the names and some information about some of our prominent ancient brethren. Many of the dates are approximations subject to change. Hellenists recalculate these matters regularly—perhaps not as often or as dramatically as modern cosmologists recalculate the age of the universe, but enough to make lay readers properly cautious.

CHRONOLOGY

Stoics Are in Bold Type

Heads of the Stoa in Athens Are Marked with an Asterisk

Early Stoa, 300–150 B.C.E.

Middle Stoa, 150–55 B.C.E.

Late (Roman) Stoa, 1st century B.C.E.–3d century C.E.

Neostoicism, 1584 C.E.–fitfully to date

BEFORE THE COMMON ERA

Socrates, c. 470–399

Plato, c. 430–347

Diogenes of Sinope (founder of the Cynics), c. 400–325
Aristotle, c. 383–322
Pyrrho of Elis (founder of the Skeptic school), c. 365–270
Epicurus, c. 341–270
*Zeno of Citium (founder of stoicism), c. 335–263
*Cleanthes of Assos, c. 331–232
*Chrysippus of Soli, c. 280–207
*Diogenes of Babylon (Seleucia), c. 240–152
*Antipater of Tarsus, 2^d century
*Panaetius of Rhodes, c. 185–109
Posidonius of Apamea, 135–55
Cicero, Marcus Tullius, 106–43

IN THE COMMON ERA
Seneca the Younger, c. 1–65
Musonius Rufus, Gaius, 1st century
Plutarch, c. 50–120
Epictetus, c. 50–130
Hierocles, c. early 2^d century
Diogenes Laertius, 2^d century?
Sextus Empiricus, 2^d century?
Marcus Aurelius, 121–180, Emperor 161–180
Galen, c. 130–201
Justus Lipsius, 1547–1606
Guillaume Du Vair, 1556–1621

Contemporary sources. Interest in Hellenistic philosophy is now very much
revived, thanks in no small measure to the work of A. A. Long, beginning in the
late 1960s. Many excellent modern summaries of stoic doctrine now exist, ranging from Gisela Striker's elegantly compressed "Stoicism" article in the *Encyclopedia of Ethics* (1992), through more detailed accounts such as the one she gives
in Striker, "Following Nature: A Study in Stoic Ethics," or the one given in Long,
Hellenistic Philosophy: Stoics, Epicureans, Skeptics, or treatises for a scholarly
audience such as Inwood, *Ethics and Human Action in Early Stoicism,* to book-
length treatments for a general readership such as Sandbach, *The Stoics.* Moreover, a great deal of illuminating philosophy based on scholarly reconstruction of
stoic doctrine has appeared since the early 1970s. A bibliography of 1,189 secondary source items in twentieth-century philosophy alone was published in the
Southern Journal of Philosophy (1985), volume 23, Supplement. Such secondary
sources will be cited throughout the commentaries to follow.

Eudaimonism. Annas, in *The Morality of Happiness,* gives an inspiring and
detailed account of the general nature of eudaimonistic theories, their limits and
possibilities, and makes a comparative study of ancient Greek versions of such
theories. The book is particularly good at characterizing the eudaimonistic "entry
point" for mature ethical reflection (how well one's life will have gone as a whole,
all-things-considered, given various ways of living), and the error of thinking that
eudaimonism is thereby structurally committed to egoism, notwithstanding its
incessant talk of virtue. On the latter point see Part III of Annas's book.

Following nature. Long, in "The Logical Basis of Stoic Ethics," shows that stoic ethics is resolutely naturalistic, in the sense of aiming to derive ethics from facts about the world, and that our general program is not in any obvious way fallacious. Striker, in "Following Nature: A Study in Stoic Ethics," is more skeptical, but the way she reads the stoic slogan about living in agreement with nature (or following it) invites such skepticism. She says (p. 3)

> As Aristotle's ethics is an investigation of virtue and what belongs to it because the end is supposed to be a life in accordance with complete virtue, so Stoic ethics, I believe, is an investigation of what it is to live in agreement with nature. The first question to ask about Stoic ethics would therefore seem to be: why is it good to follow nature?

She points out immediately (p. 4) that there was an alternative formulation, attributable to Zeno and evidently "intended to express the same doctrine." In this formulation, the aim was expressed as "leading a consistent and coherent life, one in which no conflicts occur and that is unified by adherence to a single principle." So the problem is then to "try to understand why the Stoics might have thought that consistency or harmony in one's life is the same as following nature." Striker is quite critical of the logic of stoic arguments using only the first formulation, but suggests (at pp. 48–49) that Posidonius' use of the second is more promising. Cicero, who was actually acquainted with Posidonius, and who claims to be following Panaetius by way of Posidonius, says in *De Officiis* III.iii.13 that

> when the Stoics speak of the supreme good as "living conformably to nature," they mean, as I take it, something like this: that we are always to be in accord with virtue, and from all other things that may be in harmony with nature to choose only as such are not incompatible with virtue.

Admittedly, he puts this forward in the context of discussing the conflict between expediency and moral duty. Even so, it suggests that another way to frame the issue is to ask first for an account of the sort of virtue or excellence that can be considered natural or in harmony with nature, and then to ask for an argument about why that sort of excellence should constrain all other action. This is in effect the course we pursue in Chapter 6.

Cosmic telos. There is a complex and interesting debate, among scholars of the ancient stoic texts, about whether stoic ethics is eudaimonistic through and through, or whether the stoic conception of the cosmos as a rational and purposive entity makes it difficult to assimilate stoicism straightforwardly to (other) ancient eudaimonistic theories. The debate is framed nicely in Long, "Stoic eudaimonism," and Long there and elsewhere (before and since) has argued that, although ancient stoic ethics is clearly eudaimonistic, the cosmic *telos* doctrine plays a central role in it throughout its history. See, for an early example, Long, "The Stoic Concept of Evil," 332–33. White, in "The Role of Physics in Stoic Ethics," has no doubt that many stoics claimed a central role for physics, in the sense that the sage would have to have knowledge of nature in order to act appropriately—but is dubious about whether this requirement can reasonably amount to a requirement to integrate physics fully into ethics. Irwin, in "Stoic and Aristotelian Conceptions of Happiness," explores a more Aristotelian interpretation;

and going farther along this path, Annas, in *The Morality of Happiness*, chap. 5, argues that what does the work in stoic ethical theory is an appeal only to *human* nature, not to cosmic *telos*. Engberg-Pedersen, in *The Stoic Theory of Oikeiosis*, is even more thoroughly in the antiphysics camp. Cooper, in "Eudaimonism, the Appeal to Nature, and 'Moral Duty' in Stoicism," dissents sharply from such a view insofar as it restricts what counts as eudaimonism or marginalizes the appeal to cosmic nature in stoic ethics, but see Annas's exchange with him on this point in *Philosophy and Phenomenological Research* 55 (1995): 587–610. To complicate matters further, in the way Striker, in "Following Nature: A Study in Stoic Ethics," reconstructs stoic theory its source is in theology. (We assume that in principle, ancient stoic theology would be a form of natural theology, and thus like science would be subject to revision as human knowledge changes. Indeed, we assume that our ancient brethren would not have separated physics and theology methodologically.) The issue is nearly moot here, however, since we now reject the early cosmic teleology, and since all hands agree that stoic ethical theory grows out of what we now identify as the eudaimonistic tradition, and gives a developmental account of virtue (see Chapters 5 and 6) that is thoroughly eudaimonistic. Nonetheless, our insistence that the best science (including cosmology) always shapes ethics—and that ethics thus may change in major ways when science does—effectively aligns us with the physics group.

These scholarly disputes notwithstanding, it is clear that stoics did once subscribe to the view that the cosmos as a whole was a rational, purposive being, and that in being rational creatures themselves, humans shared the most exalted property of the cosmos. Here are some representative fragments, in translations by Long and Sedley, in *The Hellenistic Philosophers* (page numbers to their text follow each fragment).

A. Sextus Empiricus, *Against the Professors* 9.332 (SVF 2–5z4, part)
The Stoic philosophers suppose that there is a difference between the 'whole' and the 'all'. For they say that the world is whole, but the external void together with the world is all. For this reason they say the 'whole' is finite, since the world is finite, but the 'all' is infinite, since the void outside the world is such. (268)

B. Diogenes Laertius 7.134 (SVF 2.300, part, 2.299)
(1) They [the Stoics] think that there are two principles of the universe, that which acts and that which is acted upon. (2) That which is acted upon is unqualified substance, i.e. matter; that which acts is the reason [*logos*] in it, i.e. god. For this, since it is everlasting, constructs every single thing throughout all matter. (268)

E. Calcidius 293
(1) And so the universal body, according to the Stoics, is limited and one and whole and substance [*essentia*]. (2) It is whole, because it does not lack any parts; it is one, because its parts are inseparable and mutually coherent with themselves; it is substance, because it is the prime matter of all bodies, and through it, they say, complete and universal reason passes, just like seed through the genital organs. (3) This reason they take to be an actual craftsman, while the cohering body they take to be without quality, i.e. matter or sub-

stance, completely passive and subject to change. (4) But while substance changes, it does not perish either as a whole or by the destruction of its parts, because it is a doctrine common to all philosophers that nothing either comes to be out of nothing or perishes into nothing. For even though all bodies disintegrate by some chance, matter still exists always and the craftsman god, that is, reason, by which it is established both at what time each thing will come to birth and when it will perish. (5) And therefore its birth arises out of existing things and passes away into what exists, because it is bounded by things which abide as immortals, i.e., that by which and that from which the generated thing comes into being. (269–70)

F. Diogenes Laertius 7.–37 (SVF 2.5z6, part) I
They [the Stoics] use 'world' [kosmos] in three ways: of god himself, the peculiarly qualified individual consisting of all substance, who is indestructible and ingenerable, since he is the manufacturer of the world-order, at set periods of time consuming all substance into himself and reproducing it again from himself; they also describe the world-order as 'world'; and thirdly, what is composed out of both [i.e., god and world-order]. (270)

B. Cicero, *On the Nature of the Gods* 1.39 (SVF 2.1077, part)
For he [Chrysippus] says that divine power resides in reason and in the mind and intellect of universal nature. He says that god is the world itself, and the universal pervasiveness of its mind; also that he is the world's own commanding-faculty, since he is located in intellect and reason; that he is the common nature of things, universal and all-embracing; also the force of fate and the necessity of future events. In addition he is fire; and the aether of which I spoke earlier; also things in a natural state of flux and mobility, like water, earth, air, sun, moon and stars; and the all-embracing whole; and even those men who have attained immortality. (323)

Physics, logic, and ethics. At least one prominent stoic in the third century B.C.E., Aristo, held that ethics alone was the proper subject matter for philosophy. His view did not prevail. For an account of its demise, brought about mainly by Chrysippus, see Striker, "Following Nature: A Study in Stoic Ethics," section 2. Diogenes Laertius, in *Lives of the Eminent Philosophers* (at 7.39–41), reports some other disputes in the Stoa about the divisions of philosophy as well. It is far from clear what the stakes were in those matters. For a detailed technical examination of them, focusing in part on the fact that Diogenes says it is philosophical "discourse" (*logos*), rather than philosophy simpliciter that has the divisions, see Ierodiakonou, "The Stoic Division of Philosophy." The disagreements seem to have been mainly about the way the branches of philosophy were to be ordered, there being near consensus on the number of them (three) and their content. This all may have been some sort of curricular debate. (We suppose teachers then as now could be interminably and comically at odds about such things.) But we follow the order attributed to Panaetius and Posidonius. See Long and Sedley, *The Hellenistic Philosophers*, section 26. We do this because it most aptly represents the logical priorities of a naturalistic system of philosophical ethics—that is, an ethics derived from reasoning about human nature and other facts about the world.

A few people want to make a case for the importance of the order in which the branches were taught in the Stoa, and of the fact that ethics was often taught first—or at least independently of physics and logic. Annas, in *The Morality of Happiness*, chap. 5, presses hard on this point. But proper pedagogy hardly ever follows the "systematic order" of the parts of a grand philosophical scheme, so we do not go down this path. Kidd, in "Stoic Intermediates and the End for Man" (157–58), lends support to this choice.

Materialism and particularism. A good way into the ancient texts on this aspect of stoic doctrine is found in sections 27–29, 45, and 48 of Long and Sedley, *The Hellenistic Philosophers*. In brief, though stoics begin their ontology with the notion of a "something,"which can be either corporeal, incorporeal (e.g., a void, time), or neither, they insist that everything that "exists" is corporeal. Bodies, however, can be understood metaphysically in four ways (under four categories, or genera): (1) in terms of their primary physical substrate; (2) in terms of the way that a primary substrate may be "qualified" by having as one of its parts another corporeal entity, such as the "breath" (active principle, god) that pervades the universe; (3) in terms of the way such qualified substrates may be "disposed" or internally arranged; and (4) in terms of the way such disposed, qualified substrates may be related to each other (relatively disposed). Every thing that exists can be understood in each of those ways. Metaphysical confusion abounds, however, when we give a name, such as prudence, to a thing considered under only one of its genera (say under the fourth, as certain patterns of behavior relative to others), and then come to identify the nature of prudence with its fourth genera aspects alone. We may thus come to ignore the fact that prudence always has a "qualified" physical substrate—that is, a substrate in a *particular* rational being. We must not forget the fact that stoics are particularists all the way to the ground. Everything that exists, and that has causal powers, is a particular. (Universals are "not-somethings" [Long and Sedley, *The Hellenistic Philosophers*, I, p. 164]. They are not corporeal. Nor are they merely shorthand names for collections of corporeal things. They are "concepts.") There are dense metaphysical thickets in all of this, but we think ethics can avoid them.

When we discuss consciousness and subjectivity in Chapter 6, we will have occasion to remind readers again that stoics are thoroughgoing materialists in the sense that we hold that there is only one kind of "stuff" or substrate of which existing things are composed. David Jones (in correspondence) has pressed the point, however, that we must make clear both that we deny substance dualism and that we decline to follow the any of the rigorously reductive or eliminative versions of materialism—versions that reject all forms of emergent property dualism, for example. We think the phenomenon of subjectivity resists all proposed reductions of that sort. (See Nagel, "What it is like to be a Bat," in *Mortal Questions*; Nagel, *The View from Nowhere*; Searle, *The Rediscovery of the Mind*). We suppose, then, that mind is an emergent entity (or perhaps set of properties) of a certain highly complex organization (or organizations) of matter—specifically, in the human case, of a healthy neurological system. In its substance, or substrate, it is a physical thing, but it is a distinctly different kind of physical thing than the bits and pieces of matter from which it emerges, and upon which its continuation depends. Jones suggests the label "compositional materialism" for this view, and that label is attractive in part because it preserves a connection with our roots. Ancient stoics were physicalistic "entity-but-not-substance-dualists," in the sense that they held that body and mind were material bodies of different sorts, blended or fused together in a conscious being. See Long, "Soul and Body in Stoicism." The difference between then and now is of course in the causal account we now suppose will one day be given about the origin of mind. Empirical science, beginning in this case at least with Galen (*On the Doctrines of Hippocrates and Plato* I–II), has convinced us that the origin of mental phenomena is to be found in neurological processes—not in the heart or the breath, certainly, and not in god either. But that sort of change in doctrine is nothing new for us. Sedley, in "Chrysippus on Psychophysical Causality" (326), argues that ancient stoic doctrines about the corporeality of the soul may be read as "attempts to update [Platonic dualism] in the light of the latest science."

Values, facts, and norms. Ancient stoic claims that virtue (or moral good) is the only thing that is genuinely good—and conversely that it is only vice or lack of virtue, rather than pain, disease, or misery, that is bad—has often been considered perverse, or at a minimum exceedingly obscure. Long, "The Stoic Concept of Evil," does much to remove the grounds for those objections, but dispute continues about how to interpret the "value" of ordinary goods—things that the stoics called "indifferent," though some of them were to be "preferred" to others. There are various ways of interpreting that doctrine to make it plausible. In our view the best are the ones given in Kidd, "Stoic Intermediates and the End for Man," and White, "Stoic Values." In effect, we offer a similar one in Chapters 6 and 7, and cite others in the commentary to chapter 6, where we quote relevant passages from White. Here we are simply concerned with reminding readers that stoics are perfectly aware of the importance of all of the things people ordinarily count as goods. Moreover, the analysis of values offered in this chapter is meant to caution against the temptation to read the stoics as denying "intrinsic" worth to all ordinary goods. We are not committed to the position that pleasurable affects, friendship, and so on are merely instrumental or "extrinsic" goods. We thus dispute Nussbaum (*The Therapy of Desire*, chap. 10, pp. 134–35) on this point.

Good lives. It is useful to divide conceptions of the good life into plural and unitary ones. A *plural* conception holds (a) that the goods realizable in a human life are genuinely diverse—that is, not reducible to a single species; (b) that genuinely diverse combinations of goods are sufficient to make a life a good one, and thus that good lives differ in kind as well as degree; and (c) that any theoretical cover to be found for the diverse array of good lives will be purely formal, or schematic, or perhaps merely heuristic. A *unitary* conception, by contrast, holds either (a′) that goods are not diverse, and thus good lives differ only in degree; or (b′) that whether goods are diverse or not, there is only one set of them sufficient for making a life a good one; or (c′) that though there may be more than one sufficient set, all of them have in common the same ordered subset of necessary goods—a set rich enough, or ordered rigidly enough, to insure that all good lives will be remarkably similar.

By those standards, stoics appear to argue for a unitary conception, since we hold that our final end is virtue, and that it, and it alone, is necessary and sufficient for a good life. So we hold (b′). Moreover, to the extent that we still hold some version of the doctrine that virtue is the only thing that is good, we evidently endorse (a') as well. Stopping there, however, would be highly misleading as to the nature of our view, because we also endorse some commonsensical considerations adduced by pluralists.

Consider, for example, the line of argument in Becker, "Good Lives: Prolegomena." Begin by observing that there is a rather long list of desiderata that people ordinarily regard as criteria for assessing whether their lives are going well, and for assessing whether, on the whole, their lives have been good ones. These "criterial goods" are plausibly regarded as distinct from one another, and all of them are either intrinsic, necessary, or widely instrumental goods. Such a list of criterial goods (so the argument goes) will include at least the following, in addition to the material conditions necessary for sustaining life and consciousness: pleasant, self-conscious experience; an understanding or knowledge of the nature, value, and meaning of things; the power of self-command; the harmonization of reason, desire, and will; excellence (being good of one's kind); meaningful opportunity, meaningful activity, meaningful necessity (in the sense of participating in endeavors in which one's actions are required); self-esteem; benevolence; mutual love; sexuality; rectitude; integrity; aesthetic value.

Stoics think that in a virtuous life, all such ordinary goods would be ordered and sought by the exercise of practical intelligence, but we suppose that the profile of such goods in virtuous lives would be very far from uniform. Indeed, while we reject the skepticism in Becker's "Good Lives" article about unitary accounts of the good life (and to make the point plain, Becker now withdraws that skepticism), we do suppose that a second major section of the article is fundamentally correct. Namely, we suppose that an examination of various standard candidates for the title of "the" good life (or the best life) will show that they are only plausible to the degree that they succeed in incorporating all or most of the criterial goods on the list, and that this is true also of the unitary account that stoics offer. Moreover, we suppose that stoic sages in different circumstances and ages will organize and pursue these criterial goods in remarkably different ways, leading to remarkably different stoic lives.

For similar (nonstoic) thoughts about the diversity of moral character, one might well begin with Nozick's famous challenge to political unifiers, in the form of a list of real people with widely divergent interests and conceptions of the good life in Nozick, Anarchy, State and Utopia. Griffin, Well-Being, is a relevant source here also, as is Kekes, The Morality of Pluralism. We note also the defense of the wide variety possible in "moral" personalities in Flanagan, Varieties of Moral Personality.

Acknowledgments

I am grateful to my students at the College of William & Mary for persuading me, during several iterations of a seminar on human good and the good life that (a) despite my protests to the contrary, I was a stoic, and that (b) a book about stoic ethics would be more interesting than the one I was planning. Work on this project began in earnest during a year of research (1993–94), funded in part by a fellowship from the National Endowment for the Humanities. Little of what I wrote that year remains in the book, except for fragments of this chapter and the technical appendix on normative logic. Discovering what will not work is valuable, however, and in the case of this book it turned out to be indispensable. Most of the published text was written from July through December of 1995, when I was on a semester's research assignment from the College of William & Mary. I am grateful to both the NEH and William & Mary for their support. An early draft was presented as a short course at the college in the spring of 1996, and the twenty students who took it made many valuable suggestions, as did my colleagues Mark Fowler and Adam Potkay, who attended the sessions. Special thanks go to Trevor Atwood, Casey Cornelius, Stephanie McClelland, and Steve Lipson from that course, and to Abbie Hattauer and Jeremy Wisnewski from a subsequent iteration of it, for their persistent queries and valuable suggestions. In the summer of 1996 Darlene Hayes provided bibliographical and clerical help in producing these commentaries. And this is also the place to thank my graduate research assistant of two years, J. Rosser Matthews, both for the usual sorts of help and for many hours of stimulating discussion. Matthews is, of course, a distinguished young historian of medicine, and it was my good luck that he decided two years ago to come to William & Mary to study public-policy analysis during a time I was teaching ethics in that graduate program.

Julia Annas gave me patient and detailed advice on several points in the section on cosmic *telos*. Confirmation of several major themes of Part One may be found in a recent paper by A. A. Long, "The Stoic Legacy on Naturalism, Rationality and the Moral Good" (unpublished manuscript). The material on the two concepts of morality is drawn from Becker, "The Finality of Moral Judgments," and Becker, *Reciprocity*. The latter, and Becker, "Community, Dominion, and Membership," elaborate the concept of a well-defined activity.

Part Two

THE WAY THINGS MIGHT GO

4

Normative Logic

THIS SHORT CHAPTER, together with its somewhat more elaborate appendix and commentary at the end of the book, lays out in a formal way the practical logic sketched informally in Part One. It tests that sketch for hidden assumptions and consistency, and is a further explanation of how stoics propose to get from "is" to "ought." Readers with limited patience for formal logic will need only the informal exposition given here. The calculus itself is confined to the Appendix, and since the commentary that would normally follow this chapter deals mostly with technical matters related to the calculus, it is also in the Appendix. Readers who are gripped by the desire to see symbols may turn directly to the calculus. Enough informal exposition is repeated there to make it intelligible, and it has the advantage of giving a fuller and more precise account.

Nothing in the arguments of subsequent chapters will involve manipulating the calculus, but everything in them depends on the existence and coherence of it (or of something like it). We think that ethics too often proceeds with unjustified confidence that the assemblage of assumptions and logical operations it employs are clear and adequate for its purposes. We are therefore committed to considering such matters in detail. We have done so, however, only with the aim of applying existing formal methods to ethics, and not with the aim of extending logic itself in a significant way. These days, stoics are as specialized as everyone else. Those of us in ethics rarely do anything original in logic, and our logicians return the favor.

We agree with Aristotle's dictum that philosophers should not seek more determinateness in their arguments than the subject matter permits—and particularly that we should not expect to get the rigor and precision of mathematical demonstrations in the arguments of ethical theory. But we also agree with Hume that the logic employed in ethics is often deeply obscure; and we agree with Brian Barry that even when the logic is clear, it often starts too close to its destination. It is our aim to avoid all three of those pitfalls.

The task of working out our normative logic in detail has satisfied us that stoic ethics does indeed have a sound method of deriving moral judgments from facts about the world—a method that meets the following tests: First, it is capable of representing the full range of behavioral norms relevant to normative judgments, and of assigning a clear meaning to "moral judgment" as opposed to other sorts of normative ones. Second, it makes very plain just how we propose to derive moral judgments from facts about the world. There is no logical sleight of hand here. And third, it shows that such derivations can be logically sound, nontrivial, and systematically coherent.

Norms and Normative Propositions

Throughout our arguments we make a sharp distinction between norms and normative propositions. In our lexicon, norms are facts about the intentional behavior of particular agents; they are facts about agents' goals, projects, or endeavors—specifically about what they believe they must do or be, ought to do or be, or may do or be. Normative propositions are assertions about norms—attempts to represent facts about norms in assertoric propositions about them. Such assertions can be true or false. Indeed, in our logic they *must* be either true or false, and cannot be both. There is no middle ground of indeterminacy (or "higher" ground of both-truth-and-falsity) about the truth value of a given representation of a norm. We thus can make use of the resources of standard, bivalent, truth-functional logic.

Types of normative propositions. Our logic diverges, however, from standard presentations of deontic logic in which the normative operators are obligation, permission, and prohibition—all interpreted in terms of the alethic modal notions of necessity, possibility, and impossibility. Instead we use normative operators of requirement, ought, and indifference, and it seems unlikely that an adequate semantic interpretation of them can be given in terms of modal logic. We make use of modal operators as well; we simply do not claim that their semantics may serve for our normative ones. Further discussion of these matters is given in the commentary to this chapter in the Appendix, and (implicitly) throughout Chapter 5.

Ought. We use "ought" in the following way: To say that an agent ought to do or be X is to say that her doing (or being) X is *advisable* (but not necessarily required) in terms of some endeavor that she has. That is, to say that she ought to do X is to say that her doing X will advance one of her endeavors along a defined trajectory toward its goals. Endeavors are intentional, goal-directed activities. Some things we do in pursuit of them are, as we say, steps in the right direction—on track, on course, on target, in accord with what we are trying to do, effective, true to our purposes, right, correct. Other things are *in*advisable, in the sense that they are deviations from the defined trajectory. Still others are neither advisable nor inadvisable, in the sense that they have no effect on our progress along the trajectory. Note that, as in navigation, deviations from a defined course do not necessarily prevent one from reaching one's destination. One can make course corrections to get back on the original path, or one can chart a new course. Moreover, to say that an act is advisable is not to say that it is unique in that regard (there may be several adequate solutions to a given navigational problem), or that it is the optimal choice (one solution may not be preferable to another).

Requirement. We use "requirement" in several distinct ways, which for convenience are harmlessly conflated in the calculus, as they are in ordinary speech. To say that an agent is required to do (or be) X is to say one or more of three things: (1) It may be to say that her doing or being X is in some sense a necessary condition for her pursuing some endeavor she has. (2) It may be to say that within the terms of some endeavor, she ought to be (or it is required that she be) sanctioned for doing or being non-X. Or (3) it may be to say that her doing or being non-X would be a "nullity" in her endeavor—would not count as pursuing that endeavor at all. (We include nullity as an alternative to make note of the cases in which the "necessity" for doing X, or the "sanction" for doing non-X, comes from the fact that non-X does not count for anything. Legal requirements that a will be witnessed are of this sort. Failing to meet them is just failing to make a valid will. This is a special case of the "necessary condition" alternative, but one that is frequently forgotten.) A prohibition is simply a requirement that one *not* do (or be) X.

For present purposes we do not think this triple disjunction needs to be broken apart to identify two or three different sorts of requirement. That is, we do not think these distinctions affect the ordinal relationships or inferences outlined below. Note that its being *required* that an agent do X is quite distinct from its being the case that she *ought* to do it. Requirements often constrain or even frustrate the pursuit of a goal.

Indifference. The indifference operator is interpreted as a logical remainder. To say that it is a matter of indifference whether an agent does X is to say that her doing X is neither advisable nor inadvisable, neither required nor prohibited.

There are important and interesting logical relationships between these normative operators and the various sorts of imperatives, endorsements, recommendations, exclamations, and other speech acts typical of ethical discourse. Imperatives, for example, often elide the distinction between requirement and ought. ("Just do it" is ambiguous in that way.) And it is challenging to try to think through the extent to which the meaning of prescriptive language in general overlaps that of the normative propositions used here. We leave all such matters for another time.

Levels of inclusiveness and dominance: moral and submoral normative propositions. An agent's endeavors, and hence the norms that are elements in them, are often related hierarchically. For example, a training regimen pursued to improve athletic performance is embedded, as it were, in the performance endeavor, and the performance norms control or dominate the training ones. Stoic normative logic defines moral norms formally as the ones that are elements of our most inclusive and controlling endeavor. See the Axioms below (p. 42). It is the task of Chapters 5–7 to describe and defend a conception of what that endeavor (virtue) is.

Possibility and necessity. Matters of possibility and necessity figure prominently in stoic ethics, and so our normative logic includes modal operators, interpreted as uncontroversially as possible. The technical issues here we leave to the Appendix, and make only this informal observation about our use of the alethic modalities. We distinguish three ranges of modality: logical, theoretical, and practical. What is logically possible may not be possible in terms of our theories of the way things work. Einsteinian physics, for example, holds that travel at speeds greater than that of light is not possible; Kohlberg's theory of moral development holds that people cannot reach stage 6 without going through stages 1–5 in order. So a proposition asserts that X is a theoretical impossibility if it asserts that it is logically inconsistent with the laws, postulates, predictions, or explanations of a given theory. Likewise, the range of practical possibility differs from both the logical and theoretical ones. It is defined by the abilities of given individuals in given circumstances. So a proposition asserts that X is a practical possibility if it is logically consistent with the abilities of the people in some referenced class. Note that theoretical and practical possibility are merely context-restricted forms of logical possibility.

Conflicts and ordinal relationships. As will be clear in the section on normative constructs below, and will be explained even more fully in Chapter 5, our logic freely represents and manipulates conflicting norms. We resolve all such conflicts, however, in three stages. First, we record whatever priorities are in fact built into the types of norms involved. For example, in general we suppose that requirements take priority over conflicting oughts, and that indifference yields to either. Second, we resolve conflicts among requirements, or among oughts or indifferences, in terms of ordinal relations of inclusiveness and dominance that are constructable from them. Third, we get closure on any remaining conflicts among norms of the same rank by constructing normative propositions (moral ones) that represent forced choices.

Normative Constructs

Certain constellations of facts, necessities, and possibilities license the construction of normative propositions. Given facts about the rules of a game, for example, and facts about the possibilities open to players, it is plain how we can legitimately construct normative propositions about what the players ought to do *strictly in terms of the game they are playing*. And it is equally plain how we can then reconstruct such normative propositions in terms of the players' more comprehensive activities—by enlarging the frame of reference to include facts about the various aims and preferences that have brought them to play the game, and the terms under which they are willing to stay in it. The normative power of such propositions is conditional: *If* we restrict ourselves simply to the rules of the "game" we are playing and the possibilities open to us, *then* we ought to. . . .

All the licit normative constructs in this logic are conditional in that sense—they are all constructed from (and thus logically tethered to) antecedents that define an ongoing activity, its participants, and their possibilities. If the antecedent conditions are all-things-considered ones—that is, if the antecedent ongoing activity in terms of which the normative judgment is constructed is simply all-things-considered practical reasoning applied to a given situation—then such constructs have some similarity to categorical imperatives. This is so because, by definition, there is no way to reconstruct all-things-considered judgments in terms of antecedents that have not been considered. Thus in effect they have the sort of finality claimed for categorical imperatives.

First-Order Constructs

The classic stoic injunction to "follow nature" is realized here as following the facts. We begin with a look at a small sampling of frequently used rules for transforming descriptive propositions about the aims, rules-of-play, and practical possibilities within a given ongoing activity into normative propositions about those activities. (For a fuller sample, see the Appendix.)

From means and ends to oughts. For stoics, means/end reasoning is the underlying form of all practical reasoning. It is implicit even in apparently noninstrumental inferences from desires or categorical commitments, for example, because those inferences depend on assumptions about their connection to eudaimonia and human happiness or flourishing. And there is no *practical* reasoning about that end, as opposed to a philosophical defense of it. However, it would not be instructive, in a normative logic, to represent all inferences simply in terms of means/end relationships. That would obscure many important distinctions. Here we will treat means/end inferences on a par with those about desires, commitments, appropriateness, and so forth.

Such means/end inferences at a given ordinal level take several forms, depending on the possibilities for action. One is what we may call the rule of the best means: If we can identify some course of action or trait X as a practically possible means to achieving one or more of the goals we are pursuing, and it is the best of the practical possibilities, then *nothing-else-considered*, we ought to do X.

That leaves the cases in which there are several routes to the same goal, none superior to the others. In such cases, though we need to avoid the indecision of Buridan's ass, immobilized between two equidistant and equally desirable piles of hay, the choice is arbitrary. So we resolve such cases with an inference that the agent ought to make an arbitrary choice between the means that are in equipoise.

Other oughts. In some endeavors the desires of the participants are allowed to trump all other considerations; the mere desire to do (or be) X counts as a sufficient reason for doing or being X, nothing-else-considered. Improvised games come to mind as an example—games in which the shifting whims of the players are allowed to overturn any of the rules, so that what begins as (say) a backyard game of croquet can mutate first into a test of love and then into an indefinite range of games that are not croquet. In other endeavors, desires are subordinate to certain considerations (e.g., efficiency), but are otherwise defined as sufficient reasons for action. And it may be that in still other endeavors, a desire to do X never counts as sufficient reason for doing it—or even counts as sufficient reason for *not* doing it.

We may represent these situations together in the following rule of inference: If the desire to do (or be) X is a sufficient reason for doing it in one of the agent's endeavors, then (nothing-else-considered) the agent ought to do or be X.

Similar rules are used to construct normative ought-propositions about ideals, guidelines, and various kinds of transactional obligations.

From commitments to requirements. A given endeavor, practice, or institution may define participants as categorically committed to various courses of action merely from the fact of their being participants in the endeavor. Such commitments are categorical in the sense that within the endeavor they are not conditioned on anything but participation—not on the desires or goals of individual participants, or the consequences of the required acts, for example. Such commitments are not optional within the endeavor. Thus our rule is that if an agent is categorically committed to X in some endeavor, then (nothing-else-considered) he is required to do or be X.

From standards to ought-nots. Many endeavors have standards of good form and appropriateness that fall short of the requiredness of categorical commitments but are nonetheless important practical considerations. Such endeavors have an etiquette as well as a set of goals, an aesthetic as well as a set of commitments, a conception of what is fitting as well as a conception of what is effective. When we disapprove of an admittedly licit and effective practice as ugly, uncouth, or tacky—or commend a failure as classy—we appeal to such standards. They are not typically employed, however, to identify a particular course of action or way of being that must or ought to be pursued. Rather they are employed to assess conduct or character in terms of some threshold of objectionability. Such appeals may be represented in a rule of inference about things we ought *not* to do or be—a rule of this general form: If X is standard or fitting conduct or character for an agent in some endeavor, then (nothing-else-considered) he ought not to to do or be anything other than X.

Escalation

Conflicts obviously arise regularly between normative propositions constructed in the way just described—that is, in terms of discrete endeavors, nothing-else-considered. We resolve such conflict in our logic by means of rules for generating superordinate normative propositions that dominate the conflicting ones. These rules do nothing more than represent ways in which our norms actually do (often) have an implicit ordinal relationship to one another.

There are two crucial ways in which such ordinal relationships occur. One we call comprehensiveness: when one endeavor is embedded in a more comprehensive and controlling one, the latter's norms are superordinate. The other we call assessment: when we recognize one endeavor as subject to assessment and correction by another, the latter's norms are superordinate.

Not every conflict is in principle resolvable in this way, however. Sometimes norms of the same ordinal rank conflict. We resolve such conflicts with forced choices—that is, with rules of the following sort: conflicting requirements at level n to choose between mutually exclusive courses of conduct generate a normative proposition that resolves the matter at level n + 1.

There are a good many technical complications in this escalation process, but the important point is getting a sound rule of closure for every case.

Transcendence

In our normative logic, normative propositions representing practical reasoning all-things-considered are defined as moral ones. We thus need rules for getting from propositions at a given level n to (unsubscripted) moral ones. Such rules are merely variants of escalation rules in which we include a premise that represents the result of all-things-considered deliberation. Together with the axioms of our logic, we may then make an inference to a moral proposition.

Axioms of Stoic Normative Logic

We conclude this swift overview of our calculus of normative logic with an informal statement of four central postulates that are specifically stoic. (There are others in the full system, but they address technical details in the calculus.) The ones listed here are given a metaethical defense in other chapters. Here they merely round out an intuitive picture of the logical ground on which our ethical arguments ultimately rest.

>   **Axiom of Encompassment.** The exercise of our agency through practical intelligence, including practical reasoning all-things-considered, is the most comprehensive and controlling of our endeavors.
>
>   **Axiom of Finality.** There is no reasoned assessment endeavor external to the exercise of practical reasoning all-things-considered.
>
>   **Axiom of Moral Priority.** Norms generated by the exercise of practical reasoning all-things-considered are superordinate to all others.
>
>   **Axiom of Futility.** Agents are required not to make direct attempts to do (or be) something that is logically, theoretically, or practically impossible.

We turn now from formal to substantive matters, including the defense of these axioms.

5

Following the Facts

SLOGANS oversimplify, and in a contentious intellectual environment they invite misunderstanding. The environment for stoics has always been a contentious one, fostered in antiquity by vigorous disputes within the tradition, and it was clear even then that stoic ethics would be much better off without its "follow nature" slogan. We are, however, too deeply branded with it to renounce it now. The best we can do is reinterpret it.

Following nature means following the facts. It means getting the facts about the physical and social world we inhabit, and the facts about our situation in it—our own powers, relationships, limitations, possibilities, motives, intentions, and endeavors—before we deliberate about normative matters. It means facing those facts—accepting them for exactly what they are, no more and no less—before we draw normative conclusions from them. It means doing ethics *from* the facts—constructing normative propositions *a posteriori*. It means adjusting those normative propositions to fit changes in the facts, and accepting those adjustments for exactly what they are, no more and no less. And it means living within the facts—within the realm of actual rather than hypothetical norms.[1]

Following nature thus has nothing to do with conjuring up a quasi-theological vision of the universe as a teleological system whose ends we are designed to serve—unless, of course, it is a fact that the universe *is* such a system and we *are* designed to serve it. And even if that were so, stoics would not now (if they ever did) finally infer that we ought, all-things-considered, to serve as designed. The fact that we had a function in a goal-directed universe would merely generate some first-order normative propositions that might or might not survive conflicts with normative propositions from other sources. Stoic ethical theory is not enslaved by nature, gods, emperors, or the status quo. Stoics have been slaves (and emperors), but have opposed the institution of slavery. Stoics have lived in parochial settings, but have argued for cosmopolitan politics and

---

[1] Recall that we use "norms" here to refer to the facts that normative propositions represent, and never to refer to the propositions themselves insofar as they are merely representations. Of course the propositional representation of a norm can itself become an object of thought for an agent, and then as an object of thought be among the facts represented by other normative propositions. But for reasons of clarity, it is important to avoid the temptation to call normative propositions themselves, as such, norms.

universal moral norms. Stoics have accepted the facts of oppression and danger for what they are, but have fought to the death. Stoics have adjusted to a changing world, but have also committed suicide as a matter of principle. Following nature—following the facts—is not quietism, conformity, or passivity.

Nor is it romanticism. Stoics do not confuse virtue with genius, heroism with metaphysical rebellion, nobility with contempt for the mundane, emotion with passion, passion with loss of control, loss of control with largeness of spirit, victory with triumph, or tragedy with death.

Impossibilities

The Axiom of Futility represents the stoic doctrine that we ought not to try to do things that are known to be impossible, and it is written as a prohibition that dominates any normative proposition to the contrary. This doctrine is merely a part of what it means to follow the facts, but it has been the source of stubborn misunderstanding. The charge against us is that, in order to avoid dashed hopes, disappointment, anxiety, and despair, stoics use the doctrine of futility to avoid projects that might fail, and in general never struggle or stretch or try to achieve anything beyond what they know they can accomplish. Thus critics say that if we were all to follow stoic advice, we would never extend ourselves to press beyond what we currently think we can achieve; we would forgo the possibility of discovering that we are not as limited as we supposed; heroism and the spirit of adventure would be lost; excellence in everything from science to sport would be forfeited; the Star Ship *Enterprise* would never be launched (etc., etc., etc.). Isolated remarks from a moral-training manual (a handbook drawn from Epictetus' teaching) are cited in support of the charge, and associated with the sort of parental cautions adolescents and other romantics reject as overly protective. (Don't set yourself up for a fall. Don't aim too high. Don't get your hopes up. Don't set your heart on it.)

There will be more about this in the discussion of detachment, in Chapters 6 and 7. Here it will suffice to point out that the Axiom of Futility says only that when we know that a given undertaking is impossible, we are prohibited from undertaking *it*. This does not imply that we ought to refrain from other efforts to make it possible. Nor does it imply that we should refrain from exploring the possibilities when we are ignorant of them. Making things possible, and exploring the possibilities, are meta-endeavors quite distinct from directly undertaking things that we currently believe to be impossible. We undertake such meta-endeavors with respect to practical, theoretical, and even logical impossibilities. Roger

Bannister trained himself to make it practically possible for him to run a four-minute mile, and then he did so. Nothing in that series of projects runs afoul of stoic doctrine. Scientists construct hypotheses about what is theoretically possible, and then explore those possibilities by testing the hypotheses—revising their theories (and hence the theoretical possibilities) in terms of what they find. There is nothing unstoic about that. Mathematicians and logicians regularly explore their understanding of coherence, consistency, and contradiction. Such exploration has led to the invention of non-Euclidean geometries and deviant logics, previously thought to be hopelessly incoherent, and to the discovery of paradoxes in areas such as transfinite mathematics that were previously thought to be coherent. Thus the range of logical possibilities expands and contracts, and stoics certainly have no doctrine that opposes creative work in logic and mathematics.

The point cannot be more straightforward: We reject the soundness of any normative proposition constructed from an agent's endeavor to do (directly) what she believes to be impossible. We do this because such endeavors are incoherent, in the sense that their propositional representation always tacitly involves an inconsistent pair of propositions: one about impossibility, to the effect that there are no available means to achieve a given end; the other about a contrary possibility, to the effect that there is a course of conduct that might be a way to achieve the same end. We do not deny the existence of such incoherence in human behavior or shrink from representing it in our logic, any more than we deny or shrink from representing conflicting norms. But the system of normative logic constitutes a formal representation of practical reasoning, and practical reasoning aims to resolve such conflict and incoherence. Thus persistent practical reasoning, while it will represent the phenomena of conflict and incoherence, will not allow them to remain as they are. It will somehow force a coherent, superordinate normative proposition from them.

Is this preferable to letting them stand? We think so. We agree that incoherent behavior can sometimes have useful results, for the agent or for us all. Agents may find it exhilarating. We may find it charming or noble; we may make it into moving narratives; it may expose errors in our beliefs about what is possible. But illness can have such results too. (It can be a liberating source of leisure; it can elicit the comforting care and concern of others; it can force us into productive new patterns of conduct.) This does not move us to recommend either incoherence or illness, especially when their beneficial effects are available in other ways. If the facts as you know them are that something is (currently) impossible for you to do, but you have good reason to think you could make it possible, and good reason to try, then you ought (at some normative level n) to try. Nothing in or implied by the Axiom of Futility says otherwise. If you do not know whether a given undertaking is possible, but have good reason to think you could find out, and good reason to try to find out, then you ought (at some normative level n) to run the investigation. All that stoic doctrine insists upon is that we distinguish such coherent meta-endeavors from incoherent direct attempts to do the impossible, and that we bring closure to practical reasoning about the incoherent ones by requiring that they not be pursued.

A *Posteriori* Normative Propositions

The axioms and rules of inference in our normative logic represent all norms as connected to the endeavors of some agent, and exclude *a priori* from moral deliberation only those normative propositions constructed (in part or in whole) from errors of fact. The short answer to why we do this is simply that we cannot find norms in matters of fact other than the endeavors of agents, and a commitment to following the facts means that (a) we must exclude falsehoods, and thus the normative propositions based on them, from our deliberations, but (b) we must not exclude, *a priori*, any normative propositions that *are* based on facts, no matter how bizarre, destructive, or repugnant they may be. Given the diversity, divergence, and conflict among human endeavors, following the facts in this way has sweeping and uncomfortable consequences for ethics. Some defense of the discomfort is in order.

Norms and individuals. Why connect all norms to facts about individual agents, and in particular the projects or endeavors of agents? We answer in three steps: first, that at least some norms do come from individual agents' endeavors; second, that endeavors conceived as "social facts" or institutions are not purposive, and thus do not generate or contain norms in the way that an individual's endeavors do; and third, that we can find no purposiveness, and no other source of norms, in anything other than the endeavors of individual agents.

About the first step we may now be very brief. It is evident that all projects or endeavors are by definition purposive, and have practices about who may participate and how participants may pursue their purposes. These features of the endeavors (goals, requirements, standards, ideals) are norm-making in the sense that, together with facts about the possibilities for a participant's conduct or character, they regulate behavior. And we represent such behavioral fact in our logic with propositions about what participants ought, or are required, to do or be, nothing-else-considered. All of the actual endeavors of individual agents, as opposed to hypothetical or fictive ones, are purposive and thus norm-making in this way, no matter whether they are as elaborate and institutionalized as trying a case in court or as evanescent as a child's solitary, improvised play. (Hypothetical or fictive endeavors have only hypothetical or fictive norm-making properties, and yield only hypothetical or fictive norms.)

Second, we insist that all actual endeavors, no matter how complex and social, are at bottom facts about the conduct and character of individual agents. Of course it may be that an endeavor like "speaking grammatical English," or "living by the rule of law," conceived of as a project common to a large number of people over many generations, will appear to have a social reality independent of the individuals participating in it. For example, participants may all believe that their understanding of the endeavor is imperfect—indeed, believe that no one individual has ever understood it completely—yet that all are participants in the same thing. Moreover, a thing may (like an economic system) have properties that can only be understood as emergent, systemic ones (as in macroeconomics). If so, then that thing—that system—does not reside, as it were, even as an intellectual object, in any individual agent. In what sense, then, are all the norms "it" generates facts about the conduct and character of individual agents? We answer that "it" generates no norms at all. Social systems are like weather systems: they are dynamic, but not purposive; they have direction, but not goals. When stoics gave up thinking of nature as a teleological system we gave up thinking of systems, period, as teleological. So it is misleading shorthand to speak of systems and social institutions as endeavors. They do not have the sort of norm-making properties that purposive agents do. When I endeavor to live by the rule of law, confess my incomplete knowledge of it, accept others (or perhaps some texts) as authorities on it and follow their edicts, the norms involved are all *my* norms, derived from *my* version of the endeavor of living by the rule of law.

Third, we assert that we can find no sets of facts about individual agents in which there are norm-making properties not attributable to their endeavors (projects, well-defined activities). For example, an affect or emotion untethered to a goal, or purpose, is normatively inert. Think of joy, or free-floating anxiety, experienced in a completely purposeless state. Or think of the recognition, in that purposeless state, that an object is beautiful, or excellent of its kind, or an effective means to some end that is not your own. We are in the normative equivalent of zero gravity in that case. We simply float along, flushing with pleasure, suffering, or appreciating a thing's value. Given some goals, such as the elimination of discomfort, and the possibility of doing that, we can generate norms easily enough. But to have the goals is to have an endeavor. We can find no norms that are untethered to endeavors, and no endeavors that are not facts about individual agents.

Particularity and truth. Stoic ethics is messy because the social world is messy. We begin (and end) our deliberations in terms of actual human beings, rather than hypothetical, idealized, or schematic ones.[2] We begin, then, by accepting every norm from every actual agent's actual endeavors as a matter of fact. We accept as matters of fact also any priorities agents attach to the norms from their own endeavors. Moreover, we make no special distinction between the norms our endeavors generate for ourselves (personal ones) and the norms those endeavors generate for others (social ones, whether their scope is local, regional, or universal). My commitment to fidelity may mean that I require it of you as well as myself, but both norms come from an endeavor of mine. They are *my* norms for us both.

We do, however, note that by definition, following the facts prohibits following false beliefs about what the facts are. Genocidal projects based on false anthropology are logically unsound, among other things. The same is true of benevolent endeavors based on false beliefs about the needs or wishes of the recipients. And in general, we may put the point this way: If any logically necessary premise in the derivation of a normative proposition is false, the derivation is unsound, and we discard any normative propositions logically implied by assuming (contrary to fact) that all the premises are true.

There is no *a priori* guarantee that the normative propositions (soundly) implied at any level n by my various endeavors will be logically consistent, and thus jointly possible to follow. For example, a single endeavor may itself make multiple, jointly unsatisfiable demands, none of which outranks another. Think of the project of giving each of several children an education optimal for intellectual development. Compare that to the project of playing favorites with those children. In the former case, if resources are scarce, the fact that the children are to be treated equally yields jointly unsatisfiable normative propositions, nothing-else-considered. In the latter case, favoritism "solves" the problem by ranking

---

[2] Thus the streamlining available to the advocates of universal, unconditional, *a priori* moral norms—the machinery that allows such theorists to rule out of account, from the beginning, a cacophony of actual human projects, such as suicide, sadism, slavery, murder, and lying, that are incompatible with some abstract standard of moral correctness—is not available to stoics. (We gladly leave that machinery to theology and its desiccated successors, such as intuitionism, natural rights theory, and various accounts of pure practical reason, including not only Kantian theories but utilitarian ones as well. Those theoretical enterprises are, as far as we can tell, purely speculative, and whatever normative force they have is due to the fact that some human beings are, as a matter of fact, engaged in these endeavors for the purpose of getting guidance for their conduct.) Human beings in their full particularity have conflicting aims, commitments, and desires. We all have such conflicts with others; most of us have them internally as well. Those are just the facts. Our logic must accommodate them all; it must follow the facts in that sense.

the competing norms. Stoics make no *a priori* rulings in favor of endeavors that give complete and determinate priorities for the norms they generate at a given level n. These conflicts are simply a matter of fact.

Similarly, it is a matter of fact that two or more of my endeavors may generate conflicting norms at level n. Let us say that endeavors are *integrated* with each other to the extent that the norms from one are hierarchically ordered with respect to the norms from the other, and that they are *isolated* from each other to the extent that their norms are of equal or indeterminate rank with respect to others. Think of the perennial conflict between career and family. It may be that for some people, these two aspects of their lives are so hierarchically arranged that no conflicts arise. But for many this is not so, because for them, in some cases at least, the requirements of their careers are neither superordinate nor subordinate to the requirements of family life. Again, stoics accept such conflicts as matters of fact about n-level norms.

Endeavors may be integrated horizontally or vertically. In our normative logic, we represent the horizontal variety with ordinal operators $(<, >)$ and the vertical variety by escalating the subscripts on the normative operators (e.g., from n to n + 1). Partial horizontal integration is a very common phenomenon. Let us say that an endeavor is *dictatorial* if its first-order norms have (for the agent) priority over norms from at least one other endeavor, and *tyrannical* if its first-order norms have priority (for the agent) over all other norms. Etiquette is an interesting example. For many agents, norms of propriety, hospitality, and common courtesy are social, not merely personal, and trump those of personal convenience and efficiency, at least at the margin. So etiquette is typically dictatorial in a way that gives an agent partial integration. In fact it is difficult to find any agent's project that is not hierarchically situated with respect to at least one other. Of course this is an empirical matter, but it is rare to find people for whom any set of first-order norms (such as etiquette) could plausibly be called tyrannical, and thus rare to find full horizontal integration among first-order norms. Suicidal religious or political zealotry might qualify, but other examples that come to mind are either fictional or highly speculative descriptions of people who seem to be relentlessly single-minded—whether in pursuit of holiness, knowledge, money, power, or glory.

Partial vertical integration is also very common. It can be achieved in two ways: First, if conflicting endeavors are embedded in a more comprehensive and controlling one, its norms will dominate. Think of the way staying trim for the sake of one's health is dominated by the more general, schematic project of staying healthy. It would be incoherent to pursue the former in a way that compromised the latter, but not vice versa. The two projects have a common goal, but staying trim is merely one way of trying to stay healthy—a way that does not always work. So when norms from the two come in conflict, such as when one gets medical advice to stop dieting, the norms from the more comprehensive and controlling of the two dominate. We represent that fact by writing them as normative propositions at level n + 1. Let us say, then, that endeavor e is more comprehensive and controlling than f for a given agent if and only if (a) they have a common goal and (b) undertaking f instantiates e for the agent—that is, f is, for the agent, a way (or part of a way) of undertaking e. Note that embedding is a matter of fact about particular agents, and not merely an abstract definitional or conceptual matter.

The second source of vertical integration is what we may call reformative assessment. It comes from the fact that some of our endeavors have the purpose of correcting errors in the norms generated by other endeavors. Judicial review of the constitutionality of statutes institutionalizes such assessment. But commentary of many sorts is reformative in this way. Art criticism, copyediting, cost-benefit analysis, ethics, political punditry, psychotherapy . . . all assess the adequacy of other endeavors. Unlike dictatorial projects, which seek to override others, these critical ones seek to improve what they assess. Thus they share (or at least do not attempt to displace) some of the aims and epistemic norms of their targets, and the norms they generate are meant to supersede others of the target. We represent this by writing them as normative propositions at level n + 1.

Practical reason. Every endeavor, because it seeks an end, poses practical problems for the agent—problems of clarifying and operationalizing the end, finding effective means for reaching the end within the constraints defined by the project, and generating norms of reformative assessment. Solving such practical problems is itself an encompassing project, which we may call practical reason, that is distinct from all others in part because it has a distinct aim (the integration of conflicting endeavors), and in part because, considered formally, as the effort to pursue ends effectively, all other projects are embedded in it. Its distinct aim, of achieving normative integration, is a consequence of its comprehensive, formal aim of implementing projects per se. Isolated endeavors, when they come into normative conflict with others, pose a practical problem that can only be solved by integrating the conflicting norms—by ranking them hierarchically with respect to one another. Without such integration, conflicts bring all the involved activities, including practical reason, to a halt. Like Buridan's ass, starving to death between piles of hay, the agent is unable to decide what to do. Practical reasoning, if it is to be adequate for its own purposes, then, must be able to integrate all the endeavors it assesses, either horizontally or vertically.

Practical reasoning achieves the normative integration of isolated endeavors in terms of its encompassing aim: to achieve success for every one of the agent's projects, over the agent's whole lifetime, and failing that, all but one, or all but two, etc. Note that this is not a maximization rule. It is rather an indiscriminate, relentless, implacable effort to implement every project, giving up on as few as possible. It is an optimization or minimization-of-loss rule, where no particular projects are favored *a priori*. All the agent's endeavors (and relevant facts about other agents and possibilities) are considered in the implementation of each endeavor, in the frame of the agent's life prospects. Thus the norms that practical reason generates are all-things-considered ones: "Given all relevant projects and possibilities throughout my whole life, I ought, now, to do (or be) *c*." The whole-life frame of reference allows an agent to solve some conflicts merely by sequencing the competing projects. The optimization rule generates efforts to redefine competing projects (e.g., by integrating them under a more comprehensive one, or by adjusting their norms so as to make them compossible), and to winnow the rest in terms of a preference for those that are most productive for the pursuit of the agent's other actual and potential aims. That much is implicit in the very concept of practical reasoning and is common to it all. We represent these things in our logic with the rules of transcendence and the axioms of encompassment and finality.

The details of the endeavor of practical reasoning vary significantly from agent to agent, however. For example, risk aversion, the discount rate for future prospects, and epistemic norms vary, and all are involved in the effort to integrate norms by sequencing endeavors. The integration a particular agent achieves in her projects, by whatever means, is a norm-generating matter of fact. Stoic ethics has no *a priori* commitment to a particular substantive account of practical reasoning, any more than it has an *a priori* commitment to a particular substantive form of economic analysis. The practical reasoning done by agents is, however, an object of intellectual inquiry about which there is a body of theory that is perpetually under construction, just as economic theory, logic, and mathematics are under development. Stoics follow the best theory they can find, or can construct, in all these matters. But we often disagree with each other about the details, and do not confuse theory with *a priori* truth.

Interpersonal integration. When my endeavor conflicts with yours in a way that makes it impossible for both to proceed, the problem is resolved for both of us if we find that, as a matter of fact, we agree on an interpersonal hierarchical ranking of the norms involved. Suppose I mow my lawn on Sunday mornings, while next door you are trying to achieve serenity, pray, and keep the day holy. If we happen to agree that your project is more important than mine, and thus dictates to mine, our problem is settled. We have interpersonal horizontal integration in that case. If we find that our conflicting Sunday morning endeavors are each embedded in a more encompassing project (tolerance in my case, neighborly love in yours), then we have the basis for another familiar sort of conflict resolution. It is a form of vertical integration to the extent that the encompassing projects are the same, or have "overlapping" elements; otherwise it is horizontal integration at n + 1. Moreover, the reformative assessment directed by the exercise of practical reason may generate norms at level n + 1 (for one or both of us) that resolve the issue. (I may find I can costlessly change my lawnmowing habits, thus avoiding unpleasant encounters with you; or you may find you can shut out the noise in some way that minimizes loss for you.)

Let us say that agents are normatively isolated from each other to the extent that neither one ranks her norms with respect to the norms of the other. Agents are in conflict if their interpersonal rankings do not agree—either because only one of the agents has such a ranking, or because their rankings differ. We will say that agents are normatively integrated to the extent that their interpersonal rankings are complete and congruent. For some agents, achieving such integration is a high priority, and utopians sometimes envision a world (or at least a moral theory) of complete harmony. Others, however, who like to fight, or compete, or be adversarial give normative integration lower priority. These conflicts appear to be endemic to human social life, and stoic ethics has no *a priori* commitment to achieving a complete integration of interpersonal norms, either in theory or in practice.

Motivated Norms

Motivation is built into our endeavors. To have a project is by that fact to be motivated to act in accord with the aims and constraints that define the project. Projects lapse, wax, and wane; they are adopted, postponed, subordinated, and abandoned; they are pursued wholeheartedly, halfheartedly, or in name only. Our motivation varies accordingly. The point is simply that the norms implicit in our endeavors are norms that we are by that fact motivated to follow. The motivation comes from two sources: from engaging in the endeavor itself, and from endeavoring to construct normative propositions from it. Almost all norms are motivated for the relevant agents in these ways (exceptions are discussed below under the heading *Heteronomous motivation*), since they are almost all tied to facts about the agents' own endeavors, and the exceptions, insofar as we exercise our agency with regard to them, are inevitably brought into our endeavors. The picture is more complex and problematic than this blunt description suggests, however.

Matched and mismatched motives. One such complexity arises from the way our projects may be unsettled by the process of constructing normative propositions about them. Sometimes, rather than being moved to follow the normative propositions we construct, we are moved to adjust or abandon the project, or adjust the logic of norm-construction in order to get normative propositions we can accept. Sometimes we abandon the process of norm-construction in order to do what we please. And in other cases we may be unable to resolve the problem at all—unable to give up norm-construction, unable to follow the normative propositions we do construct, and unable to adjust our projects or the logic of norm-construction to bring these things into accord. This suggests that there is no logical connection between pursuing a project (thus having its constitutive motivation) and being motivated to act in accord with the normative propositions that represent it.

The suggestion is misleading. The story about motivation becomes complicated only because the story about agents pursuing a project becomes complicated when they reflect on it and make explicit to themselves a propositional representation of its norms. When they do that, they may as a consequence (deliberately or not) refuse to accept or act in accord with the propositional representations of the norms, or simply find that they have no interest in acting on them. In that case the propositions are not any longer (if they ever were) accurate representations of the normative aspects of their project. This may be so because they have made an error in constructing the normative propositions. But more interestingly, it may be so because the project they are trying to represent in normative language (or the project of representing them itself) has shifted—has been changed as a consequence of their getting, or reflecting upon, an explicit propositional representation of it. The psychology of such reflexive transformation, fascinating as it may be, is not the issue here. We simply note that the norms we are concerned with are always matters of fact about agents' actual endeavors. When an endeavor is accurately represented in normative propositions, the motive constitutive of pursuing the endeavor will by that fact be a motive to act in the way represented by those normative propositions—a motive to act in accord with them. And when, for whatever reason, the normative propositions do not accurately represent the project, the motive internal to the endeavor will not be a motive to act in accord with them.

There is a further complication of some interest: Even when the normative propositions we construct from an endeavor e do not accurately represent e, we may be motivated to follow them as a consequence of the fact that we are motivated to pursue a distinct endeavor m that yields those norms "for" e. The very project of constructing normative propositions *from* e is such a distinct endeavor m, and the motive constitutive of pursuing it will by that fact be a motive to act in the way described by the normative propositions that accurately represent it. The set of normative propositions that accurately represents m will include those that are consequences of its operations on e. These normative propositions may or may not accurately represent the norms of e, and thus carry the motivation internal to e. But because they do accurately represent the norms of the distinct endeavor m, they will carry the motivation internal to that. In this way, every endeavor m to construct or assess another endeavor e may generate motivated norms for e, where the motivation comes *only* from m. Normative propositions at n + 1, and those that are unsubscripted (all-things-considered), often have this property. When they match (ratify, repeat) the lower order norms of e, then we have two sources of motivation to follow e. But when rational assessment, or norm-construction, generates normative propositions that do not accurately represent e, we have two mismatched sets of motivated norms in play for e—its own, and those constructed for it by a separate endeavor. Which set will determine our conduct?

The normative logic outlined in the Appendix contains determinate rules for dealing with mismatched norms. To the extent that our logic accurately represents an endeavor of norm-construction and assessment that people actually pursue, they will, by that fact, be motivated to resolve mismatches in the way outlined. But there is no *a priori* guarantee that the logic is descriptively accurate for everyone, and thus no guarantee that the motivational structure implicit in it will be universally or even widely applicable. Moreover, people may be motivated by the general nature of the endeavor described by the logic (or parts of it), but not by all of its details—for example, by the specifically stoic elements. We hold, however, that there is good reason to believe that the logic, even its stoic elements, is widely accurate as a description of the way practical reasoning operates in people's lives. Moreover, we hold that it generates a recommendation for itself, and on that basis, stoics recommend it to others. More argument for this will be given in the following sections, and in Chapters 6 and 7.

Motivated moral theory. Observation suggests that ad hoc practical reasoning, of a sort that involves conditional inferences, generalization, and error-correction routines, is built into human agents. The neurological capacity and propensity to process information in an instrumentally effective (and logically sound) way is evident very early in infancy, and appears to be a feature of early physiological development. Absent catastrophic limitations in our human endowments or circumstances, then—limitations of a sort that diminish or eliminate agency itself—we come equipped with, and use, logic circuits at a subconscious level, and we persist in doing so throughout our lives, much as we come equipped with and use the ability to register information through our senses. Moreover, as we acquire language, some of our subconscious information processing develops into (or perhaps is represented in) conscious instrumental reasoning in which we represent and process information about means and ends propositionally, and enter into what we have called the reformative assessment of our various projects. In the normal course of events, then, agents generate for themselves not only level-n normative propositions but many at n + 1 as well, and thus some ad hoc conceptual integration, both personal and interpersonal. Insofar as such reflection is one of the agent's projects, the integrative norms that it generates are motivated.

Furthermore, instrumental reasoning is reflexive: we can think of it as an endeavor, apply it to itself, and construct an account of its own norms. Observation also suggests that agents regularly develop, as they mature, a rough, incomplete, perhaps incoherent normative logic that they regularly use and refine. Moreover, through the iterative process of refining both the normative logic they use and the normative propositions they construct with it, many agents construct at least fragments of what might be called a normative theory—a representation of their practical reasoning in terms of formal rules of inference and assumptions, and a representation of the norms of their endeavors in terms of formal or schematic principles that more concrete normative propositions instantiate. Agents may thus introduce considerable (motivated) abstraction into their practices.

People differ considerably from one another, however, in the extent to which they follow this iterative process into its sweet theoretical reaches, and they appear to differ also in the degree to which they are motivated by the abstractions they construct from their projects, or recognize as constructable from them. After all, pursued in a thoroughgoing way, such theoretical reflection aims not only to solve ad hoc practical problems as they arise in daily life but to anticipate such problems, to take prophylactic measures to avoid them, and to represent those solutions in a logically coherent, comprehensive account of the way the agent's norms are ordered. In short, if one pursues practical reasoning in a thoroughgoing way, one aims at constructing a general theory of the normative elements of one's life all-things-considered—that is, a moral theory of one's life. The next step is to represent one's own life as an instance of a type, and to construct a moral theory for that type of life. Types of lives may then be considered as various ways in which moral agency itself may be expressed. And when one has reached the issue of normative propositions for the life of an agent as such, one has reached a form of universal moral theory.

Stoics in antiquity outlined the way they thought agents came to be motivated by universal moral theory in this sense. Their outline, reported in a compact way by Cicero in *De Finibus,* Book III.vff., is roughly consistent with contemporary developmental psychology, and is worth restating so as to remove unwarranted universalistic and metaphysical implications.

The outline begins with a thesis about the psychological primacy of narrow self-interest. The ancient stoics expressed this in terms of the infant's feeling of "attachment" for itself, impulse to preserve itself, and feelings of affection or antipathy for things according to whether they appear to help or hinder self-preservation. This sort of self-interest was distinguished sharply from mere pleasure-seeking or pain-avoidance of the sort Epicureans took to be primary. Here we will restate the point in terms of psychological egoism, without confining it to self-preservation: As infants we begin as thoroughly egocentric creatures, acting to satisfy our primal needs, drives, and impulses—including curiosity and various forms of sociability, playfulness, and task-accomplishment. We become attached to things that satisfy us, and motivated to get and keep such satisfying things; we become averse to things that dissatisfy us, and motivated to avoid them. To the extent that we experience a world that is generally satisfying, unthreatening, and predictable, we develop a basically trusting, confident, optimistic disposition. To the extent that our world is generally unsatisfying, threatening, and unpredictable, we develop a basically distrustful, anxious, pessimistic disposition. The psychological process involved here is one of "appropriation," or "attachment," or "making something our own" (*oikeiosis* in ancient stoic lingo), and it is central to every subsequent development.

The next step in the outline is the thesis that our affection for the things that satisfy our primal interests often becomes more or less independent, causally, from the things' ability to satisfy us. In antiquity there was a tendency to express this point by saying that we come to love such objects "for their own sakes." Another way to put it is to say that our egoistic affections and motivations become dispositional, and that those dispositions persist even when they no longer serve to satisfy the sort of primal self-interest that generated them. Thus our affections and motivations undergo a dramatic complication. The projects we are motivated to pursue (our interests and well-being in a wider sense) come to include not only the satisfaction of our primal needs, drives, and impulses, but the satisfaction of derivative ones that involve the creation, preservation, or enhancement of things that either impede primal need satisfaction or have no effect on it one way or the other. Thus primal needs for safety, food, comfort, social intercourse, and the like compete, for satisfaction, with needs to hold onto things that once did but no longer do satisfy those primal needs (at least in every instance).

The third step is the thesis that among the objects we develop a derivative, independent (widely self-interested) affection for is knowledge. We pursue it initially for its instrumental value in solving our immediate practical needs (including the satisfaction of curiosity, the resolution of perplexity, and the reduction of anxiety), but it soon becomes an object of independent interest. We are attracted to it, and to endeavors that generate it, independently of their connection to our narrowly egoistic concerns. We are repelled by error, ignorance, and falsehood. Modern studies of cognitive development, especially language acquisition, provide ample evidence of this.

The fourth step involves learning to translate this wide form of self-interest—our complicated affections and motivations—into "appropriate acts." Here the ancient stoics spoke in terms of developmental steps, which may be restated for present purposes in this way: We move from ad hoc narrowly self-interested pursuits to ad hoc widely self-interested pursuits (including the pursuit of knowledge), and thence to the discovery of regularities in the way things work. From these materials we formulate rules of conduct and principles of choice, which we begin to test in action. Over time, as we refine such rules and principles and use them instrumentally with increasing success, we become attached to conditioning our choices on our concept of "appropriateness"—that is, on their conformity to the rules and principles we construct. Acting appropriately (acting on principle) thus becomes for us an interest that motivates our conduct more or less independently of its effect on the pursuit of our other interests. Studies of cognitive development confirm the general accuracy of this as a (vague) description of an important feature of normal human maturation, but give us reason to be cautious in its use. In particular, we should note that mature individuals may vary widely in the strength and character of their "affection" for the pursuit of knowledge, and in their independent interest in acting on principle. We should be wary of interpreting this outline either as an account of rigidly sequential stages or as an endorsement of the idea that maturational progress is directly correlated, increment by increment, to strengthening an independent interest in acting on principle. It is nonetheless true, however, that in some individuals these normal developmental processes can (in psychological theory) motivate the pursuit of the most abstract sort of moral theory.

The final step in the outline is thus the thesis that through the operation of the ordinary, conscious psychological processes we call practical reasoning, together with the process of appropriation (*oikeiosis*), we can come to have an independent interest in moral virtue and good as such.

Even those most abstract, intellectualized norms can be motivated, and motivated strongly enough to order or override primal impulses. Does this mean that all agents become so motivated? No. Nor does it mean that all agents who are so motivated have acquired the motivation in this way. For one thing, the extent to which such motivation can be traced to conscious, intellectualized processes varies from individual to individual. And it may be that for many people, some or all of their most abstract norms are "heteronomous"—imperatives internalized from the categorical instructions of others, for example. The point is simply that agents can generate such motivated norms autonomously. Stoics have an affection for self-control—for autonomy rather than heteronomy—but the argument for cultivating that affection will come in the chapter on virtue.

Heteronomous motivation. Often we internalize norms when we are children (say, a prohibition on going to the movies on Sunday) that are part of the "project" of placating our parents—norms we conform to long after we have stopped trying to placate our parents at all, or at least to placate them in that way. Such vestigial or "orphaned" norms, untethered to the endeavors that generated them, may nonetheless continue to function as strong and exceedingly complex prohibitions, requirements, standards, ideals, or commitments. Any endeavor that we abandon or redefine can leave us with orphan norms in this way if we have pursued it to the point that acting in accord with its norms has become habitual or dispositional. The original endeavor disappears, leaving a residue of habit stripped of its original aim. In some cases we adopt these orphans into new endeavors—into an elaborate way of remembering or respecting the dead, for example, or of indulging in nostalgia, or of making arbitrary choices—in which case they cease to be orphans. In other cases they remain in their reduced state, and insofar as they intrude upon our more elaborate projects, they are a source of charming caprice, stubborn adherence to habit, or not so charming neurosis. There is a parallel in what happens with what we may call "alien" norms—those we internalize from the precepts or examples of authority figures, for instance ("Don't ever do that again!"), or from the rules or ideals we draw from traumatic or otherwise extraordinary experience. Sometimes we "naturalize" such norms by incorporating them into one or more of our other endeavors, in which case they cease to be alien. In other cases they remain unincorporated but resident, motivated prohibitions, requirements, standards, ideals, or commitments.

Both orphan and alien norms seem in a sense to govern our conduct from outside the normative logic of our endeavors. When we represent them in that logic, and must specify the endeavors from which the relevant normative propositions can be constructed, we find only a disappointing identity here: the endeavors behind the orphan or alien norms are simply identical to the norms themselves. The norms are not implicit in any project other than that constituted by their own normativity (motivational direction and momentum). Thus, insofar as that bare normativity remains orphaned or alien, it appears to come from outside any active endeavors that are genuinely our own. We may thus be tempted to regard such norms as heteronomous in the sense that the normative propositions that represent them cannot be constructed in the usual way. We would then regard a norm as autonomous if and only if it were implicit in one of our projects that was not simply identical to its own normativity.

We think this worry is resolved by the way in which following the facts captures such norms. The legitimacy of the label "heteronomous" aside, such norms are facts, and stoics do not ignore them. To "follow" such facts about one's life, however, is to be an agent with respect to them: and that involves recognizing them for what they are, no more or less. But to be an agent with respect to an orphan or alien norm is to embark on a project in which it will either be adopted or replaced. Consider the logical possibilities for agency here: (a) One is to resist the norm's motive force (reject it), thus adopting an endeavor whose aim is to resist, and in which the resisted norm is replaced by its contrary or contradictory. (b) Another is to ratify the norm's motive force (assent to it), thus adopting it into an endeavor whose aim is to act in accord with it. (c) A third is neither to resist nor ratify, reject nor assent, thus adopting an endeavor whose aim is to withhold both rejection and assent, and in which the orphan or alien is replaced either by a norm of indifference or by a conditional norm in which final judgment is explicitly reserved. Example: If I am forced to choose between x, the course of conduct prescribed by the orphan norm O, and y, which is something proscribed by O, then in terms of my endeavor e, I ought (am required) to choose x (or y), but not for the reason that it is prescribed (or proscribed) by O. (d) The last of the logical possibilities is to do some more or less complex combination of a–c. In every case the putatively heteronomous norm is incorporated in the usual way into the normative logic of our endeavors.

Heteronomous Endeavors, Autonomous Agency, and Freedom

We have considered the view that an agent's norms are autonomous if and only if the normative propositions that represent them are constructed (or constructable) from the features of that agent's own actual endeavors. We have argued that putatively heteronomous norms inevitably become, or are replaced by, autonomous ones when we exercise our agency with respect to them. But what of our ends or endeavors themselves? What of our agency? Some of our ends are autonomous in the sense that (like our genotypes) they are simply constitutive of our agency. Primal, impulse-driven, egoistic activity is an example, and so is a primitive form of practical reasoning. Other endeavors are autonomous in the sense that (like our adult bodies) they are the product of the growth and development of our natural endowments—in this case, of the interaction of the constitutive features of our agency (e.g., conflicting primal impulses ordered by primitive practical reasoning), or of the exercise of our agency either upon them or upon the external world. There are two troubling ideas raised by this picture, however. One is that many of our endeavors do not appear to be autonomous in either sense, but rather to be imposed on us from sources external to us. If so, then they are in a fairly strong sense not our own endeavors, and thus perhaps not something that should be represented in our normative logic in the same way as autonomous ones. The other troubling idea is that the whole notion of autonomy might founder on the question of agency. To the extent that autonomous endeavors are simply the determinate products of our natural endowments and circumstances, there might be no significant difference, in terms of human freedom and responsibility, between having heteronomous endeavors and having autonomous ones. Indeed, the response to the first issue shifts the whole burden onto the second.

Heteronomous ends. Any project we deliberately adopt by the exercise of our agency—that is, through carrying out some autonomous endeavor to adopt it—meets the criterion for autonomous norms. We can construct the normative propositions that represent its norms (including its ends) via the normative logic of our endeavors. Some projects do not meet that criterion, however. We acquire some of our ends unwittingly, blotting them up from parents or peers through complex learning processes (e.g., classical or operant conditioning, imitation, suggestion, submission to demands) that are largely subliminal forms of appropriation. Moreover, even when we are aware that we are being manipulated or conditioned into appropriating such ends, we may nonetheless feel compelled to adopt them. We may acquire a whole ordered set of projects—even a "vocation"—in this way. These are troubling to us as agents when we reflect on the way such heteronomous endeavors may defeat or control the successful exercise of our agency. Stoics hold, however, that when we exercise our agency upon heteronomous ends, endeavors, ordered sets of endeavors, or even a vocation or way of life, we inevitably convert heteronomy to autonomy—just as in the case of isolated heteronomous norms. We have the same four possibilities for the exercise of our agency: to endeavor to reject the alien thing, to accept it, to do neither, or to do some mixture of the three. All of the possibilities either incorporate the alien endeavor into an autonomous one, or replace it with an autonomous one.

The question that remains is whether our agency is itself autonomous—whether its exercise is within its own control.

Autonomous agency. Stoics hold that agency defines autonomy. Its every exercise is self-transformative in the sense that it captures a set of data (that which is given) and forms it into something new—for example, a discrete experience, a perception, a preference, an endeavor, a normative construct. Agency is itself a datum, a given, but when conscious of itself, it operates transformatively upon itself as well—capturing in self-consciousness a set of data about its operations and forming the data into something new, such as a self-concept, a self-image, a proprietary personal space, an endeavor about its own operations, or a logic representing those operations. In that sense agency governs or transforms everything it is given to work with, itself included. That, it seems to us, is the very definition of autonomy.

Stoics also hold that agency, like all the other properties of an individual, is generated by a deterministic process, and operates deterministically. That is, we hold that whether or not a given human being is an agent at all, or has agency with certain specific powers, is a contingent matter, wholly dependent on an elaborate conjunction of antecedent conditions. If those antecedent conditions occur, the agency will occur.

Some might think that this somehow undermines the claim that agency defines autonomy, since by stringing together a series of transitive conditionals we can create the impression that agency is no different from, say, our digestive processes. Digestion, too, operates upon what it is given, and transforms some of it (the digestible items) into something new. It can transform itself, too, as in the case of ulcers produced by gastric acid. And of course like agency, digestion is a deterministic process. It is true of both that if certain antecedent events occur, we have them, and then if we have them, certain consequences follow from that, and so on. The thought is that there is nothing autonomous in either case, since both processes arise and operate only as the determinate products of antecedent causes, and their consequences are transitively determinate products of the same antecedents.

This line of thought raises three interesting questions. Leaving aside, for the moment, whether anything we do is accurately described as autonomous, one question is whether agency has a better claim than other elements of our constitution to be identified with autonomy. Another is whether agency, when exercised, is always controlling (*nomic*), let alone *auto*nomic. The third is whether the notions of determinism and autonomy are compatible. We address the first here, and the others in subsequent sections.

On the issue of which of our powers, if any, might plausibly be identified with autonomy, we fail to see how similarities among them undermine the crucial difference between agency and the rest. To carry on with the amusing example, digestion is limited to the digestible and transforms only that. Presumably (though some of us can stomach it better than others) agency is not a digestible thing. Nothing, however, is so-to-speak unagentable for agency. The scope of its operation is in principle unlimited, though of course it does not do the same work as other elements of our nature. Thus, though indigestion may occasionally disturb or distort agency, and the digestion of hemlock may abruptly terminate it, agency is the more comprehensive process. Unlike our other constitutive powers (digestion, sensory apparatus, cardiovascular system, and so forth), agency can be exercised upon any object, and its exercise always has a self-transformative effect. It cannot replace our other powers, but it can always in principle operate transformatively on them all and on itself. Its identification with the notion of autonomy is warranted.

Weak agency. It is clear, however, that what agency can do in principle it does not always do in practice. This should not be surprising, since fully developed agency is perhaps the most complex of our constitutive powers. To see that the traditional problem of weakness of "will" is only part of the problem of weak agency, we need only consider a very sketchy account of its development.

Begin with our genetic endowments, as initially expressed in the constitutive powers of an infant. Just as one infant's sensory powers may differ widely from another's, so too there may be great variation in their hardwired conative powers—their (nondeliberative) ability and propensity to process their primal impulses into goal-oriented activities, to register and process information in a way that accurately identifies means for achieving those goals, to select one goal from among competing ones, to select one means from those available, and to stay focused upon the ones selected and pursue them. Like its sensory apparatus, an infant's hardwired conative powers can be reduced or eliminated by neurological damage. Like its primal impulses, the infant's conation is transformed by conditioning and other psychodynamic processes—in ways that introduce additional variation among individuals, especially perhaps in matters connected to the development of basic psychological "tenors," or dispositions, such as anxiety, trust, optimism, quiescence, risk aversion, aggression, and so forth. Those recursive psychodynamic processes operate throughout our lives, and coupled with the acquisition of language and the development and exercise of our cognitive and nondeliberative conative powers, typically transform conation into a conscious and deliberative, as well as nondeliberative, power.

Whether this transformation increases or decreases variation among individuals is a nice empirical question. The linguistic representation of the logic of our deliberative processes (by those who attend to this project seriously) has certainly become quite uniform at its core, and perhaps it is the case that it represents phenomena that are equally uniform, formally. But it is obvious that there are great variations in the extent to which we exercise our agency, and exercise it in deliberation; great variations in the objects upon which we exercise it, and the salience of those objects for us; great variations in the extent to which our actions are conditioned upon conscious choice, our choices are conditioned upon deliberation, and our deliberation is thorough. At each of those junctures agency may function very weakly or not all relative to our other constitutive powers. Weakness of will, understood narrowly as the extent to which action is conditioned on choice (or even deliberation and choice), is only a small part of the issue of weak agency.

A further empirical question is the extent to which agency is robust, regenerative, and self-corrective with respect to the operations of other physical and psychological processes. We know that addictions, for example, deform our deliberative powers, particularly at the juncture between deliberation and choice. We know fear and anxiety (and complex adaptations to traumatic experience) can severely inhibit deliberation—even in extreme cases apparently extinguish agency altogether, as in catatonia. We know that some kinds of neurological damage, and routine forms of conditioning, introduce systematic errors into our deliberations—both perceptual and logical errors, prejudices, and fallacious patterns of inference.

Stoics hypothesize that agency is very robust, meaning (a) that it is, in any form, highly resistant to extinction through other psychological processes; (b) that when exercised at all, no matter how weakly in relation to our other constitutive powers, it tends to increase its relative strength; and (c) that agency can thus become in material effect, through its own exercise, the most comprehensive and controlling of our constitutive powers—one that is characterized by the form of practical reasoning all-things-considered that we represent as moral reasoning in our normative logic. We hypothesize that agency is regenerative, meaning (d) that when extinguished (by physical or psychological trauma short of death or permanent coma) it is highly likely to be rebootable, and in some cases to reboot spontaneously. We hypothesize that it is self-corrective, meaning (e) that when it develops systematic errors, they tend to be reduced or corrected, rather than increased, by its further exercise. It should be emphasized that these are put forward as empirical hypotheses, not *a priori* truths. We believe they are plausible, given current findings in neurophysiology and psychology, but it is clear that, should they be falsified, we would have to rethink many matters.

Determinism. We hold that human freedom consists in the exercise of agency. We hold that agency is the determinate product of antecedent events and that its exercise has determinate outcomes. And our logic of descriptive bases is bivalent: all its propositions are either true or false, and not both or neither. Critics have held that we are thus committed to fatalism, or at least to a form of determinism incompatible with human freedom. Some stoics have (perhaps for rhetorical purposes) mistakenly agreed. The candid response is that we simply do not see any plausibility in either of these criticisms.

We are certainly not categorical fatalists. Fatalism of that sort holds that every categorical proposition about the future is either true or false, period. Whatever will be, will be, no matter what. Such a doctrine leaves out the determinate effect of antecedent events altogether. In our view, many truths about the future are truths about events that will occur as the determinate result of antecedent events, and are thus implicit conditionals: if such and such happens, then so and so happens. That is very far from the idea that so and so will happen no matter what antecedent events occur.

The remaining charge, however, is that such determinism (or conditionalized fatalism) leaves no possibility for anything to happen other than what does happen. We demur here also, by calling attention to the way we interpret the notions of necessity and possibility. As indicated in the chapter on logic, we interpret necessity in terms of logical truth—specifically the logical truth of material conditionals in a specified universe of discourse (e.g., an unrestricted, theoretical, or practical discourse). To say that, given certain antecedent events, a certain consequent event must occur (could not have been otherwise), is to say that the corresponding material conditional is logically true in a specified universe of discourse. That is, it is to say that the conditional $A \supset C$ is always true in the specified domain when A is the conjunction of propositions representing the antecedent conditions and C is the proposition representing the consequent event. That is our concept of necessary connection, causation, determined events. Note that by itself it does not imply that the only logically true conditional with C as its consequent is $A \supset C$; nor does it imply that whenever C is true some conditional of that sort is logically true.

Our view until the middle of the twentieth century was that all events were the determinate products of some particular set of antecedents. We now follow physicists in rejecting that unrestricted claim, but since we still hold that it is true about the genesis and operations of human agency, we are still apparently subject to the charge that human freedom cannot consist in the exercise of agency.

To this we respond with three by now familiar observations. The first is that if freedom is taken to mean indeterminacy, then it means that any thing that occurs freely cannot be represented as the consequent of a logically true conditional of the sort represented above by $A \supset C$. Thus it would follow that if it is true that some free human act will occur to-morrow, it is true that it will occur *no matter what its antecedents*. That is categorical fatalism again, and not a happy result for defenders of freedom.

The second observation is that it will not help to give up bivalence and to suppose that statements about our future acts are neither true nor false. That assumption, combined with freedom interpreted as indeterminacy, merely restricts categorical fatalism to the past and present: every free act that occurs, occurs no matter what its antecedents were. Thus, for exam-ple, on that view, free acts are not conditioned upon deliberation and choice—or if both those things are included in the definition of an action, then free acts in this expanded sense are not conditioned on the states of affairs that ratify the beliefs involved in deliberation. Deliberation, and thus freedom, is untethered to information. This sort of fatalism is no less problematic for freedom than the first sort.

The third observation is simply that we can avoid fatalism of both sorts by taking human freedom to consist in the determinative effect we have, through the exercise of our agency, on what happens in our lives—*including what happens with regard to the exercise of our agency itself*. Without our agency, things happen independently of our desires, prefer-ences, and purposes, whether as the product of antecedent conditions or not. Through the exercise of our agency, insofar as it has determinate effects, events are conditioned upon our desires, aims, deliberation, and choice. Since we imagine that deliberation and choice are themselves the products of antecedent events, we concede that the choices we make (or do not make) are necessary in the sense we have outlined. In that sense, each step we take by means of our agency is determined transitively by antecedents to it, and working forward by stepwise induction, there is only one journey via our agency that is possible for us—the journey defined by the complete series of steps necessitated by it and its antecedent conditions.

Notice that this is not at all conducive to the erroneous idea that some-how our destinies are fixed by particular, isolated events in the distant past. Conditional fatalism thrives on that idea, feeding despair about the power of our agency to determine our conduct. But human bodies adjust moment by moment to changes in the environment—changes in tempera-ture, light, background noise, microbes—and continue to function, often without discernable effects at the level of our gross motor activity, some-times with discernable but trivial effects. Human agency has equally pow-erful adjustment mechanisms, and the causal story of what we are doing at a particular moment can never be given in terms of a few isolated events. Rather, the story of what we are doing at a particular moment is the story of one causal thread of our whole lives to that point. (More grandly, one causal thread of the universe.) Some such threads involve the processes described as the exercise of agency, and others do not. Insofar as agency is not a causal factor, what we do is not conditioned upon our conscious pursuit of ends.

We certainly agree that such a life is not radically autonomous, or free from antecedent conditions. But consider, now, two alternatives: on the one hand a life in which agency plays no causal role, and on the other a life in which agency plays a persistent and pervasive part in the causal story of its every waking moment. We stoics simply report that we prefer our lives to be of the second sort, and find the idea of that kind of life more than sufficient to assuage our longing for autonomy and metaphysical liberty.

Responsibility. Moreover, we are not dismayed by the conception of (moral) responsibility that is implicit in this deterministic picture of the world. It is simply this: agents are fully responsible for their acts if and only if they (a) are aware of what they are doing; (b) are aware of the causes of their actions; (c) assent to acting in those ways from those causes—that is, are acting in accord with norms they recognize as their own; (d) are aware of the causes of their assent—that is, the causes of their own norms; (e) thereby introduce new causal factors into the determination of their actions through their awareness of the causal conditions that shape it; (f) are aware of this iterative, self-transformative causal process; and (g) assent to that, in the sense that they recognize that this process is normative for them.

This account of responsibility locates it squarely "inside" the agent—within a particular constellation of abilities that agents may or may not have. On this account, when the responsibility of an agent is diminished—when to some degree he lacks these abilities—then to that degree his conduct is determined by external factors operating either directly or only through his primal agency. When he is fully responsible, however (fully an agent), then his conduct is determined by his agency acting upon, through, and in terms of its primal elements and factors external to it. We have sometimes expressed this by making a distinction between things that are "up to the agent" (within the agent's control), and things that are not. This is probably a tactical error, for it erroneously suggests a paradox to our critics. They charge that on the one hand we assert that everything operates deterministically, while on the other we assert that agents somehow stand outside the causal chain of events and have some sort of radical (undefined) autonomy with respect to it. As should now be clear, we do not assert the second part of that at all. Rather, we assert that the agency generated in some links of the cosmic causal chain has remarkable causal powers *within* that chain, and that the remarkable causal powers outlined in (a)–(g) above can quite plausibly be the basis for saying that an *agent* (and not something else) is responsible for his acts. There is no paradox in that position.

A free life without metaphysical liberty. We despair of finding a way to say more to solve the riddle of determinism for people who are attracted to it. We are not attracted to it in the least. In the final analysis, perhaps, the reason for our lack of interest in it comes from our view that a life without metaphysical liberty can still be a life of undiminished virtue and happiness. If that is true, then given the aims of stoic ethics, what remains of the riddle of determinism is of no ultimate importance. Here is one line of argument for that conclusion.

Negative liberty is the absence of impediments to action. Positive liberty is the presence of the means necessary for effective choice and action. So conceived, negative liberty is not a "thing," but rather the absence of something. It is like the hole in a doughnut; take away the doughnut and it is hard to see the hole at all, let alone regard it as valuable; take away the impediments to action, and negative liberty as an "object" vanishes with them. So it may be wise to organize a discussion of the value of negative liberty by beginning with *things*, rather than the spaces they leave—in this case by looking at the impediments rather than at the space those impediments define. When we do that, it is clear that among impediments, as among doughnuts, some are good and some are bad, from the user's point of view. The friction caused by an obstacle is sometimes a necessary condition for doing what we want to do, and when it is, we see the obstacle as valuable. In fact, valuable impediments provide us with another sort of liberty—positive or material liberty. If the impediment is a good one, the corresponding negative liberty—or absence of the impediment—is derivatively bad. We should be able to learn all we need to know about the derivative values of derivative things (such as holes and other spaces) by immediate inference from the things that define them.

Positive liberty, by contrast, is not the absence of something but rather the presence of it: the presence, indeed the possession, of the means necessary for action. It is the "stuff" we require in order to act in the space provided by negative liberty. The presence of social and political institutions gives us some of the means—the liberty—to lead lives that we could not otherwise have. So do friends, courage, physical strength. We ordinarily resist labeling such things as liberty, but the description of economic resources, education, and many other things as "liberating" is surely a warrant for the label, and it is unassailable that negative liberty alone is of very little importance unless one can or might be able to use it. For using it, some resources (psychological and physical) are necessary, and we may plausibly speak of them as constituting our positive or material liberty.

Now consider the question of whether liberty of either sort is a necessary condition for a good life. Why should it be? Suppose my name is Calvin, and suppose that my creator has predestined every detail of my life, every nuance of my thought and action, including the fact that through theological study I have now discovered that my life is predetermined. Does this mean that I have not had a good life to this point, or that I cannot continue to have one? I have no genuine liberty at all to do anything other than what God has planned for me. I am, in effect, a total slave to God. But I certainly *think* I have a good life. I remember, and feel, and feel joy, anticipation, fear, responsibility, pride, guilt, shame, and obligation. I fear judgment. I do not know how things will turn out for me, but I suspect I am one of the elect, and am glad for that. In any case, I know that whatever happens, it will be exactly as God has planned. In the meantime, I will live the life that I have been given. Given God's will, nothing else could have happened. I was never at liberty to do other than I did in fact do. I had a life without liberty. But I rejoice in it, and affirm it anew every day.

End of story. Now what is wrong with it? It surely does not suggest that we cannot have good lives without liberty. Negative liberty, in general terms, is the space left to us by the political, social, personal, and metaphysical impediments that surround us; positive liberty is the stuff that enables us to act in that space. What Calvin imagines is that *the space and stuff available to him are enough for exactly one life*—the one God has given him to live, without liberty.

Enough for one life is enough.

Commentary

Naturalism. The sense in which stoicism, and ancient Greek ethical theories generally, are forms of ethical naturalism, is described succinctly in Annas, *The Morality of Happiness*, 135ff. She notes that if we define naturalism by contrasting it with intuitionism, and draw that contrast in terms of whether the theory treats moral terms and properties as definable in or reducible to nonmoral ones, then treating ancient moral theories as naturalistic is problematic at best. But she continues:

> Ethical naturalism can of course be taken more generously. . . . If we reject the demand to be reductive . . . we can still be left with something that can fairly be called ethical naturalism, namely a position which insists on grounding ethical claims in facts about nature that support those ethical claims. This is general enough to form a spectrum of positions, of which reductive versions would merely form one extreme. . . . (136)

We are certainly not reductivists about meaning or concept formation, for example in a way that follows the early logical positivists. But in one respect at least we advance a form of naturalism that is closer to a "reductive" extreme than some will find comfortable, for we do insist that normative propositions can be soundly constructed only from facts about the purposive endeavors of agents. But that sort of reductivism (if the label is apt) is simply a consequence of three things that are unavoidable for stoicism today. One is the development of the empirical method, which of course began to affect stoicism even in antiquity, and to turn it away from flippant speculation about physical processes. (For Galen's scathing and hilarious critique of *a priori* arguments by Zeno, Chrysippus, and Diogenes of Babylon to the effect that the heart, rather than the brain, was the source of speech, and thus discourse, and thus the mind, see Galen, *On the Doctrines of Hippocrates and Plato* II.5) A second thing is the collapse of the notion that the cosmos, or Nature as a whole, can most plausibly be understood as a rational being. And the third is what we have learned from the exacting metaethical investigations pursued by philosophers in the twentieth century.

Annas argues that for the Greeks generally, the notion of nature—in particular human nature—that figured most strongly in ethical theory was not one of "neutral, 'brute' fact; it [was] strongly normative" (137). It concerned

> the goal or end of human development; the natural life [was] the life led by humans who have developed in a natural way, this being understood as a way in which the potentialities which for us are given develop without interference from other, external factors. It is obvious that this . . . use of nature presupposes two things. One is that we can in fact distinguish between the thing's or person's nature and outside influences that count as interferences with that nature. . . . The second assumption is that we can distinguish between what forms an expression of a person's nature and what forms a corruption of it—between a natural and an *un*natural development. (136)

See also on this point Long "The Logical Basis of Stoic Ethics," (88), and Gill, "The Human Being as an Ethical Norm." This sort of claim is implicitly unpacked here (some might say unraveled) in the section on motivated norms, and in the account in Chapter 6 of how a preference for health over ill health, fitness over mere health, and virtuosity over fitness leads to the identification of virtue with perfected agency, and motivates a commitment to virtue as one's final end.

Oikeiosis *and the cradle argument.* Brunschwig, in "The Cradle Argument in Epicureanism and Stoicism," reminds us that cradle arguments, with varying premises, were common currency in Hellenistic ethics. He is rather dubious of the worth of the arguments as he pieces them together, but his comments on Hierocles, at pp.138–40—particularly on the way Hierocles complicates his version of the cradle argument by introducing a premise about the developmental effects of the child's powers of representation—are intriguing.

In any case, in our view the linchpin of the stoic account of moral development is the psychological process through which the newborn's self-interest becomes the infant's interest in and affection for things that serve self-interest and other primal impulses, which thence becomes the child's interest in and affection for such things independent of whether they serve those impulses, which in turn becomes an affection for acting appropriately, and so forth. See White, "The Basis of Stoic Ethics"; Striker, "The Role of Oikeiosis in Stoic Ethics"; and Engberg-Pedersen, *The Stoic Theory of Oikeiosis,* on this point as it relates to the ancient texts. In each developmental step toward the sage's eventual attachment to virtue as the final end, the causal process is the same. The ancient stoics called this psychological process *oikeiosis,* which has variously been translated as endearment, making a thing belong to the agent, familiarization, attachment, incorporation, or appropriation. (*Oikeion* is opposed to *allotrion,* what is alien. *Oikeiosis* descends from the word for house, in an extended sense of household that includes virtually anything and anyone closely related to the house. See Pembroke, "Oikeiosis," for an account of the history of the term, the distinctive stoic use of it, and the thought that "if there had been no *oikeiosis,* there would have been no Stoa.") Striker, in "The Role of Oikeiosis in Stoic Ethics" (145), says "The Greek term is usually not translated, but transliterated; not because it is untranslatable, but because any translation would seem to be intolerably clumsy. What it means can perhaps be rendered as 'recognition and appreciation of something as belonging to one'; the corresponding verb . . . as 'coming to be (or being made to be) well-disposed toward something.' " We often use the metaphor of attachment in our text because it seems a good fit with contemporary psychological theory. But Long and Sedley, in *The Hellenistic Philosophers* (351), make a strong case that "appropriation" better suits the ancient texts:

> 'Alienation' and 'appropriation' are literal translations of the Greek terms *allotriosis* and *oikeiosis.* Their English associations with property ownership capture the main force of the Stoic concepts here, though any translation will miss something of the original. The advantage of 'appropriation' is its providing a means, through the verb or adjective 'appropriate', of rendering grammatically related forms of the Greek root *oik-.* This connotes ownership, what belongs to something, but in Stoic usage that notion is also conceived as an affective dispo-

sition relative to the thing which is owned or belongs. Hence the English associations of 'appropriation' with forcible possession are to be discounted in our translations. Correspondingly, the notion of claiming or desiring ownership needs to be read in our translation of the adjective *oikeion* by 'appropriate'. So [for example] the 'first thing appropriate to every animal', means the first thing 'fitting' or 'suitable', but the relevant suitability is like that of a house to its owner, a recognition of ownership, or like that of a kinsman to a blood relation, a recognition of affinity coupled with affection.

This is sobering, and suggests that our use of attachment in this context might be too weak.

We think the best source in the ancient texts for a summary of this developmental story is in Cicero, *De Finibus* III. The story was told and retold in many texts. Long, in "The Logical Basis of Stoic Ethics," reconstructs and analyzes the logic of the version in Diogenes Laertius, *Lives of the Eminent Philosophers* VII. 85–88, in detail. And as one might guess, a variety of texts on this point are excerpted and compared helpfully in Long and Sedley, *The Hellenistic Philosophers*, section 58ff. But that otherwise admirable book presents stoic ethics in conformity with an ancient stoic "division" of ethics that (in our view) obscures and dilutes the continuity and power of the developmental story.

Even a straight run through Cicero's exposition, however, shows that a good deal of work needs to be done to dig out the structure of the argument. Engberg-Pederson, in "Discovering the Good: Oikeiosis and Kathekonta in Stoic Ethics," has done this thoroughly and lucidly, though we think his disputes with Striker ("The Role of Oikeiosis in Stoic Ethics") and Long ("The Logical Basis of Stoic Ethics") are unhelpful. Engberg-Pedersen, in "Stoic Philosophy and the Concept of Person," has a useful discussion of the conception of subjectivity, objectivity, and the concept of the person implicit in this developmental story. We are less at ease with his book-length study (Engberg-Pedersen, *The Stoic Theory of Oikeiosis*) in several respects, though we certainly agree with the general line in chapter 4 of his book that there is no great trick to getting a moral argument (in addition to a description of development) out of *oikeiosis* and the cradle argument. Moreover, we agree with him that the key to doing this lies in noticing the way agents reflect upon and generalize beliefs about themselves. His reconstruction is limited by the terms of his project, which is primarily historical, but is refreshing and illuminating on many points. Our endorsement of the central point about the reflexive, iterative processes of rationality comes from cognitive psychology, however (e.g., the work of Piaget; see Flavell, *Cognitive Development*, 2d ed.), and not from an analysis of the ancient texts.

It is worth quoting Cicero's text at some length, so it can be conveniently compared to the version of the cradle argument offered here in Chapters 5 and 6. The quotation is from Cicero, *De Finibus* III.v–vi, in the Loeb translation by H. Rackham. Cato is speaking to Cicero on behalf of stoicism.

V. [Cato] began: "It is the view of those whose system I adopt, that immediately upon birth (for that is the proper point to start from) a living creature feels an attachment for itself, and an impulse to preserve itself and to feel affection for its own constitution and for those things which tend to preserve that constitution; while on the other hand it conceives an antipathy to destruction and to those things which appear to threaten destruction. In proof of this opinion [stoics] urge that infants desire things conducive to their health and reject things that are the opposite before they have ever felt pleasure or pain; this would not be the case, unless they felt an affection for their own constitution and were afraid of destruction. But it would be impossible that they should feel desire at all unless they possessed self-consciousness, and consequently felt affection for themselves. This leads to the conclusion that it is love of self which supplies the primary impulse to action. Pleasure on the contrary, according to most Stoics, is not to be reckoned among the primary objects of natural impulse; and I very strongly agree with them, for fear lest many immoral consequences would follow if we held that nature has placed pleasure among the earliest objects of desire. But the fact of our affection for the objects first adopted at nature's prompting seems to require no further proof than this, that there is no one who, given the choice, would not prefer to have all the parts of his body sound and whole, rather than maimed or distorted although equally serviceable.

"Again, acts of cognition (which we may term comprehensions or perceptions, or, if these words are distasteful or obscure, *katalepseis*),—these we consider meet to be adopted for their own sake, because they possess an element that so to speak embraces and contains the truth. This can be seen in the case of children, whom we may observe to take pleasure in finding something out for themselves by the use of reason, even though they gain nothing by it. The sciences also, we consider, are things to be chosen for their own sake, partly because there is in them something worthy of choice, partly because they consist of acts of cognition and contain an element of fact established by methodical reasoning. The mental assent to what is false, as the Stoics believe, is more repugnant to us than all the other things that are contrary to nature.

"(Again, of the members or parts of the body, some appear to have been bestowed on us by nature for the sake of their use, for example the hands, legs, feet, and the internal organs, as to the degree of whose utility even physicians are not agreed; while others serve no useful purpose, but appear to be intended for ornament: for instance the peacock's tail, the plumage of the dove with its shifting colours, and the breasts and beard of the male human being.) All this is perhaps somewhat baldly expressed; for it deals with what may be called the primary elements of nature, to which any embellishment of style can scarcely be applied, nor am I for my part concerned to attempt it. On the other hand, when one is treating of more majestic topics the style instinctively rises with the subject, and the brilliance of the language increases with the dignity of the theme."
"True," [Cicero] rejoined; "but to my mind, any clear statement of an important topic possesses excellence of style. It would be childish to desire an ornate style in subjects of the kind with which you are dealing. A man of sense and education will be content to be able to express his meaning plainly and clearly."
VI. "To proceed then," [Cato] continued, "for we have been digressing from the primary impulses of nature; and with these the later stages must be in harmony. The next step is the following fundamental classification: That which is in itself in accordance with nature, or which produces something else that is so,

and which therefore is deserving of choice as possessing a certain amount of positive value—*axia* as the Stoics call it—this they pronounce to be 'valuable' (for so I suppose we may translate it); and on the other hand that which is the contrary of the former they term 'valueless.' The initial principle being thus established that things in accordance with nature are 'things to be taken' for their own sake, and their opposites similarly things to be 'rejected,' the first 'appropriate act' (for so I render the Greek *kathekon*) is to preserve oneself in one's natural constitution; the next is to retain those things which are in accordance with nature and to repel those that are the contrary; then when this principle of choice and also of rejection has been discovered, there follows next in order choice conditioned by 'appropriate action'; then, such choice becomes a fixed habit; and finally, choice fully rationalized and in harmony with nature. It is at this final stage that the Good properly so called first emerges and comes to be understood in its true nature. Man's first attraction is towards the things in accordance with nature; but as soon as he has understanding, or rather has become capable of 'conception'—in Stoic phraseology *ennoia*—and has discerned the order and so to speak harmony that governs conduct, he thereupon esteems this harmony far more highly than all the things for which he originally felt an affection, and by exercise of intelligence and reason infers the conclusion that herein resides the Chief Good of man, the thing that is praiseworthy and desirable for its own sake; and that inasmuch as this consists in what the Stoics term *homologia* and we with your approval may call 'conformity'—inasmuch I say as in this resides that Good which is the End to which all else is a means, moral conduct and Moral Worth itself which alone is counted as a good, although of subsequent development, is nevertheless the sole thing that is for its own efficacy and value desirable, whereas none of the primary objects of nature is desirable for its own sake. But since those actions which I have termed 'appropriate acts' are based on the primary natural objects, it follows that the former are means to the latter. Hence it may correctly be said that all 'appropriate acts' are means to the end of attaining the primary needs of nature. Yet it must not be inferred that their attainment is the ultimate Good, inasmuch as moral action is not one of the primary natural attractions, but is an outgrowth of these, a later development, as I have said. At the same time moral action is in accordance with nature, and stimulates our desire far more strongly than all the objects that attracted us earlier. But at this point a caution is necessary at the outset. It will be an error to infer that this view implies two Ultimate Goods. For though if a man were to make it his purpose to take a true aim with a spear or arrow at some mark, his ultimate end, corresponding to the ultimate good as we pronounce it, would be to do all he could to aim straight: the man in this illustration would have to do everything to aim straight, and yet, although he did everything to attain his purpose, his 'ultimate End,' so to speak, could be what corresponded to what we call the Chief Good in the conduct of life, whereas the actual hitting of the mark would be in our phrase 'to be chosen' but not 'to be desired.' "

The obscurities in this outline have made heavy weather for scholars on several points—for example, on the issue of how self-interest can generate genuine altruism, whether cosmic *telos* plays a logically necessary role in the argument, or whether Cicero is giving an argument in ethical theory at all, as opposed to a description of psychological development. On the last point see Striker, "The Role of Oikeiosis in Stoic Ethics," versus Engberg-Pedersen, "Discovering the Good: Oikeiosis and Kathekonta in Stoic Ethics," and then Striker, "Following Nature: A Study in Stoic Ethics" (esp. 6–13), and Engberg-Pedersen, *The Stoic Theory of Oikeiosis.*

Some people draw the inference, from what remains of Hierocles' *Ethics,* that he used the cradle argument to argue that the sage ultimately comes to regard the welfare of others as "belonging" to her just as surely as her own does. The reconstructed text includes this famous passage, here translated by Annas, in *The Morality of Happiness* (267–68):

> In general each of us is as it were circumscribed by many circles, some smaller, others larger, some enclosing and others enclosed, depending on their differing and unequal relations to one another. The first and nearest circle is the one which a person has drawn around his own mind as a centre; in this circle is included the body and things got for the body's sake. This circle is the smallest and all but touches its centre. Second, further from the centre and enclosing the first one, is the one in which are placed parents, siblings, wife, and children. Third is the one in which are uncles and aunts, grandfathers and grandmothers, siblings' children and also cousins. Next the circle including other relatives. And next the one including fellow-demesmen; then the one of fellow-tribesmen; then the one of fellow-citizens and then in the same way the circle of people from towns nearby and the circle of people of the same ethnic group. The furthest and largest, which includes all the circles, is that of the whole human race.
>
> When this has been considered, it is for the person striving for the proper use of each thing to draw the circles somehow towards the centre and to make efforts to move people from the including circles into the included ones. It is for someone with familial love to [treat] parents and siblings, [wife and children, like oneself; grandfathers, grandmothers, uncles and aunts like parents, siblings' children like one's own, cousins like siblings] and so by the same analogy treat older relatives, male and female, like grandfathers or uncles and aunts; those of one's own age like cousins, and the younger ones like cousins' children.
>
> I have thus briefly given clear instructions as to how to behave to one's relatives, once we have learnt how to treat oneself, parents and siblings, and also wife and children. But there remains the point that we should treat people from the third circle similarly to those in the second, and our [further] relatives similarly to those from the third circle. For the distance in blood, which is rather great, removes some of one's goodwill, but nonetheless we must make efforts towards equating them. We would hit a reasonable mark, if through our own initiative, we reduce the distance of this relationship to each person. The basic practical point has been stated; but we should add more, in the ways we address people, calling cousins siblings and uncles and aunts fathers and mothers, and among our further relatives calling some uncles, others nephews and others cousins, extending the use of the name to fit the age they happen to be. For this mode of address would be no mean sign of the efforts we make in each case, and

at the same time would stimulate and intensify the drawing-in of the circles we have suggested.

However, now we have got so far, it occurs to me to remember something which is not irrelevant to the division of parents that has been given. We said about that, when we were at the place where we were comparing a mother with a father, that we should allot more affection to one's mother and more respect to one's father. Consistently with this we should now establish that it is fitting to give relatives on one's mother's side greater affection, and those on the father's side greater respect.

On the face of it, this is very thin evidence of Hierocles' giving a developmental account of "social" *oikeiosis* from a basis in self-love alone, and Sandbach, in *The Stoics* (34), says of it that

> it has been objected that it is superfluous to suppose a progress through these circles to a final recognition of affinity for all men, since there are many passages [in stoic texts] which indicate a belief that man has a natural tendency to love and assist his fellows, from which his *oikeiôsis* to them can be immediately derived.

Annas (*The Morality of Happiness*, 283) affirms that grounding social *oikeiosis* in a natural affection for others is the standard stoic account of the matter. And her account of the debate between Aristotelians and stoics about whether morality has a single primal source (self-love) or twin sources is instructive (288–90).

Cicero (*De Officiis* I.iv) elaborates the stoic account of the sources of moral duty in terms of six or seven elements of primal agency:

> IV. First of all, Nature has endowed every species of living creature with the instinct of self-preservation, of avoiding what seems likely to cause injury and to life or limb, and of procuring and providing everything needful for life—food, shelter, and the like. A common property of all creatures is also the reproductive instinct (the purpose of which is the propagation of the species) and also a certain amount of concern for their offspring. But the most marked difference between man and beast is this: the beast, just as far as it is moved by the senses and with very little perception of past or future, adapts itself to that alone which is present at the moment; while man—because he is endowed with reason, by which he comprehends the chain of consequences, perceives the causes of things, understands the relation of cause to effect and of effect to cause, draws analogies, and connects and associates the present and the future—easily surveys the course of his whole life and makes the necessary preparations for its conduct.
>
> Nature likewise by the power of reason associates man with man in the common bonds of speech and life; she implants in him above all, I may say, a consistency . . . [a carefulness] to do nothing in an improper or unmanly fashion, and in every thought and deed to do or think nothing capriciously.
>
> It is from these elements that is forged and fashioned that moral goodness which is the subject of this inquiry—something that, even though it be not generally ennobled, is still worthy of all honour; and by its own nature, we correctly maintain, it merits praise, even though it be praised by none.

Cicero does not say this directly, but we assume it is plausible to think that these are all operative elements in the developmental story in which *oikeiosis* is the linchpin.

In this stoic text we too follow the cradle argument all the way from primal affection for self and others out to social justice for "the remotest Mysian." We do not propose that what develops is ultimately a universalistic sort of fellow feeling, love, or Kantian awe about the dignity and infinite worth of rational agency—though we suppose that happens in some cases. Rather, we argue that in *all* cases in the normal development of healthy agency, the process of *oikeiosis* works through successive approximations to produce an eventual appropriation of consistent, principled action. Whether those principles must all be of a completely impartialist sort—for example, universal impartial beneficence—or whether some or all of them may properly remain a sort of radiating beneficence (hot near the core of the dear self and cooling as it moves farther from the core) remains a disputed point.

Psychology. The psychology used here is the textbook variety. That is, the psychology is the sort that represents settled findings in the field, and whose careful description has passed the critical scrutiny of many professionals who are using it to report results to their students (and not, for example, merely to serve as a provocation). This is in keeping with the stoic project. Ethics should be sensitive to changes in science, but understandably declines to be blown about by hot ideas that have not yet been thoroughly tested and integrated into existing knowledge. The psychological material employed in this chapter and the next can be gleaned from several standard (and massive) texts in developmental psychology. A useful way to approach this is to look at successive editions of well-regarded and widely used texts. For example, Brown, *Social Psychology* (1985), went through many printings, and then there was a major revision. (Brown, *Social Psychology*, 1986). The comparison is instructive. Flanagan, *Varieties of Moral Personality*, is also an extraordinarily useful resource. More of this literature will be cited in the commentary to Chapter 6, where the cradle argument is developed in more detail.

Internalism. The terms externalism and internalism, as applied to moral theories, have been used in a variety of ways. For especially clear guidance through the ensuing confusion, see the article "Externalism and Internalism," by John Robertson and Michael Stocker in the *Encyclopedia of Ethics*, Lawrence C. Becker and Charlotte B. Becker, eds. (New York: Garland, 1992), and for an important criticism of conventional wisdom on the subject, see Korsgaard, "Skepticism About Practical Reason." The issue arises here because we insist that motivated norms are to be found *only* within the psychological structures of the actual endeavors of individual agents. In that sense we are thoroughgoing internalists. Norms do not exist in some realm "external" to the particular psychology of a particular agent, such that the agent's moral task is to work up the motivation to conform to an external standard or rule. Rather, the agent's moral task is to "get it right, all-things-considered"—to act appropriately, meaning to act so as to optimize the achievement of all her goals, given her resources and situation.

This naturally raises the following objection of an externalist sort. "Don't we want to say that the norms that come from an agent's murderous projects are just *wrong*? And that what makes them wrong is that they are morally unjustifiable—regardless of whether or not they accurately reflect the agent's internal, all-things-considered norms? And regardless of whether the agent has some project that motivates her to conform to them?"

Our answer to these questions is no. Every norm (as a fact about the world) is internal to *some* agent's project. We simply cannot *find* any norms—*as opposed to sentences about them in writing or speech*—that are external to agents in this sense. Even in antiquity, when we thought we had found norms in the cosmos itself, this was because we believed the cosmos was a rational being (god). We thought its norms were in fact the norms of individual human agents also because we thought such agents were parts of the cosmic being, infused with its rationality. So even then we were internalists in the sense described. (For a dissenting view on whether to call this an appeal to "external" reasons, see Cooper, "Eudaimonism, the Appeal to Nature, and 'Moral Duty' in Stoicism.") So the answer is no. Even in our now abandoned theology, there were no norms external to all particular agents. Of course any agent can have norms (from her projects) about how others ought to behave. And god can have norms for us all. Those norms are external to the targeted agent, certainly, but they are facts about the lives of other agents. It remains to be determined whether it is appropriate for the targeted agent, in terms of her own endeavors, to conform. (As the title of the Werner Herzog film has it, every man for himself and God against all.)

On the other hand, we certainly think that an agent can be mistaken in various ways about the norms internal to his endeavors. There is always a truth of the matter with respect to what conduct is appropriate for him—a truth that he may often miss. More to the point, we hold that when healthy agents come to be attached to (or to appropriate) the endeavor of "getting it right," then they will by that fact be motivated to do x simply by coming to believe that x is the appropriate thing to do. And their motive will be to do the right thing just because it is right. This sounds to some ears similar to the sort of internalism ascribed to Kant. For reasons to be skeptical of intimations of Kant, see the commentary to Chapter 6.

Tying norms to endeavors of particular agents is hardly a novel approach. For a discussion of some of its advocates, and its difficulties, see Griffin, *Well-Being* (chap. 8, sec. 3). Bernard Williams, in particular, has argued forcefully for this sort of internalism in "Internal and External Reasons" in Williams, *Moral Luck*, pp. 101–13. What these "personal aims" accounts typically lack, in our view, is exactly what the stoic developmental story provides—an account of how healthy agents come to be motivated by moral norms just because they are moral norms.

In recent correspondence, Alasdair MacIntyre has raised additional concerns about these matters, suggesting that the concept of an endeavor needs further attention. In particular, he remarks on the fact that this chapter makes rather little of the distinction between endeavors of a very primal sort and the other, much more elaborate sorts of endeavors we typically identify with moral action. The suggestion is that this distinction might be relevant to the debate about internalism, perhaps by providing an opening for externalism. We do not think this is so, but hope to address the issue at length at a later time.

Autonomy, determinism and fate. Long, in "Freedom and Determinism in the Stoic Theory of Human Action," ably defends the ancient stoics on these topics against charges of incoherence. Botros, in "Freedom, Causality, Fatalism and Early Stoic Philosophy," places the discussion of the ancient doctrines in the context of contemporary discussions of Humean and necessitarian causation, compatiblism and incompatiblism, and free will. Though she holds that ancient stoics had a "defective" view of freedom, she nonetheless argues vigorously that they had original and defensible positions on these issues that are not adequately captured by assimilating them to contemporary doctrines such as soft (compatibilist) determinism. Here is part of her summation, footnotes omitted:

> We can now perhaps attempt a first shot at stating the differences, as so far revealed, between the early Stoic and the modern soft determinist accounts of freedom and responsibility, and suggest why these accounts are so easily and frequently confused. The *Stoic* account comprises two inter-connected parts. Human action, or what is (in our power), is distinguished from mere happening in terms of its special causal structure, of which assent and impulse (the nearest equivalents of the soft determinists' 'choice' and 'desire') are the most important constituent elements.
>
> The charge that Stoic fatalism rules out human influence upon events is then answered by asserting the causal indispensability of action to certain kinds of outcome. But, it would seem, the only power granted to us by Chrysippus . . . is the power to do what we *must* do in order that destiny be accomplished. It is perhaps hardly surprising then that the Stoic position has puzzled commentators, and has even led to charges of disingenuousness; for, disregarding the teleological, and possibly also the necessitarian, overtones, it is precisely this way of representing the human situation in a determined world that *hard* determinists exploit in order to show how *im*plausible it is to regard the individual as free in such a world.
>
> Now the modern soft determinist, like the Stoics, asserts that actions caused by our choices or desires are in our power. But, unlike them, he is not here elucidating the causal structure of action in general (i.e. as opposed to mere happening), but is distinguishing actions which are, from those which are *not* within our power. Moreover, in construing this distinction in terms of whether or not we are *compelled* to act as we do (or, with omissions, whether or not we are prevented from doing what we fail to do) he attempts to represent the power thus accorded (or denied) us as entailing, even within a deterministic framework, that we could do *otherwise* than we do or, in other words, that we are presented in some sense with alternative possibilities of action.
>
> Thus it is that, under one ambiguous and misleading formulation, the soft determinist account of freedom may seem to resemble that of the early Stoics. But to substantiate the claim that these ancient thinkers *were* soft determinists, in anything like the traditional sense, it would be necessary to show, not just that the Stoics *happened* to propound a theory of possibility, as well as of freedom, but that they *used* this account of possibility (whether explicitly, like Moore and Ayer, or implicitly, like Schlick, i.e. merely through the ideas of compulsion and constraint) to show how men may still be regarded as free in a determined world. No modern commentator has yet demonstrated that such a connection exists between the Stoic theories of freedom and possibility. (288–89)

Long, in "Freedom and Determinism in the Stoic Theory of Human Action" (175), makes a useful observation when he says, "What matters to the Stoic sage is his disposition, how he is inside. He is free because he feels free, because he makes up his own mind about moral action in accordance with the values prescribed by *orthos logos*." Inwood, in *Ethics and Human Action in Early Stoicism* (95), notes helpfully that "[The stoics] wanted to be able to say that an agent is responsible because he realized and accepted what he was doing." Frankfurt, "Freedom of the Will and the Concept of a Person," on second-order desires, is obviously relevant to what we say about iterative causal processes and awareness.

On fatalism, we must take note of the so-called Master Argument, famous in antiquity and attributed to Diodorus Cronus. Epictetus gives this exposition in *The Discourses* (II.xix.1), in the translation by William and Martha Kneale (Kneale and Kneale, *The Development of Logic*, 119):

> The Master Argument seems to have been formulated with some such starting points as these. There is an incompatibility between the three following propositions, "Everything that is past and true is necessary", "The impossible does not follow from the possible", "What neither is nor will be is possible". Seeing this incompatibility, Diodorus used the convincingness of the first two propositions to establish the thesis that nothing is possible which neither is nor will be true.

The Kneales say of this: "It is difficult to understand either why the first statement should have been found generally acceptable or why the first two should have been held to entail the denial of the third" (Kneale and Kneale, *The Development of Logic*, 119). Their criticism of it (119–28) summarizes the standard objections to it, both ancient and modern.

Additional textual material and commentary are in sections 38 and 55–62 of Long and Sedley, eds., *The Hellenistic Philosophers*. This is their translation of an apt passage about the equally famous Lazy Argument, advanced by critics to embarrass the stoics (339–40):

Cicero, *On Fate* (28–30)

(1) Nor will we be blocked by the so called 'Lazy Argument' (the *argos logos*, as the philosophers entitle it). If we gave in to it, we would do nothing whatever in life. They pose it as follows: 'If it is your fate to recover from this illness, you will recover, regardless of whether or not you call the doctor. Likewise, if it is your fate not to recover from this illness, you will not recover, regardless of whether or not you call the doctor. And one or the other is your fate. Therefore it is pointless to call the doctor.' . . . (2) This argument is criticized by Chrysippus. Some events in the world are simple, he says, others are complex. 'Socrates will die on such and such a day' is simple: his day of dying is fixed, regardless of what he may do or not do. But if a fate is of the form 'Oedipus will be born to Laius', it will not be possible to add 'regardless of whether or not Laius has intercourse with a woman'. For the event is complex and 'co-fated'. He uses this term because what is fated is both that Laius will have intercourse with his wife and that by her he will beget Oedipus. Likewise, suppose it has been said 'Milo will wrestle at the Olympic Games.' If someone replied 'Will he then wrestle

regardless of whether or not he has an opponent?' he would be mistaken. For 'He will wrestle' is complex, because there is no wrestling without an opponent. (3) All fallacies of this kind, then, are refuted in the same way. 'You will recover, regardless of whether or not you call the doctor' is fallacious. For it is just as much fated for you to call the doctor as for you to recover. His term for these cases is, as I said, 'co-fated'.

We now reject Chrysippus' example of a "simple" event—without prejudice to the issue of whether their might be a better one (perhaps the moment nothing became something, or the moment that the initial something exploded in a big bang). But we are happy to develop the remainder.

Richard Taylor has formulated what may be seen as a successor of the Master Argument in Taylor, *Metaphysics* (chap. 6). His version makes the connection to fatalism clear, but it also makes clear how far such an argument strays from our views in this section. For a trenchant and witty critique of this and related versions of fatalism, see Cargile, "Some Comments on Fatalism."

Acknowledgments

An early draft of this chapter was presented to a graduate seminar on Stoic and Cartesian Ethics, run jointly by Daniel Devereux and John Marshall of the University of Virginia in the fall of 1995. The whole book was improved as a result, but this chapter in particular was subject to acute criticism by John Marshall (on heteronomous norms), James Cargile (on futility, and on fatalism), and Daniel Devereux (on the ancient texts). John Cooper read his paper "Posidonious on Emotions" at the University of Virginia that term, and it illuminated much about the moral psychology employed by ancient stoics. I am also grateful to Paulette Parker for her able assistance in the UVa libraries. A later draft of the chapter benefited from comments by Stephen Darwall (on motivated norms).

For many years my thinking about moral argument has benefited from a course of lectures given by Philippa Foot at Oxford in 1971–72—lectures distilled in a justly famous article (Foot, "Morality as a System of Hypothetical Imperatives"). Among other things, that article makes etiquette into a theoretically illuminating example. My reply in Becker, "The Finality of Moral Judgments," is developed in more detail in Becker, *Reciprocity* (chap. 1). I have profited in a similar way from Searle, "How to Derive Ought from Is," and the work by G.E.M. Anscombe, "On Brute Fact," on which it builds.

6

Virtue

In antiquity, stoics were notorious for their hard doctrines about virtue: that it was one thing, not many; that it, and not happiness, was the proper end of all activity; that it alone was good, all other things being merely rank-ordered relative to each other (as "preferred" or not) for the sake of the good; that virtue was sufficient for happiness even on the rack; and that it did not admit of degrees. Such slogans are treasures for publicists and caricaturists, and distractions for philosophers. Nonetheless, in a cool intellectual climate we can harmlessly connect them to the account of virtue we now offer.

The Development of Virtue as the Perfection of Agency

As biological organisms we arc through the processes of generation, growth, development, reproduction, and degeneration. Each of these processes has its own distinct and final terminus (creation, increase, elaboration, replication, disintegration) toward which its subordinate processes work, and each functions alongside the others throughout our biological lives. These processes are not coordinated in the same way, or even very well, in every life. They are subject to lethal genetic mutations, gestational malformations, defective growth mechanisms, deficits in development, and disease. Nonetheless, we suppose it is plausible to say they are all in fact coordinated on mortality; they are coordinated on completing the life, not perfecting the organism to the point of immortality. The ultimate destination of every biological organism, insofar as it is a unified system, is its own death.

As agents, however, we are purposive. We have intentional goals, aims, ends, as well as a biological terminus. We ceaselessly organize and reorganize our biological lives into endeavors—into unconnected sets of them; into more or less coordinated sets of them running parallel to each other; perhaps into a coherent way of life; even into a life-plan or a deliberately constructed life. Agency is not oriented toward its own completion. Its end is not to finish but ceaselessly to optimize the number of endeavors that are successfully pursued, which is to say that agency is oriented toward the end of perfecting-in-use the power of agency itself. We hold that, considered as an end, virtue consists in perfected agency, something that does not admit of degrees. This is the end toward which agency, considered as an activity, is oriented. To the extent that this activity—the exercise of our agency—is our maximally comprehensive and controlling endeavor, its end is our final end. To the extent that this activity achieves its end, we may call it virtuous. Virtuous activity, unlike virtue itself, thus is a matter of degree.

The Structure of Agency

The agency of a mature human being is an exceedingly complex set of powers (capacities, abilities, propensities), and the set varies greatly from person to person. People differ in their perceptual abilities, in the salience various kinds of information has for them, in the strength and frequency of their primal impulses, in the way they deliberate, and so forth. For theoretical purposes, whether scientific or ethical, we need to make this bewildering complexity perspicuous, so that we can survey its full range and construct explanations, predictions, or prescriptions of some general or even universal applicability. The standard way of doing this is to work with a schematic account of agency that we may plausibly suppose covers at least the full range of actual (as opposed to hypothetical or fictive) variations we have encountered, either directly or by description. That is, we want a schema such that every actual variation of agency we find in the world will be an instantiation of that schema.

In doing this for ethical theory, we should be wary of two pitfalls. One is the philosopher's impulse to seek tight conceptual connections—in this case to construct a schematic model of agency from which substantive normative propositions can be derived *a priori*. In the worst cases this leads to circularity: The schematic account of agency is subtly moralized—that is, constructed from features or varieties of agency that will yield (nothing-else-considered) pretheoretically defined moral principles. The other pitfall is simply the theorist's bias for simplicity, combined with the philosopher's remarkable tolerance for abstraction. In the worst cases this leads to triviality: The schematic account of agency is so abstract that it yields nothing of interest in concrete cases.

Stoics hold that modern moral philosophy has often fallen into one or both of these traps. Ethical theorists now know in great detail, for example, much of what can and cannot be done theoretically with a single formal feature of reasoned argument—universalizability. Some have tried to build the whole edifice, like a perfectly balanced inverted pyramid, on that point. Others have built equally elaborate theories upon the single substantive idea of maximizing expected utility, under various definitions of utility. Still others are developing a body of theory about coordinated and cooperative rational choice, under a variety of motivational and cognitive assumptions. All of this work is immensely valuable, and we have learned as much from it (for the purposes of ethics) as from modern science. We reject, however, the ruthlessly pruned accounts of agency employed in it. We speculate that the seemingly intractable disputes between Kantians, utilitarians, contractarians, intuitionists, and so forth are ultimately traceable to the differing and overly simple or even formal accounts of agency they employ.

We offer here a terse, schematic description of agency in the form of what has been called a cradle argument—an account that treats agency as something that emerges in the normal course of psychological development, beginning with the behavior of infants in the cradle, and whose mature (standard) form is what we then parse to find the structure we want to perfect. Schematic though it is, we believe our description is nonetheless fairly close to the ground in psychological theory. What we say below will necessarily repeat some things outlined earlier in Chapters 3 and 5, but it will elaborate and reorganize those remarks. It should be noted that our intent is to give an account that is wholly unmoralized, except for the leading way in which its elements are ordered.

The organization of our cradle argument is meant to do two things, both of which serve our theoretical aims. One is to emphasize the recursive, hegemonic nature of agency. We suppose that, as a matter of empirical fact, every exercise of agency in the pursuit of some endeavor has consequences for the structure of one's agency itself. Moreover, we suppose that under favorable circumstances, every exercise of one's agency strengthens its structure—by improving its power to help us achieve our aims, and by making more dominant the norms generated by the application of our agency powers to practical problems. We think that these suppositions are well supported by psychological investigations of the elements of agency we describe here.

The other thing the cradle argument is meant to do is to suggest the futility of using extremely reductive or abstract notions of its constitutive elements for the purposes of ethical theory. Reductiveness is a special temptation because the proposal to give an account of agency appears to be a proposal to describe one among many features of our psychology. Thus the temptation is to identify agency as the power of action (as opposed to mere motion), and then to parse the concept of action to get the account of agency *a priori*. This yields useful discussion of the formal characteristics of desire, intention, deliberation, and choice, but it does not yield enough for stoic ethical theory. For our purposes we must have an account of agency that reminds us, even if only schematically, of the scope, variety, and complexity of the ways in which the formal features of action operate in human lives. (Our ethical theory is a naturalistic one, after all, about the lives of human beings. Other sorts of agents exist in the animal world, and still others are imaginable, but the price of thinning out the account of agency to cover them all is a purely formalistic ethic.) To get the account we need we will treat the formal features of action as formal operations upon objects in a domain (agency), and our task here will be to survey not only those formal operations but the sorts of objects they range over. We will treat both the objects and the operations as constitutive elements of agency.

Suppose we begin by sorting the constitutive elements of agency into two categories. Let us say that an element of one's agency is *received* if it is generated or acquired without the exercise of one's agency; it is *constructed* if it is produced through the exercise of one's agency.

RECEIVED ELEMENTS

The received elements are quite diverse, and they arise, erupt, develop, and are acquired anew throughout our lives, providing constant fodder for the constructive function of agency. For expository purposes we may divide received elements into two groups. In one group are all the elements that are part of our original equipment as human beings—our endowments. In the other group are those elements we acquire in ways subliminal to agency.

Endowments include many kinds of "impulses," as the ancient stoics would have called them, as well as many dispositions to react or respond in a patterned way. We will also include under the heading of endowments some of the formal features of the operation of those traits (such as neurologically fixed information-processing routines), along with consciousness and mechanisms that generate and control the level of what we may call pure agent-energy. We will also include, as part of the constitutive elements of agency, all of the other anatomical and physiological properties that enable or limit its exercise—from height, weight, and opposable thumbs to redundant neurological structures. That is, we will remind ourselves and others that in our view agents are material objects. Indeed, we will begin with a brief reminder to that effect, which would be trivial if it were not for the sort of mind-body dualism that infects ordinary speech and incautious philosophical use of it.

Bodies. Stoics are materialists. When we speak carefully on this point, we do not want to say that agents "have" or "inhabit" physical bodies, because that might suggest that agency is not itself a physical thing. We believe that 'agency' refers to a physical entity (or perhaps set of properties) that emerges from the neural processes of some particular beings.

(Not of all beings. Not, as far as we can tell, of rocks, or of dead humans.) We believe that consciousness itself is at bottom a physical thing, though of a quite distinctive sort, and we will say more about that below. But here we merely want to mention our view about the physicality of agency in order to explain our resistance to *a priori* accounts of it. If we were to allow ourselves to speak as though agency were something *non*physical that is somehow "embodied" in various ways here and there (here in a six-foot, seventy-year-old, one-legged man, there in a six-foot, twenty-year-old, two-legged woman), we would soon be drawn to the thought that the body is incidental—that one and the same agency could theoretically have inhabited a different body from the one it does, or perhaps could even exist independently of embodiment altogether. We might then come to think that the body an agent inhabits merely defines practical possibilities for the exercise of agency by defining the practical limits on action in a particular case, but that agency itself, considered abstractly as something that can be the same thing in different embodiments, can be analyzed formally—that is, without reference to any particular embodiment. Thus we might also come to believe that we can discuss the perfection of agency without tying that notion to an account of physical development. We might even get the remarkable idea that we can make useful *a priori* normative remarks about all possible forms of rational agency, and discard the notion of following the facts. We see no warrant for doing this, because we see no warrant for venturing into the metaphysical wilderness of mind-body *substance* dualism. What we say instead, when we are speaking carefully, is that agency is a material feature of some material bodies and that there is no reason to suppose *a priori* that the formal properties of agency per se (the properties that allow us to identify particular things as instances of agency) are adequate for the ends of ethical theory. Thus we insist on considering agency as a material reality—one that undergoes characteristic and dramatic development in human beings. The differences in the material realities of different agents may be as important for ethics as their common formal properties.

Impulses. Studies of infant and child development suggest that standard agency equipment for humans includes many active traits, variously described as drives, instinctual impulses, or propensities to act. Even very young infants appear to initiate certain sorts of endeavors, including information seeking, and soon develop remarkable information-processing abilities and the propensity to use them. They soon begin to make persistent, active efforts to satisfy or reduce their biological needs, to seek sensation, comfort, or pleasure, to identify objects and make (probably subliminal) inferences about them, to explore and define the boundaries between self and other, to act upon the other and upon the self, and to *inter*act with others. One thing we can say with confidence about the behavior of children prior to their acquisition of language is that it is characterized by persistent, goal-directed initiatives. Moreover, those initiatives are not reducible, in a theoretically useful way, to variations on a single kind of goal-directed activity or unified set of endeavors. Primal curiosity has quite a different aim than primal sensation-seeking.

Responsive activity. Studies of human learning, beginning with classical and operant conditioning, have yielded a great deal of information about our characteristic reactive endowments. They describe notable stimulus-response patterns of arousal and readiness to act, for example. Some of these are telic or goal-directed and others are not (compare a flight-or-fight response to watchful alertness). Arousal readies us for further responses of all sorts, including those that engage basic learning mechanisms such as behavior reinforcement and extinction, and stimulus and response generalization. These basic processes shape our agency powers in fundamental ways throughout our lives. (For a particularly riveting example, consider the phenomenon of learned helplessness.) Similarly, the received responsive processes that underlie self-development and social interaction are important to note here. Among these is a host of what we might call "mirroring" responses, in which our behavior reflects or mimics things around us. We vocalize in response to sounds of certain sorts, and attempt to replicate them. We mirror the movement of objects in our vicinity, or follow them with our gaze. We have sympathetic responses to others' sensations and affects: delight, fear, dismay, tears, shudders, twinges, pangs that simply mirror what we see in others. In addition to mirroring, we seem as well to be endowed with an array of basic reciprocating responses that we employ in interactions—responses that return rather than replicate what we get from others. We are disposed to return the gaze or attention of others, their care and concern, their hostility, and so forth. These responses are quite labile, but constitute a basic, uncalibrated form of reciprocal sociality. What might be called boundary-keeping should also be given special mention here. We impulsively initiate the making of the self/other boundary and the definition of a personal space or "proprium," but then respond to things that crowd or cross those borders in ways ranging from violent repulsion of the invasion (akin to a sphincter reflex) to greedy welcome (e.g., for food).

Formal features of information processing. Neuroscience has begun to yield tantalizing data and hypotheses about the ways in which the central nervous system is structured to process sensory information. Structural linguistics offers hypotheses about the formal features of our "language acquisition device." Stage-theories of cognitive development suggest that such structures undergo maturational transformations. The science is far from settled on the details, but strongly suggests four things of special

concern here. One is that some important forms of information processing are neurologically fixed, that these fixed items include various ways of
parsing, sorting, interpolating, and extrapolating information, and that
such processing may be of different forms for different sorts of data (different in form for visual and for auditory data, for example). Another is
that these fixed features of information processing may produce persistent errors, either in the sense that the logical representation of a given
part of the process shows it to be formally invalid or in the sense that a
given part of the process persistently yields the prelinguistic equivalent
of false beliefs. A third is that cognitive development is relentlessly recursive—"leg over leg" as Piagetians say—in the sense that whatever conceptual schemas we develop and whatever content we acquire in them
themselves become the objects of (and determinants of) our subsequent
development. And a fourth is a built-in motivational pressure for reducing cognitive dissonance—for achieving logical consistency and connectedness (integration) among the objects of thought.

Consciousness. As might be expected from the remarks about materialism above, stoics reject any account of mental events or consciousness
that depends upon a dual-substance view of the distinction between mind
and body. We do not, however, endorse the view that the mind and the
body are identical. We follow John Searle in thinking that the phenomenon of subjectivity cannot be explained *away* by such a reductive account
(in the way, for example, that the phenomenon of the sun "rising and
setting" can be explained away by heliocentric orbital mechanics). And
we think that the explanation eventually to be given is likely to be of a
sort that treats mental events as emergent physical processes. On this
view, the mind, like the heat produced by running an electrical appliance,
is distinct from the neural processes that generate it, operates in ways that
require explanation of a different sort than we give for its generative processes, and has distinct causal powers and an independent existence.
(Think of the way undissipated heat affects the running motor, and lin-
gers after the motor stops. Note that this analogy does nothing to illumi-
nate the phenomenon of subjectivity or consciousness, however.) This is
very deep philosophical water, and although recent work in neuroscience
with respect to memory, body-image, and emergent properties of neural
nets is fascinating, there is little in it so far to suggest how neural processes could cause conscious (subjective, mental) states. The crucial thing
for present purposes, however, is not to explore the metaphysical mys-
teries of the mind-body problem. Rather, we simply need to note that
what we have in the way of neural structure evidently allows us to register
and process information in two importantly different ways: in or through
our awareness of it (i.e., consciously), and without our awareness of it
(i.e., subconsciously). In either case the information gets recorded and

processed, but the existence of two levels of processing raises the possibility that we might get inconsistent results from them. That is, the information processing done at the subconscious level may not always be congruent with the sort of practical reasoning done at the conscious level. If it were the case that such inconsistencies were fixed (e.g., by unalterable physiological processes on the one hand, and the unalterable formal properties of the logic of our conscious representation of our experience on the other), the notion of perfecting our agency would be considerably complicated. As it is, our consciousness—and even more our self-consciousness—complicates the notion of agency substantially. The ancient stoics were clear that agency was as much a matter of character—the nondeliberative expression of behavioral dispositions—as it was a matter of conscious deliberation and choice. But one gets the impression from the ancient texts that, in general, behavioral dispositions were supposed to arise through (or at least, in the mature agent, be brought under the control of) the process of habituation—a process in which deliberate, conscious choice becomes routinized, nondeliberative, habitual conduct. Moreover, the picture of mature agency that usually emerges in philosophical writing is one in which conscious processes have normative priority over subconscious ones and in fact ultimately control them. In contrast, we follow contemporary psychology in holding that many elements of our agency are subconscious through and through: they are not generated by conscious processes, and they remain *sub*conscious processes even in the most mature form of agency. More surprisingly, perhaps, we have no a priori commitment to a way of living in which the conscious exercise of agency, and the conscious control of subconscious processes predominates.

Agent-energy. A final element of our endowments that must be mentioned in any discussion of the structure of agency is what we will call agent-energy. In ordinary language the metaphor of exhaustion is often employed to describe states in which we feel unable to exercise much in the way of agency—states in which we cannot "bring" ourselves to "do" anything very much. Weariness after prolonged exertion is one form of this, but there are many others that are equally familiar: grogginess due to lack of sleep; depression; the fever, weakness, and torpor associated with some diseases; and so on. We know from medical science that these states can be explained (and manipulated) physiologically. We can raise or lower people's ability to exercise their agency, for example, by manipulating their energy level through their blood chemistry. And it is clear enough that some features of our physiological endowments (e.g., those involved in oxygenating the brain) will define a baseline, received-energy level that will dramatically affect the development and exercise of agency.

Let us now contrast endowments (bodies, primal impulses . . . energy) with what might be called received, nonmaturational developments of them. Endowments are part of our original equipment, so to speak, though of course some of them, such as our reproductive systems and the apparatus for our higher cognitive functions, are immature at first and their maturation is shaped by the physical and social environment in which we live. (Growth in certain parts of the central nervous system, for example, is influenced not only by nutrition but by the way we are held and handled in infancy by those who nurture us.) But development is a more complex phenomenon than can be described with the notions of the growth, maturation, and degeneration of our original equipment. It also involves the emergence of traits that are received (rather than constructed) but are not, properly speaking, endowments.

Routines. Patterns of behavior and affect soon begin to emerge out of the infant's persistent, largely uncoordinated, multiform activity. Impulses are frustrated or sated. Responses are reciprocated or not. These events register, and have affective consequences. Active curiosity and startle responses, for example, sometimes resolve into pain or discontent, and sometimes into pleasure or satisfaction. Our behavior is conditioned by such events, and we generalize from them subconsciously. Such generalization—in cognition, affect, and conation—is then refined and fixed by further experience. Even simple iteration has this effect, but its potency increases dramatically when some of the iterations are traumatic, or framed (e.g., by an unpredictable reinforcement schedule) so as to arouse, before the fact, anxiety or anticipation, fear or eagerness. Among the earliest and most common "developments" we acquire in this way are behavioral routines—settled sequences of ideation, affect, or action through which our primal impulses or responses are expressed. Infants as well as adults are creatures of habit. The things we undertake repeatedly, from taking milk to taking our ease, quickly become routinized; and in the absence of distracting circumstances or adverse consequences, we proceed with them in much the same sequence of steps time after time. Such routines can, of course, become pathologically insensitive to consequences—obsessions or compulsions that have morbid or even lethal results. And it may be that we feel slightly uneasy or unsatisfied—as though something were not quite right—whenever we deviate from a well-established routine under "normal" circumstances. ("I don't remember whether I brushed my teeth this morning?"—Well, brush them now.—"It's not the same.") Nonetheless routines often increase efficiency dramatically, and routinized behavior can often be kept compatible with attention to the full range of purposive behavior in which it is embedded, and sensitive to situations in which deviation from routine would be prudent. This is a happy result, since the development of settled routines seems to be a pervasive and irrepressible feature of our lives.

Salience. To say that routinized behaviors, or dispositions generally, are sensitive to circumstance is to say that they are structured so that certain events trigger the operation of the disposition, others trigger its suspension, still others prompt temporary deviations, and still others engage learning mechanisms that work permanent changes in the routine. That is, the "context-sensitive" routines we develop may be described as dispositions for which certain events are especially salient in various ways. Just which events will become salient for a given agent is not something that can be predicted from the nature of the agent's dispositions alone. In congested central city traffic, for example, where drivers must be alert for other cars making sudden or aggressive lane changes, one driver may learn to watch the head and arm movements of the other drivers, another may watch the front wheels of the cars, still another may factor in the types of cars in view (battered taxicab; immaculate old Volvo), and yet another may operate with only global expectations (Is this Williamsburg in New York City or Williamsburg in Virginia?). Good drivers have a large repertoire of dispositions with highly discriminating and accurate arrays of salients—many of which are learned and employed subconsciously, or at least nondeliberatively. And what is true of driving skill is true of context-sensitive dispositions generally: through standard, nondeliberative learning mechanisms we acquire more or less elaborate and more or less accurate arrays of salients for them.

Two things about this are of special significance for the exercise of agency. One is the extent to which, and the frequency with which, such salients are acquired and employed subconsciously. The other is the way in which persistent disagreements between agents can be traced, psychologically, to differences in the subconscious salients that are factors in their deliberations. We may think of this in terms of the complexities of pattern recognition. The cold-eyed "look" of the city bank clerk, who thinks she is merely being efficient and professional, may register with me as discourteous or actively hostile behavior, and contribute to my dislike of the city. More generally, what she regards as the marvelously coordinated, energetic, focused, productive, and richly civilized nature of city life I may see as chaotic, dangerous, dirty, and barbaric. She and I can argue about this, and consider the same long list of things characteristic of city life, but as long as the items on my list of grievances have no salience for her, she will simply not "see" my point. Even though she understands it intellectually, she will not "get it," in the sense that it will not trigger in her any disposition to be wary, or fearful, or dismayed with city life. And to the extent that such differences between us depend on salients that are so deeply buried, or so complex, that we are not fully aware of them, we may be so baffled by the disagreement that we come to regard each other as irrational—or worse, as vicious. Ethnic conflict, racism, anti-Semitism, and sexism give us disheartening examples of this.

Affects. Salience is a phenomenon of cognition and conation, but not necessarily of affect. The fact that something triggers a dispositional routine does not mean that it generates an affective response in the agent as well. So separate notice must be taken of the obvious: that among the most prominent nonmaturational developments in our lives are the affective states that become linked, dispositionally, to objects in our memory, experience, and imagination. Such linked affects make objects salient for us, or alter their salience, but it is worthwhile to note that they play a much more direct role in our deliberations as well. Objects linked to affects in this way are by that fact valued, and thus figure prominently in our endeavors, either as means to achieving or avoiding the affect, or as ends. As we mature, these linkages—these affective associations—become deeply ingrained and richly nuanced. For aesthetes, refining, organizing, and reflecting on them escalates to a way of life. For ascetics the links are deliberately broken or ignored.

So much has been written on this topic that little needs to be added here, except perhaps for two reminders. One is just that stoics are not committed, *a priori*, either to endorsing an ascetic way of life or to rejecting the life of an aesthete. The other is a caution about reductivism. Some philosophers reduce the concept of value to pro and con affects, in aid of making a sharp distinction between fact and value. For reasons that can be gleaned from Chapter 3, we think this obscures matters important to ethics.

Attachments. Another structural development of agency is the pattern and strength of the attachments we form with objects of various sorts—with our bodies, other people, inanimate objects, our affects, states of consciousness, or objects of thought. Attachment is a metaphor for a psychological phenomenon in which an agent first identifies something as an object that is conceptually or physically distinct from him and then comes to be more or less internally related to it, in the sense that loss of or damage to the object is loss or damage to the self. The nonagency processes through which attachments develop are complex. In ordinary speech we describe them with a variety of metaphors: we say we appropriate the object, or incorporate it, bond with it, adhere to it, are bound to it. Whatever the processes may be, and however different they may be from person to person (for example, in a person who is deeply insecure, possessive, and introverted versus someone who has the opposite traits), attachments play a central role in the subsequent exercise of our agency. Normatively, they define categorical commitments that, because they are part of the very comprehensive project of self-preservation, are controlling for many of our other endeavors. What particularly interests stoics, however, is the relation between our contingent attachments, virtue, and happiness.

Representations and logical operations. Some of the pieces that we eventually put together into what we call reasoning are evidently hard-wired into our neurological structures. Object recognition and some primitive forms of generalization and inference may be in this category. Other elements may arise spontaneously in the process of maturation. Perhaps the "language acquisition device" is among these. We know, however, that the actual acquisition of language is a development that occurs only through social learning. And it appears that certain other fundamental elements of reasoning depend on the developed ability to represent objects symbolically. Symbolic representation enlarges memory and imagination. Representational memory and imagination make possible the development of set theoretic and logical operations (counting, class inclusion and exclusion, union, intersection, conditional inferences), and those operations in turn make possible (indeed are equivalent to) the propositional representation of experience, and the subsequent development of propositional inferences. The propositional representation of experience infects and transforms everything it touches by putting it into consciousness in a definite form—a form that facilitates communication because it is common to everyone who shares our language, and a form that remakes our agency into a consciously reflexive process of assenting to or rejecting the propositions that represent it. These are the seeds from which the full-fledged reflexive aspect of agency is constructed.

Basic tenors of personality. What we have been considering as "developments" here are traits that we acquire (rather than receive as endowments) but do not construct through the exercise of our agency. Among the most potent things we acquire in this way are traits of temperament or personality that the ancients sometimes referred to as basic "tenors"— fundamental frames of mind, forms of conduct, kinds and degrees of affect that shape every aspect of the exercise of our agency. Some data suggest that basic elements of some temperamental differences ("shyness," for example) may be inborn. But it is also clear that through the iterative learning processes mentioned above some of us become basically trusting, optimistic, confident, outgoing, benevolent, nonaggressive children with high self-esteem. Others become basically distrustful, pessimistic, anxious, introverted, malevolent, and aggressive, with low self-esteem. Some become tenacious, others persistent, still others yielding. Some develop temerity, others caution, still others timidity. Some become increasingly impulsive, others increasingly deliberative. The number of combinations of traits and degrees of traits is very large (perhaps as large as the number of human beings), and strikingly nuanced with respect to what sorts of feelings, thoughts, and conduct are evoked by a given situation.

Two questions arise immediately for our purposes. One is whether, and to what degree, such basic tenors control the development and exercise of our agency. The other is whether we can identify a "healthy" tenor, and if so what its relation is to the perfection of agency. (It would be circular merely to define a psychologically healthy tenor as one that is conducive to the perfection of agency.) We will postpone the discussion of those issues to the relevant sections below.

CONSTRUCTED ELEMENTS

Constructed agency, deliberation, and choice. We receive, from our endowments and developments, a moment-by-moment supply of purposive activity—aims defined by consciousness of primal impulses or patterns of response, organized around affects and attachments of various sorts, regulated by our energy levels and basic tenors of personality, structured and implemented by dispositions to act that are triggered by salient experience. This is a primal form of agency, consisting initially of uncoordinated, easily interruptible activity. As we develop and begin to use the ability to represent this purposive activity symbolically, however, and begin to manipulate those symbolic representations logically, a secondary form of agency arises, driven by this representational and logical activity. The process seems to go in more or less the following way, in the absence of disease, injury, or oppressive conditions.

First, the increased ability to remember and imagine that comes with these powers makes clear to us the multiplicity of our projects, and allows us to be aware of the history of our attempts to carry them out and to become aware of patterns of success and failure. We also actively look for patterns in our activities, and represent them in generalizations. (Studies of language acquisition, for example, show that children learn their first few irregular verbs accurately, by imitation, but soon begin to "correct" themselves by generalizing from the far more numerous regular verbs they are learning.) We then begin to represent those patterns in conditional propositions. This crucial development allows us to represent some features of our activities as consequences of others, as means to our ends, as necessary or sufficient conditions for them. We are also able to represent the operation of salients in triggering our dispositions to act. (The propositional schema 'If S then A' represents the conditional form of the dispositional relation between my recognition of some salient S and my acting in a given way A. Thus when I recognize the salient and then act, the form of the whole process is represented by 'If S then A, and S. Then A.') Mapping the dispositional structure of our activities onto logical operations in this way represents them as forms of elementary practical reasoning.

Next come several simultaneous and equally important developments of practical reasoning. We become profligate in our efforts to understand every aspect of our experience in propositional terms. (So profligate, say the advocates of right-brain living and other romantics, that we begin to distort or lose contact with our intuitive, spontaneous, emotional side.) We generalize compulsively about our activities and the world around us, and construct elaborate representations of the structure of our projects—perhaps in narrative terms, perhaps in terms of rule-governed endeavors. We just as compulsively revise those generalizations, narratives, and rules when for whatever reason we become dissatisfied with them. (Perhaps, for example, because irregular verbs persist in the speech of people we are trying to imitate.) Uncertainty and anxiety about our ability to get these representations "right" arises, but at the same time we develop routines that incorporate elementary practical reasoning into more and more of our other activities, and we strive for congruence between the conclusions we reach and the results we achieve. When we achieve such congruence regularly in some area, we often begin to use the conclusions of our practical reasoning routines to guide our conduct—either in place of or as a retrospective assessment of subliminal determinates of action. That is, the process of deliberation and choice becomes a determinative condition of (some of) our conduct.

In particular, deliberation and choice become reflexive, determinative conditions of revisions of their own routines. The effort to get the practical reasoning right is in part the attempt to generalize, regularize, and make practical inferences about the reasoning process itself. Success in this reflexive effort to improve the congruence between practical conclusions and outcomes motivates the wider, and more deeply dispositional, incorporation of practical reasoning routines into the determinative conditions of action in our various endeavors. Thus, unhindered primal agents construct and recursively reconstruct themselves into agents who deliberate and choose in an increasingly determinative way in an increasing number of their endeavors.

It should be noted, of course, that the notion of unhindered agency, like that of frictionless motion, is a theoretical fiction. The self-constructive exercise of agency is often hindered even by the simplest forms of conditioning and social learning, especially when routine failures are coupled with a pessimistic, passive, or anxious basic tenor of personality.

Constructed traits. Nonetheless, in whatever endeavors deliberation and choice (henceforth, agency or full-fledged agency, as opposed to primal agency) become determinative conditions of our conduct, we begin to construct rather than merely to develop all of the elements of our agency that play a part in those endeavors. That is, we begin to deliberate about and undertake to shape or control our primal impulses, patterned responses, affects, attachments, and so on, as well as the logical operations of our agency itself. And agency is robust. Even if its initial self-constructive activity is greatly hindered, when it operates in any of our reasonably complex activities it will exert persistent infiltrative pressure on many others. This is so because complex endeavors—especially if they are either long-lasting or frequently repeated—will be entangled with a wide assortment of primal impulses, responses, and attachments that also enter as determinants into many other endeavors. If, through the exercise of our agency, we shape or control those things in one endeavor, we will (through mechanisms of generalization in both primal and full-fledged agency) try to do the same in closely analogous endeavors, and if successful there, continue in this stepwise fashion.

Consider the way an infant learns impulse control. First, perhaps, he is simply trained—conditioned—to sit rather than squirm in the restraints of a high chair for meals. Mechanisms of stimulus and response generalization may then more or less automatically extend this to similar situations. (The high chair for play; an infant seat in the car.) The infant becomes a child, and begins to do elementary practical reasoning—suppose by cooperating (fitfully) with his parents' efforts to train him to sit in a normal chair for meals. Suppose that (unbeknownst to his parents) his agency becomes a determinant of his behavior in this matter. He experiments with various policies: squirm when the adults are distracted, because you can get away with it; sit still when the aunts visit because father punishes every little infraction then; squirm when you are sick, because that just increases mother's loving concern; sit especially still at special meals in the dining room when the good china is being used, unless you really want to provoke a scene, in which case the best tactic is to be jittery, to slump, to spill food on the tablecloth, to kick the table legs accidentally on purpose, and when rebuked, to dive under the table and refuse to move. Notice that acting on these rules takes considerable control of a wide variety of impulses and responses. For example, if you really want to provoke a scene in front of company, you have to be pitiless about your parents' embarrassment, and ready to deflect their most ingenious attempts to interfere. Incentives of unimaginable attractiveness may be offered; horrific punishments threatened. All of these things must be as nothing to you. That kind of control at a formal dinner prepares you in an outstanding way for similar ventures in church, or school, or the doctor's office. Agency infiltrates these analogous activities. And so on. In this way, starting even with badly hindered or restricted agency, we soon construct (i.e., reform and deliberately control) a very wide range of our primal behavioral dispositions.

There is every reason to suppose, moreover, that while the general outlines of the dispositions we construct for ourselves will be similar to those that other similarly situated and equipped agents construct for themselves, the details will vary remarkably from person to person. This is a deterministic process, but subtle differences in the antecedents that generate each step can generate remarkable diversity even in the ways children provoke their parents, let alone the ways in which adults goad each other. We will comment here only on the general outlines of some traits that are especially prominent in human personality generally.

Reciprocity. Reciprocity is one of these traits. Beginning from the patterns of reciprocal response built into and developed in our primal agency, we typically construct and dispositionalize intricate generalizations about when and how to respond to the benefits and harms we receive at the hands of others. Autistics, and pathologically withdrawn children are exceptions, but exceptions that show how unusual—how extreme—the antecedent conditions must be to inhibit the development and eventual construction of this fundamental trait. What happens under even very harsh conditions is not that we fail to construct the trait but that we construct it to fit our harsh circumstances. We generalize from the experience we have with reciprocation, and that means some of us become literalistic about what is fitting and proportionate (returning a kiss with a kiss, a slap with a slap), while others become much more imaginative (a warm letter for a kiss, hard words for a slap). Some of us give up proportionality, becoming extravagantly generous in response to benefits or implacably vengeful about injuries. Some of us adopt indirect forms of reciprocity as well as direct ones; some of us cultivate a wide form of reciprocity that is triggered by all the goods others provide rather than just those we invite or eventually accept.

Benevolence. This is a related trait. We may begin life as greedy little egoists, but it is clear enough that we soon spontaneously develop matching affective responses to what we read as signs of others' pleasures and pains. In a reasonably rich social environment we then begin to have a significant amount of vicarious affective experience, which is either pleasant or unpleasant in itself, and some of which is useful in anticipating the behavior of others. It thus behooves us to learn to read others' affects accurately, so that we can anticipate their behavior correctly, and it behooves us to do what we can to elicit positive experience in others, so we can share it (rather than its opposite) vicariously. These empathic responses develop and are refined initially in primal agency. In that sphere also we develop an independent affection for others' having positive affective experience. But when we exercise full-fledged agency on these matters, we represent our vicarious experience propositionally, by thinking of it as being a (nonpropositional) representation of others' experience in our own. And that thought both intensifies our vicarious experience and licenses a host of analogical arguments about the nature (and value to them) of others' affects. Others then become substitution instances in universalizable rules we make about our own behavior. If my thought is that you ought to help me (or please me) just because I am suffering (or desire to be pleased), then logically that holds for anyone who is like me, and who is suffering (or desires to be pleased) like me. We are alike. So if our situations are reversed, it follows that I ought to help you (or please you) when you suffer (or desire to be pleased). That and similar principles of active benevolence or beneficence are routinely constructed and dispositionalized by agents. Some of us construct heavy restrictions on who is like us (local humans only, for example); others generalize to all humans, or to humans and some animals as well. Some of us link this disposition to reciprocity in such a way that bad behavior from others quickly suspends it; others persist in their active benevolence without reciprocation. And so on.

Emotionality. In general, this is also a constructed trait. What begins as spontaneous affect is soon shaped in the arena of social learning. Just as we are taught to sit still at meals, we are taught when and where various sorts of emotional outbursts are permissible—or required. From early in childhood, our rage, glee, fear, erotic delight, pain, and so on are all elaborately tailored by punishment, reinforcement, and imitation of the behavior of others. We learn not only how to control the expression of the feelings we have, but we learn how and when to have those feelings. Consider the response of a toddler who trips and falls suddenly, skinning his knee. What will he do if his mother shows happy surprise, scoops him up encouragingly in her arms in a way that reinforces his interest in playing, distracts him momentarily by straightening his shirt, and then helps him examine the wound with clinical interest? By contrast, what will he do if his mother shrieks in alarm, scoops him up protectively in a way that focuses his attention on his pain, and mirrors his fear and pain by responding sympathetically to his cries? We have all seen the difference, and it is a remarkable one. It is a difference not only in how much (or whether) the toddlers cry and stop playing to devote themselves to this new endeavor, but evidently in how much pain they experience as well. (Think of the use of distraction and counterirritants in medical practice. The alcohol wipe and firm pinch of flesh before the needle-stick have more than one use.) When we begin to deliberate and choose in our activities, we add a powerful new determinant to the process of our sentimental education. We begin to construct our emotions along several dimensions—by reflecting on the *occasions* when certain emotions are appropriate, the appropriate *amplitude* of the emotion, the *duration* of it, the manner in which it is *expressed*, and the ways in which it is a *determinant* of our conduct in other endeavors. (Is it appropriate to be sexually aroused by someone at the funeral of a mutual friend? How strongly, or persistently, aroused? How overtly can such arousal be expressed in such a case? Should you allow it to interfere with the rituals of mourning your friend?) We make decisions about such things across the whole emotional field, and through repetition and habituation we construct both the interior nature of our emotional lives and our expression of it. The extraordinary variety in the ways people construct their emotions is a large part of what makes social life interesting. But it should also be noted that social and personal life cannot be very satisfying overall unless we have emotional dispositions that broadly serve the purposes of our endeavors. (We ask our neurosurgeons to leave their grief and sexual arousal outside the operating room.) This is the point that has so often been distorted in hostile discussions of stoic doctrine. Stoics do not recommend a toned-down emotional life for everyone. We recommend an artfully constructed emotional life that enhances rather than obstructs the full range of our endeavors, in the full range of circumstances in which we pursue them. This is compatible with recommending a very intense and expressive emotional life in conditions where it is prudent and productive for the agent, as long as the agent is dispositionally equipped to modulate those emotions when circumstances change. Impulsive wailing in fear and grief is not something you want when you are hiding from the enemy.

Courage, endurance, and perseverance. These are traits about which we make a different point. Courage we define simply as the ability to act—to exercise our agency—despite fear. Thus deliberately fleeing, or surrendering, can be as courageous as fighting if it (rather than fighting) is what you fear. Endurance is the ability to act despite pain, discomfort, weariness, or difficulty. Perseverance is the ability to act despite failure. These traits simply strengthen agency and enlarge the realm of possibility for its exercise. Thus they contribute to its perfection, and hence to virtue. One cannot be excessively courageous, or excessively able to endure or persevere. One might use such abilities inappropriately, but that is a different matter. (Fearlessness is by definition not courage at all, and whatever the excessive element is in reckless abandon, it is not excessive courage as defined here. Similar points can be made about endurance and perseverance. The excessive elements in pointless suffering or intransigence are in the use of the abilities, not the abilities themselves.) These abilities are in part developments, through subliminal learning, of primal agent energy and basic tenors of personality. But they are also heavily constructed. We rehearse ourselves into courage by deliberately putting ourselves in scary but controlled situations. We build endurance and perseverance in protracted, competitive or adversarial endeavors. Stoics thoroughly approve of this, and that fact has often been ignored in attacks on the Axiom of Futility.

Attachment. This trait is also subject to construction, and stoic recommendations on the matter have been systematically misunderstood in the modern era. (It is worthwhile noting that the antistoic polemics of antiquity do not typically attack stoic doctrines about dispassionate detachment.) To understand them properly, modern readers should take care to reflect, not only on the sort of attachments characteristic of loving personal relationships but also on the sort characteristic of vendettas, holy wars, genocidal campaigns of ethnic cleansing, and mindless loyalty. Properly understood, the motivation for stoic concerns here is not controversial.

In the normal course of development we become attached to many sorts of objects—parents, security blankets, beliefs, body images, lovers, land, houses, institutions, and so on. These attachments are all shaped by social learning, just as our emotional responses are. And when we begin to exercise our agency with respect to them we notice that they can differ importantly in strength, depth, and dissemination throughout the structure of our personalities. We may be very firmly attached to something, be prepared to resist its loss fiercely, and yet find that when we do lose it the wound is only superficial. Think of the way a child may fight wildly to keep his favorite jeans, now too small for him, from going to his little brother for whom they are still too big. As long as this strong attachment is superficial, so that the child is easily assuaged by a replacement pair, we are typically not too concerned. But if the attachment is not only strong but deep, so that the loss has a profound, enduring effect on the child, perhaps such that he feels aggrieved for days or weeks whenever he thinks of it, we may reasonably think this is pathological. (Or that the jeans are not the issue after all.) And if the attachment to the jeans is not only strong and deep but is also widely disseminated in the child's personality, so that he feels the loss in connection to almost everything he does, we will be even more concerned for his mental health (or for getting a better understanding of what is going on). Adults train children with respect to the appropriate strength, depth, and dissemination of various attachments. Some of us are trained to have the sort of attachments to kin that equip us to carry on obsessive blood feuds, or the sort of attachments to church doctrine that equip us to torture heretics into professions of faith, or the sort of attachments to holy lands that equip us to wage perpetual war and to assassinate those who give up portions of the land for peace. Some of us are trained to have the sort of attachments to our parents, children, spouses, or lovers that equip us to be psychologically crippled by losing them—inconsolable, unable to cease our mourning or even suspend it to carry on daily routines. Some of us are trained to have no deep or disseminated attachments at all, just as some of us are trained to have only chilly emotions. When we begin to deliberate and choose with respect to our attachments, we inevitably begin to construct them. Stoics have arguments to offer about how these elements of our personalities should be constructed. I will say more about them in the discussions of perfected agency, virtuous activity, and happiness that follow, but for the moment, a cursory summary will suffice.

We simply hold that it is wise to calibrate the strength, depth, and dissemination of our attachments to the fragility and transience of the objects involved. (The ancients were fond of expressing this in terms of the distinction between things that are within our control, or are "up to us," and those that are not. But this is misleading.) Irremovable, unchangeable objects, such as the number 1, are fair game for any sort of attachment. Since such objects cannot be lost, our attachments to them (as opposed to our affects for them) can never become a practical problem. People may attach themselves, with our blessing, in whatever way they please to numbers (as opposed to numeric nursery blocks). We dispute the wisdom, however, of developing any attachments at all to particular mayflies or subatomic particles. Between those poles we oppose unconditionally only one sort of attachment: the sort whose rupture makes us incapable of exercising our agency. That means we are very reluctant to endorse any attachment that is maximally strong, deep, and disseminated. It does not mean, however, that we endorse only weak, superficial attachments. On the contrary, strong and deep attachments can be so encapsulated (undisseminated) in our personalities that we can continue to exercise our agency despite their rupture. (One child is dead, and another needs rescue. Parents who can rescue the living child despite the loss of the other have encapsulated attachments, nonetheless strong or deep—and we add virtuous—for being so.)

Rationality. The motivation to generalize is found in the most primitive processes of primal agency—that is, in the stimulus and response generalization phenomena of classical and operant conditioning. The process of language acquisition shapes and amplifies such generalization by giving it a propositional representation that can be used in deliberation and choice. And language acquisition adds another new element to this process: rule making, or regularization. (Recall the child's attempts to regularize verbs.) When such generalization and regularization are then themselves represented in further deliberation and choice—that is, in the exercise of our agency upon the processes of generalization and regularization—they are soon constructed through trial and error into an elaborate endeavor to think and act consistently. That endeavor, in turn, involves representing generalizations and rules as the consequents of quantified conditionals—conditionals that specify the antecedent conditions under which the consequents are true and whether they are true for one, some, all, or a particular number or percentage of instances. That then involves constructing a way of assessing the truth of conditionals, and the validity of inferences based on them. All of this routinely happens in childhood when, unless they are extremely deprived, people commonly construct a serviceable set of elementary argument forms and criteria for truth—though not of course in the rigorous way employed by logicians and epistemologists. For most human beings, this informal, unsystematic yet serviceable sort of rationality (that is, simply the endeavor to think and act *consistently*, in the rudimentary way indicated) is a very robust trait. It is robust in the sense that even a little practical success with it tends to disseminate its use quickly and widely in our endeavors.

Practical rationality, integration, unified activity. As we begin to rationalize our deliberative processes and apply them in various endeavors, we often find ourselves at dead ends. Even within a single endeavor our deliberation may be deadlocked by conflicting goals, requirements, goods, attachments, and so forth that are not hierarchically ordered, or norms that are too vague to be determinate. Moreover, when deliberative processes begin to be widely disseminated across the whole range of our endeavors, we find that some of them are isolated from others in the sense that we have no way of ordering the norms of one with respect to the norms of another. Thus conflicts between normative demands from different endeavors cannot be resolved by deliberation. Insofar as we are motivated to persist in exercising our agency through deliberation and choice in all these situations, we are motivated to construct ways of breaking deadlocks. That means we must construct ways of assessing endeavors so as to get determinate results from our deliberations within them. And that, in turn, means that we must find ways to make the ordinal relationships between norms, both within and across endeavors, complete, as well as to bring closure to deliberations in which norms are undeterminative for other reasons. Further, we are motivated to generalize and regularize these matters, so that we are not always deliberating case by case. All of this generates impressive and persistent attempts to make our endeavors internally coherent, to integrate various endeavors both vertically and horizontally, and to do this in terms of general principles or rules. We accomplish this in part by constructing various kinds of "critical" endeavors through which we embed one in another, order their norms, amend them, and so on. The theoretical end point of this form of practical rationality is a complete, consistent, and determinate decision procedure for ordering all of the elements of our activity, present and future. In practice, the end point is typically far short of this.

Constructed self-concept, integrity. Among the first stirrings of primal agency is the exploration of the boundaries between the self and the other with the formation of what some neuroscientists call a body-image—the mapping, in consciousness, of various tactile sensations (pressure, heat, etc.) onto locations in our body parts. Concurrently we develop ways of identifying objects that occur repeatedly in our experience—in effect, some criteria of sameness, difference, and continuity, both with respect to the self and to other objects. We also develop boundary-making and boundary-keeping behavioral dispositions (expulsion, incorporation) that further define the self-other distinction, and the consciousness of ourselves as agents (self-consciousness) adds still another element. By the time we develop the ability to represent the self-other distinction symbolically, we not only have a sharply defined body to refer to as the self but a growing assortment of memories, attachments, projects, emotions, and behavioral dispositions as well that we include in our consciousness of ourselves as agents. As we then begin to construct rather than merely to receive the elements of our agency, we construct a self-concept as well, by deliberating about, selecting, and helping circumstances to train ourselves to regard some things (including, perhaps, some imaginary or idealized things) as constitutive of the self, and other things (perhaps some of our actual traits) as not constitutive of it. Moreover, this constructed self-concept is something to which we typically become attached, even when, perhaps as a consequence of the basic tenors of our personality and conditioning, what we have constructed is a thing we fear or loathe. Once we become attached to our self-concept, the maintenance of it becomes a practical issue—an issue that arises whenever we see in ourselves traits or behavior that we recognize as inconsistent with it. Such inconsistency makes it difficult (in the presence of the rationality we have also acquired) to continue to regard our favored self-concept as what it was constructed to be; namely, an accurate representation of the self as it is. Thus one sort of "integrity project" arises: an endeavor to exercise our agency in ways that are consistent with our image of ourselves. Moreover, insofar as we integrate our endeavors vertically and horizontally, by pursuing the project of making them internally coherent and mutually consistent, and insofar as the level of integration that we achieve (or aim for) is incorporated into our self-concept, then an additional integrity project arises: an endeavor to maintain an integrated or unified array of activities.

These integrity projects should be sharply distinguished from endeavors simply to protect, burnish, and revel in one's self-image. A concern about integrity is not simply a concern about image; it is rather a concern about consistency—about the match between the image and the reality. It is vulnerable to virulent pathogens—for instance, various forms of self-deception and narcissism. But it is also one of the principal ways in which agency is exercised to create stable traits of character, consistent patterns of behavior, and a coherent way of life.

Agency Constructed and Perfected

Health. We can give an account of healthy human agency in much the same way we can give an account of a healthy human body. Stoics are materialists, and in this case that means we regard healthy agency, and a healthy psychology generally, as aspects of physical health. The circumstances of healthy agency (i.e., the conditions under which it is practically possible to achieve and sustain it) are thus a subset of the circumstances of physical health. In particular, these are the conditions under which the elements of primal agency can thrive, develop into agency proper, and then continue to provide material for its constructive processes. (Without the continued workings of the elements of primal agency, agency proper soon becomes inert.) This requires, among other things, the nutrition necessary for agent energy, protection from predators and the elements, scope for unhindered activity, and enough success and benevolent, reciprocating care and concern from other agents to ensure that the elements of primal agency are not extinguished by conditioning or social learning mechanisms.

A perfectly healthy human body has a complete and intact structure, standardly configured; all the parts of that structure, from skeleton to skin, function in their nominal ways (lungs as lungs, for example, not merely as bellows); the integrated systems of parts necessary for sustaining life (respiration, digestion, and so on) also function nominally and homeostatically; growth and development of the structure is timely and complete; disease is absent; the body thrives. A perfectly healthy agency likewise has a complete inventory of intact, nominally functional elements and integrated, homeostatic systems whose development is timely and complete. Among other things this means that its endowments (body, primal impulses and responses, consciousness, information processing, and so on) enable rather than hinder developed traits (basic tenors of personality and so on), which in turn both preserve endowments and enable rather than hinder the exercise of agency in constructing the elements of agency proper (benevolence, reciprocity, affect, emotions, and so forth). These constructed traits, moreover, both preserve agency's received elements and enable rather than hinder the continued exercise of agency proper.

Thus the picture of healthy agency that emerges here is just the picture of psychological health, with special reference to its agency powers. And naturalists that we are, stoics think it is no coincidence that the picture of psychological health maps so well onto the ordinary conception of moral character or virtue, while psychopathology has correlates in vice. A healthy psychology is capable of a very large number of variations of course, but all of them will exclude the basic personality tenors (phobias, distrust, pessimism, depression) that paralyze agency or render agents unable to feel or express empathy, or unable to take a benevolent interest in others. All of the healthy variations will exclude the extremely asocial (autistic or introverted) dispositions that prevent the development of cooperation, reciprocity, conviviality, and benevolent initiatives. All of them will exclude the extremely antisocial dispositions that generate acting out unprovoked malice, hostility, and deliberately injurious attacks on others. All of them will exclude the sort of ungovernable impulsiveness and emotionality that make the self-protective exercise of agency impossible. All of them will exclude the sort of extreme anhedonia and detachment that caricaturists (falsely) attribute to the stoic sage. Moreover, the picture of psychological health will *in*clude effective powers of deliberation and choice, and the disposition to use them. It will include curiosity, abundant agent energy, a developed self-concept, and a disposition to regularize, to seek consistency and integration within and among one's endeavors.

All of this is of course consistent with a personality that is far from ideal by the standards of ordinary morality. It is, for example, consistent with a good deal of weakness in the dispositions that characterize agency—weakness that is not evident in fortunate circumstances but which may have damaging or even lethal consequences in especially stressful, threatening, or extreme situations. (The comparable point on the side of bodily health is a more or less weak constitution—one sufficient for health in ordinary circumstances, but vulnerable to disease or injury in unusually stressful ones.) Agency can be healthy, then, in a way that maps nicely onto ordinary morality in ordinary circumstances, and yet can yield to impulsiveness, prejudice, thoughtlessness, or malice. Weak but healthy agency is consistent with a good deal of criminal conduct, and so is a broader notion than virtue. But we should not ignore the extent to which the boundaries of popular conceptions of minimally acceptable moral behavior and character simply retrace the line between psychopathology and psychological health.

We assume that agents characteristically prefer health to the lack of it, and thus that the endeavor to become and remain healthy is always motivated for us all—even though in particular circumstances the motivation may be quite weak. In what sorts of cases is it plausible to imagine the reverse? Suppose we say, uncharitably in order to test the assumption, that hysterics and hypochondriacs more or less deliberately make themselves ill; half-hearted suicides deliberately injure themselves; anorexics and bulemics deliberately ignore their health; malingerers deliberately prolong their disabilities. Is it plausible to think that these cases reflect a preference for ill health over health? Note that, as typically understood, they are not cases in which the agent seeks ill health for its own sake. Rather, illness or injury is sought as a means for achieving some other end—for gaining the attention, love, and care of others, for example— and it seems plausible to think that if the agents involved could find ways to both achieve these other ends and preserve their health, then they would (other things equal) prefer to do so. That leaves us with the question of whether there are more exotic cases in which agents seek ill health for its own sake. We can imagine such cases (or rather, we can see that they are logically possible), but we cannot find convincing ones in our experience, nor are the imaginary ones consistent with plausible psychological theories. Weak as the motivation for preserving our health may sometimes be, the persistent preference for health is enough to license the general claim that an agent's endeavor to perfect her agency will in part be the endeavor to perfect its health.

Fitness, virtuosity, and versatility. A powerful feature of healthy agency that Rawls labels the Aristotelian Principle licenses some further claims. Rawls puts the principle this way: "Other things equal, human beings enjoy the exercise of their realized capacities . . ., and this enjoyment increases the more the capacity is realized, or the greater its complexity" (Rawls, *A Theory of Justice*, 426). We join him in taking this motivational assumption to be well supported (however indirectly) by various findings of modern psychology. And the principle supports the view that just as agents persistently prefer health to the lack of it, they prefer fitness to health and virtuosity to fitness—where fitness is defined as excellence for a given circumstance or purpose, and virtuosity maximizes various properties of fitness. Moreover, when agents construct and exercise practical rationality in a variety of endeavors, they come to prefer versatile, adaptable versions of fitness and virtuosity to specialized, unadaptable forms of those things. A continuation of the physical health example will illustrate this and help explicate its connection to virtue.

Physical fitness is the result of training a more or less healthy body to function especially well for a given purpose. The purpose may be the prevention of cardiovascular disease; the development of work-related abilities, athletic prowess, self-esteem, or beauty; the attempt to compensate for a disability, and so forth. Whatever the purpose, the training is designed to adjust the size, strength, flexibility, speed, skill, stability, or control of one's body well beyond the minimum required for physical health, up to a level of excellence or fitness for the purpose. Psychological fitness is analogous, and fitness in the case of agency proper is the result of increasing the scope, strength, speed, accuracy, stability, control, and effectiveness of one's powers of deliberation and choice—and of the traits constructed through the exercise of those powers—for practical purposes generally. That means making one's agency powers effective (i.e., adequately engaged, strong, quick, accurate, and so on) across the whole range of one's endeavors, and part of that is making sure that all the considerations practically relevant to the joint success of all our pursuits enter into the process of undertaking each of them. The motivation to be a fit agent is thus in part the motive to make the effective exercise of agency comprehensive and controlling. And when the exercise of agency proper actually becomes comprehensively effective in our lives, we may plausibly say that we are satisfying in practice the Axiom of Encompassment and the Axiom of Finality (Chapter 4, p. 42). This is so because we are then, in effect, making practical reasoning all-things-considered our most comprehensive and controlling endeavor, even if it is often employed subconsciously, or only as a retrospective corrective to intuitive or routinized behavior.

It is worth sketching quickly here what this comprehensive sort of fitness might require for a given agent. In part we need to do this to clarify the connection between fit agency and explicit practical reasoning. But the main point is to call attention to the fact that what counts as agency-fitness varies greatly across the population. It is determined by (and thus varies widely with respect to) the range and character of the agent's *actual* endeavors. Effective hostage negotiators need rather different agency powers than members of an assault team; people who sell used cars on commission need a different psychological profile than pediatric nurses; logicians need specialized knowledge and skills that are largely irrelevant to plumbers; citizens of a stable, wealthy, postindustrial, liberal democracy need rather different deliberative powers than homesteaders on a dangerous frontier. We should note that one thing that varies especially widely as we move from negotiators to soldiers to nurses to logicians and so on is the extent to which they need agency powers fit for sustained, explicit deliberation before action, as opposed to agency fitted with expert routines that are then subject to retrospective assessment. Even among deliberative types, the need for quick conclusions varies widely. (Tenured philosophers who can write good articles in medical ethics cannot necessarily do good work as consultants in a clinical setting.) Similarly, the extent to which fit agency requires a theoretical understanding of practical reasoning (say of the problem of cyclical or intransitive preferences) is equally dependent on the nature of our activities.

Beyond fitness, but along the same line of improvement over mere health, lies virtuosity—an ability developed to the upper limit of some human capacity. The standard here is not the limit of the agent's own capacity, but the limit of (known) practical possibilities for human beings as such. And virtuosos often set new standards. The intensity of general admiration and interest in them is evidence for a general preference for virtuosity over mere fitness, and thus its pursuit is typically and persistently motivated for agents generally. Two things work against the effective incorporation of this motive into the endeavors of most agents, however. One is just that virtuosity in endeavors that are significant to a given agent is not typically available to that agent. But a more interesting one is the way in which virtuosity is sometimes incompatible with versatility and adaptability. The bulked-up muscles of a virtuoso bodybuilder may exclude her from many other pursuits (ballet, or competitive swimming, for example). The intellectual dispositions of a virtuoso rational-choice theorist may likewise exclude him from polite company. And even when virtuosity in one thing (say, singing grand opera) does not actually exclude the agent from another (say, singing the blues), it sometimes diminishes her fitness for it in a significant and irreversible way. If to save your life you cannot disguise the operatic or bluesy nature of your voice, then if you have to save your life by singing, you may regret your inflexibility.

Versatility and adaptability is fitness for a wide range of practical possibilities, particularly unanticipated or unwanted ones. To the extent that we have a wide range of projects, or our circumstances are unsettled, we may have a strong preference for versatility and adaptability over the sort of virtuosity that dramatically limits our options or threatens to diminish, rather than optimize, the success of our endeavors generally. There are, however, cases in which virtuosity necessarily includes versatility and adaptability. Athletes fit for the decathlon must be versatile, and while virtuosos of this sport do not typically hold world records in any one of the ten events, they typically outperform any of the world record holders overall. That is the point of the sport. What is of interest here is the sense in which virtuoso agency is also, and necessarily, as versatile and adaptable as is required for the optimization of the agent's practically possible endeavors. That is the point of agency proper. There is thus no opportunity for motivational conflict here between virtuosity and versatility. For agency, health is preferred to the lack of it, fitness is preferred to health, and because virtuosity requires versatility, it is unproblematically the end beyond fitness.

Ideal agency is virtuoso agency. The standard here, as with virtuosity generally, is that of an ability developed to the limit of human capability, and not merely to the limit of a given agent's capability. The elements of such ability in this case, then, are ones that would be available only to the most favorably endowed and situated human beings, whose agency (to meet the requirement of virtuosic versatility and adaptability) has been developed and constructed to contend successfully with the widest array of endeavors that are practically possible for such humans in the widest possible range of both favorable and unfavorable circumstances. It is true that ideal agency is not the magnification of pathological traits—for instance, of autism, paralyzing anxiety or depression, physical or cognitive deficits. Rather, it is a product of the activity of healthy primal agency, made fit and coordinated into completely integrated endeavors that are then optimized and effectively controlled by the exercise of healthy agency proper (by way of the traits it constructs), and subsequently raised beyond fitness to the limit of success that is humanly possible. So the "widest possible range of endeavors" referred to here obviously does not include the sorts of deficits and ill health that prevent the development of healthy (and thence fit) agency. But virtuoso agents are made, not born, and they are made by having to learn to cope with passion, fear, pain, loss, depression, disappointment, malevolence, failure, and so on as well as the opposites. Powers of imagination and generalization greatly reduce the amount of direct experience necessary for such learning. One does not have to commit violent crimes, or be the victim of them, in order to develop the sort of agency needed to cope with one's criminal impulses and others' crimes. But one does have to have experience of a sort that generalizes adequately, where the test of adequacy ultimately rests on what happens in other people's direct experience. Severely sheltered lives thus stunt the development of agency, and it is reasonable to think that even a rather loose approximation of ideal agency would require a long, full, complex, challenging, and worldly life.

It is not plausible to think that ideal agents, let alone loose approximations of them, must all live even roughly the same kind of life. They must all be perfectly wise—that is, sages—and that is a significant kind of uniformity (by itself enough to put sagehood permanently in the category of a thought experiment for everyone we know). Not that wisdom requires omniscience. But sages must know as much as is humanly possible about things relevant to integrating all of the endeavors that they themselves might have, and about optimizing their success in the entire range of circumstances they might possibly face. That, in turn, means having an enormous range of both theoretical and practical knowledge—about oneself, about others, about possible physical and social environments, and about dealing with other agents of all sorts in all sorts of environments. Ideal agents must have not only the knowledge but also the skill and toughness it takes to cope successfully with immature, ignorant, and pathological agents as well as healthy ones, or other ideal ones. Coping means being able to thrive, or at any rate being able to survive with one's agency intact, at the theoretical limits of human possibility: in extremities of abuse, neglect, malevolence, and competition from others; fear, loss, sudden reduction or reversal of fortune; crushing duties and lack of opportunity; and at the other extreme, the corrosive effects of great wealth, good fortune, fame, adulation, and an overabundance of opportunity. (The emperor says, wistfully, in *Meditations* V.17, that it ought to be possible for a sage to live happily even in a palace.)

N.B.: Tragedians are pinned by the thought that admirable people might bring down whole houses, not from some flaw in their characters but rather from the way their very perfection plays out in unlucky circumstances. It is a short step from this to the notion that the sort of virtuosic strength and competence we are describing might not be ideal—that some sorts of "fragility," to use Nussbaum's memorable metaphor, might be necessary to excellence of character. We reject that notion, and invite those who are attracted to it to consider this thought experiment: Imagine in some detail two cases: one in which a physically healthy person is vulnerable to a crippling disease, and another in which a healthy agent is vulnerable to a crippling breakdown in adversity. Now consider ways in which each of these healthy people could be made fit to withstand the bad fortune. Suppose, for example, that a vaccine were available to prevent the crippling disease, and strengthening certain behavioral dispositions would prevent the crippling breakdown, both without offsetting ill effects. Would we not recommend them? Would we recommend strengthening the immune system but not the agency? And if we could strengthen both to the point that they could withstand anything, without offsetting effects, is that not preferable to their being vulnerable? (Is there some good reason for wanting people to be hurtable?) Critics of stoicism think these are not rhetorical questions, at least not in the case of psychological health and agency, because they think the limiting case at the end of this strengthening process is a cold, dispassionate, calculating creature who is altogether incapable of profound love, commitment, and attachment. Thus even loose approximations of perfect strength have no appeal. We think arguments for this position fail by ignoring one or more of three things. First, we should not expect immunization—physical or psychological—to be costless. Vaccines sometimes cause mild paralysis, but that is surely preferable to the severe kind; and modulated affect that cuts off extremely high frequencies of manic euphoria is a small price to pay for avoiding extreme depression. Pointing to the fact that stoic moral training has an emotional price is not sufficient for establishing that the cost offsets or outweighs the benefit. Second, we should remember that the immunity stoics recommend is dispositional. The emotional detachment or coldness it involves, for example, is triggered only by salient circumstances (for an airline pilot, flight emergencies). That does not mean that an agent who is psychologically equipped to be detached and unfeeling must always be so. Third, stoics have always recommended a life filled with "good" feeling and passion. The fact that ancient preoccupations with self-sufficiency caused some of us to describe the sage in a way that is repugnant to many modern readers does not invalidate our project. The sage we imagine now is made of strong stuff, to be sure, but it is not inflexible, impermeable, or especially hard.

Sages have stable character traits, which dispositionalize all of the elements constructed by healthy agency (rationality, reciprocity, benevolence, commitments, affects, attachments, emotions, and so forth), as well as the normative principles or rules logically constructed from them. Given the range of possibilities generated by life in a social and physical environment filled with uncertainties, those dispositions must be enormously complex, subtle, and responsive to unanticipated events. Sages will thus be persistently benevolent but also reciprocal, cooperative but committed to their own agendas, principled but not rigoristic. However, there is no developmental story we can tell, running from healthy to virtuosic agency, that eliminates the possibility of radical differences among people who equally approximate the ideal. Some may have world-historical ambitions, others not; some may be quickly moved to tears, others never; some may be theoretically inclined and contemplative, others relentlessly practical; some may be artists of the first rank, others merely dilettantes, ascetics and bon vivants, jocks and aesthetes, philosophers and lens grinders. Social life within a community of ideal agents, while we suppose it would be free of violence and deceit, would not be free of persistent conflict. Such virtuosos would coordinate their endeavors, but we can find no plausible developmental story in which this coordination would necessarily be more than a stable, peaceful *modus vivendi* for people with fundamentally different ways of life.

N.B.: For millennia, pictures of sages have typically been pictures of men—men suspiciously similar to the ones with the drawing pencils. This would be amusing except for the fact that aristocrats, racists, ethnic or religious zealots, and misogynists have consistently used such pictures to obscure and distort facts about the distribution of human endowments. We think modern science has decisively clarified most of these matters with respect to the potential for healthy, fit, and virtuosic agency. There is no longer any reason to believe that the array of endowments necessary to launch development into a close approximation of virtuoso agency is limited to members of a particular sex, race, or ethnic, religious, or social group. It is not practically possible for anyone we know ever to achieve more than a close approximation. But for the thought experiment, the appropriate picture of the ideal agent is a separate issue, and we are obliged to mention (with some pleasure in the sudden reversal of the model) that the only interesting question along these lines that appears to remain open is whether or not the picture of the sage must necessarily be the picture of a woman. We think not, but the considerations that keep the question open are the following:

As we said, sagehood is a developmental achievement that requires learning to cope successfully with the widest array of endeavors that are practically possible for humans. This requires learning from direct experience everything necessary for the appropriate generalizations and imaginative experience. The open issue is simply whether the significant physiological changes, opportunities, risks, and experience that are unique to women during their reproductive years are both imaginatively inaccessible to men and importantly connected to virtuosic agency. If so, and if men do not have important, uniquely male experience that is imaginatively inaccessible to women, then our picture of the sage should be the picture of a woman. The reason we put the issue in this way, rather than asking whether there must be separate ideals for men and women, is that only the reproductive differences between the sexes seem to us to be candidates for complicating the notion of ideal agency in this way, and it seems implausible that anything about the male role in it would be both imaginatively inaccessible to women and crucial to ideal agency. It seems clear enough, for example, that many statistical physiological differences between the sexes (e.g., in height, weight, upper-body strength, hormone levels) are not relevant here, since such differences do nothing to prevent members of either sex from becoming virtuoso agents in coping with passion, aggression, violence, deep attachments, tests of strength or endurance, and so forth. And it is equally clear that neither the reason, objectivity, or public, military, and athletic virtues cited by misogynists, nor the intuition, feeling, connectivity, or collaborative virtues cited by misandrists, are relevant here. Whatever the statistical distributions of these traits may be, they do not remotely raise the possibility that ideal agency is theoretically inaccessible to members of one sex. Relevant social learning, moreover, seems equally accessible in theory (though social structures that segregate people create differences in practice). It is true that some accounts of early childhood psychodynamics (e.g., those in the Freudian tradition) suggest that men and women have profoundly different sexual experience that is mutually inaccessible, but we are not aware of any evidence that such differences are importantly connected to the perfection of agency as we define it. Brain imaging studies that show sex-linked differences in the distribution of neural activity likewise fail to show a plausible connection to virtuosic agency. But is there such a connection in the case of motherhood? Perhaps. If, as even many misogynists suppose, the healthy mother's bond with her child is especially powerful and complex, and if such experience gives mothers the opportunity to perfect their agency in ways inaccessible to men (for example in making and sustaining complex intimate relationships), then there is such a connection. We do not believe the case for it has yet been made, however, and so we will keep our picture of the sage androgynous.

Virtue as Ideal Agency

Ideal agents will clearly have many of the traits that are standardly called virtues. They will act in a principled way toward others, treating similar cases similarly by criteria of fittingness and proportionality. That fits an ordinary description of a narrow sense of justice, and is a trait that healthy agents will construct (and ideal ones will perfect) from primal reciprocal responses, generalization, and rationality. They will exhibit justice in a wider sense of the term as well, for they will construct cooperative dispositions from the persistent need to integrate and optimize endeavors that arise from both their primal benevolence and their narrow self-interest, and to find solutions to distributive questions that are rational and stable in a given social environment with a given set of resources. Wisdom in two senses is also included in the notion of ideal agency. Such agency is the practical ability to optimize the success of one's endeavors, and means having wisdom in the narrow sense of practical intelligence (*phronesis*), along with the knowledge necessary for effective deliberation and choice. But the move from healthy to fit agency, and then to the limit of versatility for it, inevitably means that ideal agents will frame their deliberations in terms of what is best for their whole lives. That frame of reference, together with the enormous breadth and depth of knowledge required to make practical intelligence effective in it, surely qualifies as wisdom in a broad sense (*sophia*). Courage, endurance, and perseverance are also parts of fit agency, as we mentioned earlier. And temperance or moderation (*sophrosyne*) will be evident in the modulation of passion, affect, emotion, attachments, and purposes necessary to integrate one's endeavors (personally and socially) in terms of an optimal whole life. Those are the traditional cardinal virtues, and it is not hard to see in equally general terms how versions of many other familiar virtues would be constructed in the move from fit to ideal agency. Compassion, generosity, conviviality, civility, conscientiousness, honesty, fidelity, and others are all in some form or other inevitable outgrowths of the move from healthy to fit to ideal agency. How uniform such traits must be in ideal agents is a difficult philosophical question—difficult enough to warrant many books longer than this, and so we will not consider it further here. (It will be interesting to see whether the most plausible ideal of justice that we can construct with a stoic agenda, for example, resembles any one of the competing contemporary theories more than another. It is not immediately clear whether it will be closest to Hume's, Kant's, Mill's, Rawls's, or some other modern theory, though it is clear enough that it will converge, as they all do, on a great many elements of the commonsense conception of justice.)

The notion of ideal agency we have described also supports all but one of the notoriously hard doctrines about virtue that stoics held in antiquity. (The one it does not support—namely, the view that virtue as the perfection of reason is the only good—will be considered separately in the final section of this chapter.)

Virtue as the final end. Happiness considered as an affective mental state—pleasure, contentment, pleasant excitement, euphoria, ecstasy, a richly varied succession of such states, or whatever—is clearly not the end for the sake of which healthy agents do everything else that they do. It is not our final end. This is clear because achieving a given affective state is only one of the many powerful and persistent aims of healthy primal agency, and one that even young children regularly sacrifice (not merely postpone) in order to pursue other things. For an ideal agent, the appropriate exercise of healthy agency proper is her most comprehensive and controlling endeavor. That is, her controlling aim in every circumstance is to "get it right"—where that means ordering and defining the norms of whatever "it" she faces with respect to all of her endeavors, so as to achieve optimal integration and success over a whole life replete with projects and beset by difficulties. Moreover, she will have come to value "getting it right" for its own sake, and not just for its instrumental value, and because it is her most comprehensive and controlling aim, it will have a comparable (comparative) value for her. It will be supremely valuable, for its own sake. Thus, for an ideal agent, any other given aim or endeavor (other than acting appropriately; getting it right) will be a subordinate one. The virtuosic exercise of agency will be her final end, not because every (or even any) other endeavor is aimed at achieving it, but because every other endeavor is intentionally pursued only in ways that are compatible with achieving it.

Virtue as an activity. Agency is a set of abilities. Those abilities are dispositional states that generate activity. The aim of that activity is to optimize endeavors in the way just mentioned. That aim, in turn, entails perfecting the operations of agency itself. When we aim at achieving ideal agency, then, we aim at achieving those perfected operations, or activities, as generated by the appropriate dispositional states. The perfected dispositional activity, then, is our final end. The often repeated analogy in antiquity is to the expert archer, whose endeavor is to make a perfect shot. That *endeavor* can be successful even if an unpredictable gust of wind blows the arrow away from the target at the last second, and it will fail if the arrow hits the target only because a similar accident occurs.

The unity of virtue. If virtue is ideal agency, then it is by definition unified in two senses. It is one thing—one endeavor—not a collection of them. It is thus a unity. Moreover that single endeavor is unified, in the sense that all of the other endeavors it governs are perfectly integrated in the activities that issue from its exercise. The separately named virtues (justice, wisdom, courage, temperance, and so forth) are dispositions that are likewise coordinated in ideal agency; and conflicts that are generated by them are resolved in deliberation and choice. Note that our picture of perfected agency is not monochromatic. We do not imagine, as perhaps Chyrsippus did, that the sage's very motivations are harmonized, with the result that desire and passion are unified with reason and will, thus producing tranquility by removing conflicts at their roots. Rather we follow Posidonius in supposing that conflict remains constitutive of healthy, mature agency, and that the function of agency proper is to cope with it, not necessarily to root it out. The tranquility produced by ideal agency, then, is prospectively the serenity generated by confidence in one's ability to cope, and retrospectively the lack of regret generated by knowing that one has shot perfectly, even if the arrow has missed the target.

Mutually entailing virtues. It is also a (trivial) consequence of our views here that the separately named virtues are unified, in virtue proper, in yet another sense that interested the ancients—namely, that the existence of any one of them implies the existence of all the others. Courage, ideally speaking, is just that version of the ability to act despite fear that is possessed by ideal agents. That means it is the version produced by integrating all the traits constructed by ideal agency—including all of the separately named virtues it constructs—into a coherent set of traits that realizes our final end. So to have one of these traits ideally integrated with the others will necessarily be to have all of them, similarly integrated, with it. The reason that this trivial result may nonetheless be provocative has to do with the temptation to think that somehow having an incomplete or underdeveloped inventory of "virtuous" traits can make an agent worse, not better. (Stalin's ability to act despite fear, for example, enabled him to perpetrate atrocities on a massive scale, and this makes some people reluctant to call it a virtue in that case.) In antiquity, some of our brethren were attached to a related doctrine.

The Argument for Virtue as the Perfection of Agency

In recent years some critics have charged that stoics have at most a *description* of how we might come to have certain moral motivations, and that what we lack is a moral *argument* for virtue. We think there is an argument clearly implicit in the developmental account just given, but it may be worthwhile to lay out that argument's structure in a compact and explicit way here. We will carry it most of the way through in the first person, to make clear that this is an argument that particular agents (of a certain sort) make from the inside, so to speak. But it is a reasoned argument whose premises and conclusions can be universalized for the domain of such agents. As follows.

1. I have many endeavors—many things I want to do—and each of those endeavors warrants normative propositions about what I ought (or am required) to do or be, nothing-else-considered. While it is logically possible for an agent of some sort (a shark beyond his reproductive years, perhaps) to have one and only one aim, I am not that sort of agent. There are always many things I ought to do and be.

2. One of my endeavors is practical reasoning *nothing*-else-considered—practical reasoning devoted solely to the task of implementing any occurrent endeavor I might have—including itself. Its norms for the pursuit of any endeavor it assesses typically dominate the norms arising immediately from the assessed endeavor itself—by identifying the best means to that project's end, by sequencing and correcting activity in pursuit of it, and so on. So the norms of practical reasoning nothing-else-considered typically warrant superordinate requirements or oughts about projects it assesses. While it is logically possible for an agent of some sort (a very impulsive one, perhaps) to have no such endeavor of practical reasoning—or at least none whose norms dominate those of its targets—I am not that sort of agent. What I ought to do to pursue a given endeavor (when I have time to deliberate about it) is to follow my normative practical reasoning about it.

3. My normative practical reasoning about my endeavors, done serially, routinely generates a welter of conflicting requirements and oughts. That is, even though some of my endeavors are vertically or horizontally integrated from the beginning and thus raise no conflicts, many are mutually incompatible with some range of my other endeavors, and will remain so unless I sequence or otherwise modify some of my pursuits. While it is logically possible for an agent of some sort (a god or a devil, perhaps) to have a completely integrated set of aims, I am not that sort of agent.

4. However, none of my endeavors, considered separately, routinely claims all of the resources available for the exercise of my agency—even for a single day. That is, none of my endeavors typically warrants requirements or oughts whose satisfaction demands all of my time, energy, attention, opportunity, or ability over an extended period of time. While it is logically possible for some sort of agent to have a project that is, nothing-else-considered, tyrannical and all-consuming ("pray without ceasing," perhaps), I am not that sort of agent. Each of my endeavors claims only a fraction of my resources and is indifferent to the rest.

5. Thus even the sequential application of practical reasoning nothing-else-considered to a long, arbitrarily selected series of target endeavors will routinely face local optimization problems—conflicts between two endeavors that can be solved by integrating them so that both of them can be pursued successfully. And a norm to the effect that more (success) is better than less is built into

my endeavor of practical reasoning. While it is logically possible for an agent of some sort (someone with a comprehensive will to fail, perhaps) to operate briefly with a version of practical reasoning that does not have such an optimization norm, I am not that sort of agent. What I am required to do, as a necessary condition of exercising my agency, is to (try to) optimize the success of multiple endeavors.

6. The indefinitely repeated, stepwise solution of local optimization problems eventually results in global optimization, but as I reflect on this process in the course of integrating any two projects, I see that I may fail in my local endeavor if I do not *now* consider matters globally. This is so because the local sacrifices I might be prepared to make now, *nothing*-else-considered, might not be necessary or effective given conflicts with endeavors of mine that are not yet under consideration. So it is clear just in terms of a reflective application of the optimization norm of practical reasoning to local problems that the norm itself warrants a requirement to widen the range of considerations to everything that might be relevant to the local problem. That is, on reflection, the norms of practical reasoning nothing-else-considered soon warrant the proposition that I am required, as a necessary condition of exercising my agency, to do my practical reasoning *all*-things-considered. While it is logically possible for an agent of some sort (an extremely manic one, perhaps) to lack this sort of reflectiveness, I am not that sort of agent.

7. When I reason all-things-considered, however, I am no longer engaging in an endeavor whose aim is local optimization. Rather, every endeavor that I consider (because it defines an aim for me; is normative for me) becomes a target for the optimizing work of practical reasoning. The norms of practical reasoning all-things-considered warrant the proposition that I ought to optimize over the full range of my occurrent endeavors. And persistent reflection on the danger of paying attention only to my occurrent projects eventually forces me to (try to) consider all the sorts of projects I might plausibly pursue over the various courses my whole life might take. This is the sort of deliberation I am required to do. While it is logically possible for an agent of some sort (a very impatient one, perhaps) to lack the sort of reflectiveness that warrants that normative proposition, I am not that sort of agent. What I am required to do, as a necessary condition of exercising my agency, is to aim, through my practical reasoning, at the global optimization of my projects current and future.

8. Further reflection reveals that *even* if my most comprehensive and controlling endeavor is *solely* to perfect the exercise of my agency based upon the sort of practical reasoning I ought to do, and if I succeed in *that* endeavor, then I will by definition succeed in optimizing the success of all my endeavors—over my whole life. Moreover, reflection reveals that if I have any *other* ultimate aim, practical reasoning in aid of *it* will by definition *not* be directed at global optimization, and I will not be doing the sort of reasoning I am required to do. Thus the norms of this extended sort of practical reasoning warrant the propo-

sition that I am required, as a necessary condition of exercising my agency, to take solely the perfection of (the exercise of) my agency based on practical reasoning all-things-considered as my most comprehensive and controlling endeavor. While it is possible for an agent of some sort (a follower of the dreadful Epicurus, perhaps) to lack the sort of extended reflectiveness that warrants that normative proposition, I am not that sort of agent.

9. Any normative proposition that is sound in my case is sound also for anyone who is relevantly similar to me. Thus all those whose agency is similar to mine, in the respects described in steps 1–8 above, are required to make the perfection of their agency their most comprehensive and controlling aim.

10. As noted in the account of the development of virtue, healthy agents will acquire strong norms corresponding to the usual notions of wisdom, justice, benevolence, beneficence, courage, temperance, and other traits that are standardly called virtues. Indeed, developing such traits is a necessary condition for developing one's agency from health to fitness to virtuosity. Those norms warrant corresponding normative propositions for each such agent, and can be universalized in that domain. Thus the proposition that all such agents are required to make the perfection of their agency their most comprehensive and controlling aim, is *a fortiori* the proposition that they are required to develop the traits necessary to pursue that endeavor, some of which traits are commonly called virtues.

11. Finally, since any normative proposition warranted by our the endeavor to perfect our agency is ultimately traceable to a requirement that we make this our most comprehensive and controlling endeavor, it will dominate any conflicting requirement from any other endeavor.

Readers interested in a more formal representation of this argument are cordially invited to plug it into the calculus outlined in the Appendix. Hint: in the calculus, the rules for transcendent assessment generate requirements (rather than oughts) in steps 5–9, and those requirements together with the axioms of encompassment and finality secure step 11.

Agency, not rationality. It is important to keep in mind, however, that this argument is sound only for agents of the sort described in our developmental story, and that it is a mistake to characterize them solely in terms of rationality. Pure practical reason, shorn of the rest of the psychology of healthy human agency, does not yield the normative propositions described in 1–11 (at least, we cannot see how it could). Rather, the argument outlined here depends crucially, at every step, on the normative content found in the multiple, less-than-fully-integrated endeavors of healthy agents, and on the operation of *oikeiosis* in their psychological development. Rational agents with a significantly different psychology (for example, rational agents who are primarily pleasure seekers, or who have only a very limited and thoroughly integrated repertoire of endeavors) fall outside the scope of this argument. It is clear that the operation of practical reason in some of those radically different psychologies would not lead to step 9 above, and would not yield the normative proposition that the agents acquire the traits commonly called virtues. This is a fact about the requirements and oughts those agents can soundly construct (about what they and we should do or be) from the resources of their psychology—and then universalize in the domain of agents like themselves. Their requirements and oughts, however, are no more than that: theirs, not ours.

Dealing with different sorts of agents. There is a very wide range of character-types among healthy human agents. Should we try to make them more alike? Certainly, if that means acting on the universalized normative propositions of 1–11. All such agents are required to seek to perfect their agency—to be virtuous. And just as we ought to develop an independent interest in the welfare of others, and are required to develop virtues of beneficence and justice, we ought to help other healthy human agents (as well as ourselves) to become virtuous. A serious commitment to do that, together with the opportunity to do so, would have enormous social consequences, especially in endeavors to ensure the development of healthy agency in human infants, children, and other immature agents. But nothing in 1–11 warrants the proposition that we should strive for a harmonious kingdom of ends all the way to the ground, on matters indifferent to virtue.

That leaves the question of requirements and oughts about agents whose psychology is radically different from our own. Should we simply deal with them strategically, in the pursuit of our own welfare? Ought we to help them pursue their own ends? Or should we try to make them more like healthy human agents? Here the argument sketched in 1–11 is largely silent. But it is clear that the answers to such questions will turn on particular cases, and on at least three matters about them. One matter obviously has to do with the other agent's own welfare. Domesticating animals is a good example. Domestication often appears to run counter to profound and persistent needs or endeavors of the animals, and when it does, the stoic doctrine of following the facts would argue against it. Another relevant matter, however, has to do with consequences for the development of our own agency. Even if velociraptors genuinely, profoundly want to become better practical reasoners, it is not clear *we* should want that unless at the same time they develop strong vegetarian norms. And finally, there is the matter of possibility. Teaching a stone to talk, as someone once remarked, is slow work. For stoics, it runs afoul of the Axiom of Futility.[1]

---

[1] "... when a man who has been trapped in an argument hardens to stone, how shall one any longer deal with him by argument?" Epictetus, *Discourses* I.v.2.

Exalted Virtue

For those who like their ethical doctrines hard as nails, here is one to consider: Virtue is the only good, and it is an all-or-nothing affair. No one who falls short of being a sage has any trait that can be called good at all, nor can one such person be any better or more virtuous than another. There are sages, and then there are the rest of us. Sages are equally virtuous; the rest of us (serial killers and mild-mannered reporters, mass murderers and their innocent victims) are all equally vicious. You can drown, as the writers of the Early and Middle Stoa were fond of saying, face down on the calm surface of the sea as surely as at the bottom. (Yes, but you can more easily be rescued at the surface.) We follow later colleagues in thinking these doctrines are untenable. But the concerns that underlie them are worthy of attention.

Virtue as all-or-nothing. Try this: The coping mechanism used by agency proper is practical intelligence, operating sometimes at the level of conscious deliberation and choice, sometimes subliminally, but always in terms of inferences. Inferences are either valid or not; this property is not a matter of degree. Neither is soundness. One false proposition in an argument makes the inference unsound, period. Below the level of ideal agency, invalid or otherwise unsound inferences may have merely local effects. Imperfect agency may be incompletely integrated, for example, and less than comprehensively controlling. If so, and if we do not exercise agency properly or at all in some areas, then we may not notice conflicts between our endeavors, or attempt to generalize from one to another. This has obvious disadvantages for learning, of course, but it also has the peculiar advantage that the effects of our errors are limited simply because we fail to apply those errors widely. Thus, short of achieving perfection itself, the closer we get to ideal agency with respect to integrating all our endeavors and controlling them all with practical intelligence, the more likely it is that errors in anything we do will invalidate everything we do. (Recall that perfect agency is perfectly unified.) Thus in one sense, as we "advance" from health through fitness toward ideal agency, we get no "better" at all, because the benefits we reap by developing our agency are offset by the increasing damage its remaining imperfections can do. So only ideal agency (virtue) will do. Short of that, we are all equal, equally wretched, equally subject to drowning in our circumstances, but from different causes. For some of us, the cause is weak agency; for others, the cause is strong but defective agency. We prefer strong to weak, then, not because one is better than the other, but because it gets us closer to the only thing that is good—virtue. (It does not follow from this that we must treat mass murderers the same way we treat pillars of the community. Quite the reverse follows.)

There is something in that argument that we should face squarely, even though we may think its rhetoric is indefensible. The advantages of agency that we are motivated to pursue, as we move from mere health to fitness and beyond, are not guaranteed to us, *to any degree*, until we achieve ideal agency. Until then, no matter how far from the seabed we have come, depending on our luck we may have just as much difficulty breathing as when we began. Partial virtue does not make life easier, or more tranquil. In that sense, virtue is an all-or-nothing affair; not a matter of degree.

That is a hard hypothesis to entertain, made harder by reflecting on the fact that for most of us, ideal agency does not seem to be a practical possibility. If it is not, then in the logic of stoic ethics, we are required not to pursue it directly at all, but only at most to pursue endeavors to make it possible. That weakens the way in which virtue is the final end of the exercise of agency, and hence is motivated for us. If the ideal is very far out of reach, and indirect efforts to bring it closer are also beset with difficulties, we may lose motivation for it altogether. Healthy agency is robust, however, if not quite irrepressible. The traits we construct by exercising it, under a very wide range of circumstances, are enough to keep us persistently attracted to its improvement, both in ourselves and others. In very favorable circumstances, perhaps the leisure for philosophical reflection together with stoic moral training can do the rest.

The Value of Virtue

So far, this is not a very satisfying approach to accounting for the exalted status virtue has in stoic ethical theory—a status that has persistently tempted us to say (misleadingly) that it is the *only* thing that is good. We will perhaps be able to make this temptation intelligible if we consider the possibility that virtue might be uniquely, unconditionally, and incommensurably good.

Virtue as uniquely and unconditionally a good. For a healthy agent, no matter what her circumstances, virtue as a set of dispositional powers is unconditionally a good, right up to the moment of death. We can think of no circumstances in which a mature, healthy agent could plausibly hold that the ability to act appropriately, as understood here, is a bad or indifferent thing, all-things-considered. And this is not the formal, tautological claim that what is appropriate and good is appropriate and good. Acting appropriately, as understood here, is a special kind of optimization project—one that it is logically possible to reject. (And which many people with compulsive, obsessive, or addictive personalities do in fact reject.) Our claim is only that healthy agents, at least those well along the road to fitness in their deliberative powers, cannot plausibly reject it.

What could be a counterexample? Reckless love? Selfless courage? Kantian respect for the moral law? Any deliberative defense of these things, from a healthy agent, is surely going to turn on the claim that, properly considered, those things just *are* instances of an agent's acting appropriately in terms of her own projects. There are thus no implicit conditions attached to the value of virtue in this sense. It is a good in sickness and in health, in war and peace, poverty or plenty, hate or love. It is a good independently of how things turn out (recall the archer). It is a good independently of others' attitudes, actions, virtues, and vices.

Moreover, virtue appears to be unique in this regard. Everything else (pleasure, for example) is only conditionally good. Apparent counterexamples turn out to depend implicitly on the circumstances; usually on the virtue of others. Consider benevolence, kindness, friendship, love. Can those ever be bad or indifferent things? Surely not, we want to say. But in doing so we also want to exclude busybody benevolence, fussy friends, smothering love, and so on from what we are endorsing. In excluding them, we sometimes directly acknowledge the conditional nature of the goods involved. We say, in effect, that loving concern from others is good *if* it does not include x, y, or z. At other times, however, the exclusions may be wrapped up in the very concepts involved—as when we claim, perhaps, that "true" friendship, "proper" care, and so forth exclude all the objectionable possibilities, and thus by definition are unconditional goods. But then it is clear that we have simply hidden a condition of appropriateness (in the form of virtue in the friend or lover) in the concepts. What is it, after all, that makes having the friendship of a sage seem to be an unconditional good, when having the "friendship" of a fool or a knave is so clearly a conditional one? The difference lies in the fact that the friendly sage always acts appropriately. The good of her friendship thus turns out to depend on her virtue. And virtue alone is unconditionally a good.

Virtue as an incommensurable good. The development of agency from its primal stage to its maturity requires many goods—food, shelter, the care of others. But what happens in the course of such development, for healthy primal agents in even minimally favorable circumstances, is that they develop a superordinate affection for virtue—for the exercise of the sort of agency that optimally coordinates, integrates, and implements their endeavors. The exercise of that kind of agency becomes their most comprehensive and controlling endeavor. And the value that the exercise of such agency (virtue) then has for them is independent of the value of any other, ordinary good that they may or may not have. Virtue is no less (or more) valuable in reduced circumstances than in plenty, no more (or less) valuable for the genius than for the mediocre intellect. Its value is constant. And more to the point here, once virtue becomes our most comprehensive and controlling endeavor its value for us will be incommensurable with that of other things in the sense that nothing will be an adequate substitute for virtue; no other good or combination of goods will "add up" to its good, or be something that could conceivably compensate for its loss. Virtue will then be off the balance scales of value for us. It will be of incomparable value.

The dignity of virtue. In many ancient Greek texts, not just stoic ones, there is the contention that reason (or rational agency) distinguishes human beings from other mortal forms of life, and somehow elevates us above them—makes us superior to them. It is clear enough, in terms of the developmental story we have given, how a virtuoso agent inevitably comes to believe that her own worth as a human being is ultimately determined *only* by the quality of her agency—and is not determined to any extent whatsoever by wealth, fame, good fortune, or any good other than the good of virtue. And it is clear how such an agent would, by generalizing, inevitably come to believe the same thing about other human beings. It is not clear at all, however, how further claims about the superiority of rational beings per se could logically be inferred from this.[2] Nor is it clear how we can plausibly infer from it that rational agents possess a special sort of (godlike) dignity. Such matters are perhaps best left in the hands of theologians, rationalists, and romantics—or people who practice all three callings simultaneously.

Nonetheless, it is fair to recast some of the sage's beliefs about human agency in rhetoric that is reminiscent of Kant. It is fair to say that stoic sages come to believe that the dignity and moral worth of healthy, mature human beings reside wholly in their virtue, and not in any other goods or good qualities they may possess. Wrenched out of the context of the developmental account of virtue outlined here, such rhetoric is misleading. In context, however, it seems a plausible way to summarize the exalted status that virtue should have in contemporary stoic ethics.

---

[2] Arguments such as this seem to come out of thin air (or prior theological commitments):

What employs reason is better than what does not employ reason.
But nothing is better than the universe.
Therefore the universe employs reason.

This is attributed to Zeno by Cicero in *On the Nature of the Gods* II.20. My thanks to Julia Annas for the reference and the translation. She adds helpfully, "It is most charitable to take this not to be a serious argument from premises which an opponent might be expected to share, but rather an encapsulation of Stoic doctrine, using premises which are already accepted." See Annas, *The Morality of Happiness*, 161, and 161 n. 9. But what imaginable grounds are there for accepting them?

Commentary

Psychology. Here, as in Chapter 5, we take a very conservative approach to the literature in psychology, relying fundamentally on standard, long-run textbooks currently in use by academic psychologists, especially by those who describe their endeavor as scientific psychology. Chaplin and Krawiec, *Systems and Theories of Psychology*, 4th ed., is an example. Nothing in the argument depends, as far as we know, on unreplicated or controverted studies, and none of the empirical premises is in dispute among the various competing approaches to studying psychological phenomena scientifically. Further, we have deliberately avoided taking positions in two areas of fundamental theoretical dispute among developmental psychologists. One dispute is about the range and extent of cognitive ability that is hardwired or preformed as opposed to acquired in adaptive interaction with one's environment. There is consensus that both sorts of processes are at work in every healthy human agent. But there is considerable difficulty in identifying which of the two regulates which specific developments (and to what degree some elements of adaptive development might be idiosyncratic or culture-bound). The other basic dispute we have avoided concerns (a) whether to proceed on the theory that human cognitive (and moral) development occurs in more or less discrete stages that necessarily occur in a certain order and which impose distinct schemas or frames on the data, or (b) whether it is better to think of cognitive development as a continuous and somewhat disorderly "acquisition of expertise" by the repeated, reflexive use of a fixed repertoire of frames, and information-processing routines, that are fitted with feedback functions.

Flanagan, *Varieties of Moral Personality*, is useful in checking our descriptive claims in several ways: for the detailed philosophical and scientific evaluation he provides of some controversial studies (e.g., Kohlberg's, Milgram's); for his evaluation of motivational principles employed by moral philosophers (e.g., Rawls's Aristotelian Principle); and for the wealth of entry points he provides into the literature of empirical psychology.

The psychology of the person, or self, is clearly one area to explore. For the early work, Gordon Allport is a sensible and rewarding guide, both in his classic book, Allport, *Becoming: Basic Considerations for a Psychology of Personality*, and in his systematic summation, Allport, *Pattern and Growth in Personality*. His useful essay, "Traits Revisited," is in Allport, *The Person in Psychology*, and for obvious reasons, any argument based on the concept of *oikeiosis* will find Allport's concept of the "proprium" and "propriate striving" very helpful. Some inadvertent similarity between our account of healthy agency and Carl Rogers's concept of a "normal, fully functioning person" may also be of interest. For a convenient summary statement of Rogers's view, see Chaplin and Krawiec, *Systems and Theories of Psychology*, 4th ed. (552–56).

For an overview of cognitive development, blending sophisticated versions of Piagetian stage-theory and information-processing approaches, see Flavell, *Cognitive Development*, 2d ed. His classic full-length exposition of Piaget is Flavell, *The Developmental Psychology of Jean Piaget*. Since the development of representational and linguistic abilities figures prominently in our account of *oikeiosis*, the literature on language acquisition is also relevant. See, for example, Brown, *Social Psychology*. On inference—especially systematic divergence between "normative" and "intuitive" inferential processes—see Kahneman and Tversky, eds., *Judgment under Uncertainty: Heuristics and Biases*, and Nisbett and Ross, *Human Inference: Strategies and Shortcomings of Social Judgment*. And for a sensible overview of matters concerning the integration and stability of character traits, see Flanagan, *Varieties of Moral Personality* (chap. 13). We note with special interest this remark (p. 276):

> We tend to think that integration is achieved mostly through a top-down control mechanism. But a high degree of vertical coordination, without any overarching control mechanism, is also a possibility. Indeed it now seems most likely that consciousness notices and regulates a unity that emerges from other sources as much as it creates whatever unity exists in the first place. In any case there is a strong presumption—possibly greater than the facts will bear—that some sort of integration, coordination, unity or wholeness of being is both more or less inevitable and a necessary and sufficient condition for personhood. Minimal persons possess . . . personality.

Flanagan argues that moral theories must be assessed in part by whether they satisfy the Principle of Minimal Psychological Realism: "Make sure, when constructing a moral theory or projecting a moral ideal that the character, decision processing, and behavior prescribed are possible, or perceived to be possible, for creatures like us" (32). Despite the formidably virtuosic character of the stoic sage (who is, after all, a kind of theoretical limit or convergence point at infinity), we believe stoic moral psychology satisfies Flanagan's principle, especially in the way he unpacks its four requirements (54–55). (1) We certainly give a scientifically defensible "*general picture* of how, in rudimentary terms, persons are put together." (2) We use that psychological picture to define "constraints on [our] conception" of moral personality, and "to give a picture of the motivational structure required for its realization and an argument for believing that this motivational structure is possible." (3) We use psychology to assess the degree of difficulty in carrying out our moral program. And (4) we do not confuse or conflate "social or narrow" psychological traits (ones that are socially determined) and "natural" traits (ones that are biologically determined). The sticking point is clearly the ideal of the sage. Here we think it is sufficient, to meet the requirement of minimal psychological realism, to have shown that the motivational structure needed to *pursue* the ideal is practically possible, and that achieving the ideal is theoretically possible. In fact, we think our account is realistic in much stronger ways than that.

The analogy to health. The ancient stoics were fond of medical analogies. Chrysippus reportedly wrote a book called *Emotional Therapy*, and it is not a quirk that Galen discusses stoic views extensively in a treatise: Galen, *On the Doctrines of Hippocrates and Plato*. Here is an interesting passage about how to diagnose "inferior men" from Book V, section 2.

> Chrysippus says that their soul is analogous to a body which is apt to fall into fever or diarrhoea or something else of that kind from a small and chance cause.

Posidonius is critical of this comparison; he says that the soul of inferior persons should not be compared to these (bodies) but simply to healthy bodies. For with respect to their experiencing the affection and being led to suffer it in any way whatever, it makes no difference whether the cause of their fever is large or small; the difference between them is that the one kind (of body) contracts the disease easily, while the other does so with difficulty. Thus Chrysippus erred, he says, in his comparison of health of soul to health of body, and disease (of soul) to a bodily state that easily falls into disease, for there is a soul—that of the wise man, obviously—that becomes immune to affection, whereas no body is immune to disease; it would be more correct to compare the souls of inferior persons "either to physical health with a proneness to disease"—that is Posidonius' phrase—"or to the disease itself"; for there is a constitution that is either sickly or already laboring from a disease. But he himself agrees with Chrysippus to the extent of saying that all inferior men are diseased in soul and that their disease is comparable to the above-mentioned states of the body. His actual words are as follows: "Therefore the disease of the soul does not resemble, as Chrysippus had supposed, the sickly constitution of the body, whereby it is carried off in such a way as to fall into irregular, non-periodic, fevers; rather, disease of the soul resembles either physical health with a proneness to disease, or the disease itself. For disease of the body is a state already diseased, but what Chrysippus calls disease resembles rather a proneness to fever."

Nussbaum, in *The Therapy of Desire*, makes heavy use of the fact that the medical analogy figures prominently in stoic texts. For an illuminating discussion of the intersection of "Philosophy and Medicine in Antiquity," see Frede, *Essays in Ancient Philosophy* (225–42). For an account of the extent to which virtue does and does not track psychological health as that notion is now employed in psychology, see Flanagan, *Varieties of Moral Personality* (chap. 15). Our discussion is consistent with what he says about health. He does not consider what we call fitness and virtuosity.

Weak agency. It is clear from the discussion in the text that on our account, agency below the level of sagehood can be weak, and action *akratic*, in a variety of ways. But one way in which action cannot be *akratic* and still be agency (or action) proper is if passion simply "overwhelms" agency—renders it inoperative. Gosling, in "The Stoics and 'Akrasia,'" (esp. at 186–87), argues helpfully that ancient stoics may have been making a similar point about *akrasia*, which their critics failed to see. He says:

> Suppose we take the example, which was popular in the ancient disputes, of Medea torn between her desire for revenge against Jason, urging her to kill their children, and her judgment (of reason?) that that would be a wicked act. . . . Critics of Stoicism tended to interpret this example in Platonic terms of the (real) agent being overwhelmed by passion. The oddity of this way of talking is that it risks undermining the supposition that Medea acts intentionally.

But on the supposition that even the most passionate acts are intentional, thus involving the exercise of agency (or reason, as the ancients would say), then our account of *akrasia* must be an account of defective agency or reason, and it follows that perfected agency cannot be *akratic*.

Ordinary goods. The ancient stoics held that there were two sorts of things that had worth, but that only one of them (virtue) could be called good. Things of the other sort were "preferred indifferents." The fragmentary nature of the texts on this point, its seeming oddity, the fact that other ancient philosophers attacked it so vigorously, and the impression we glean that our forebears ultimately yielded ground to their critics on the matter have combined to generate a persistent puzzle for scholars. The puzzle concerns not only how to make sense of the notion of the worth or value of a preferred indifferent, but how to explain the connection, if any, between such ordinary goods and the exalted value of virtue. White, in "Stoic Values," lays out the problem carefully, and solves it elegantly, by distinguishing acts that are merely appropriate (in our lingo, submoral requirements or oughts) from acts that are "right" in the full sense. The solution anticipates some matters we will argue for in Chapter 7, but here is White's summary statement (White, "Stoic Values," 50–53).

> The crucial fact is that even when the sage and the ordinary person perform what is outwardly the very same act, they conceive of that act in quite different ways. To the ordinary person, the act will be seen as falling under a type, such as honoring one's parents, for which there is a "reasonable defense." These types include those that appear in the various precepts that we employ in ordinary deliberation and teaching. Thus for the ordinary person a particular action will seem justified *qua* falling under the concept or predicate, *honoring one's parents*, or perhaps some wider predicate under which it is subsumed. For the sage, on the other hand, it will recommend itself in a rather different way. It will be seen primarily under the very general notion: *fitting into the whole structure of acts that it is appropriate for him (and others) to perform.* And it will be seen in this way only by the sage, because only the sage, according to the Stoics, is in a position to comprehend all of his actions within a systematic and coherent picture. . . .
>
> But if this is so, then clearly the sage can have two simultaneous attitudes toward one and the same act. He approves of the act *qua* fitting into the pattern that he comprehends, which gives it its status as a "right act," but he is indifferent toward it *qua* merely falling under the type, e.g., "honoring one's parents," that gives it its status as a merely "appropriate act." The Stoic claims about the end of life make it inevitable that the sage will have this dual attitude toward acts (and, *mutatis mutandis*, things that are preferred and dispreferred). The end, we saw, was "living in accord with nature."
>
> But so far we only have part of the answer to our problem. For to see that the same thing can be regarded both as indifferent and nevertheless also as preferable, under two different concepts, is still not to see the connection between these two concepts. As I have insisted, we must still ask why virtue involves the propensity to choose certain things even though they are indifferent.
>
> For the sage, i.e., the perfectly virtuous person, the answer is straightforward. The sage's appropriate acts are simultaneously right acts. For him the particular acts that have a reasonable defense are precisely the acts that are

done with a full understanding of the correct pattern of acts into which they fit. So for him the propensity to perform particular appropriate acts is extensionally equivalent to the propensity to act from full understanding. But the sage's reason for performing those acts is that they satisfy the latter condition, not that they satisfy the former. *Qua* conforming to nature, these acts are not indifferent at all. When chosen as such, they are "right acts," not merely "appropriate acts," and so there is no reason to wonder how it could be the human end, or rational, or virtuous, for the sage to perform them.

External goods and happiness: stoics versus Aristotle. Ancient critics of stoicism sometimes took the line that what was true in stoic ethics was not new, and that what was new was not true. Current critics are more generous. For example, most now grant that the notion of *oikeiosis* and its role in moral development are important stoic contributions, not to be found in predecessors despite what some later Peripatetics claimed. But the issue that has drawn the most sustained attention, almost all of it unfavorable to us, and almost all of it couched in terms of a comparison to Aristotle, is the thesis that virtue is sufficient for happiness (or "identical" to it). In one sense, of course, Aristotle also identifies virtue with happiness (e.g., at 1098a. 16–20 of the *Nicomachean Ethics*) when he says that the highest good for humans is the activity of the soul in accordance with virtue in a complete life. And as Annas, in *The Morality of Happiness* (369–70), says, for Aristotle,

> There is . . . a sense in which virtue is the only aim of the virtuous person. She will go for health, money and so on in the normal course of things; but if she is fully virtuous, and virtue demands ignoring or losing these things, she will not only perform the virtuous action but she will be completely motivated to do it. She will note the losses, and may regret them for many reasons, but they do not so much as tempt her to reject the virtuous course. To be fully virtuous, from both the affective and the intellectual side, is to be someone who does what virtue requires just for that reason and not for any ulterior reason, without having to battle down counter-motivation. And to be this sort of person is to be a person who aims at the life of virtuous activity for its own sake.

Yet Aristotle famously insists that a life of virtuous activity cannot be "complete" (and thus be identical to happiness, our final end) without an adequate supply of "external" goods such as wealth, power, and good luck (e.g., at 1101a. 14–16 of the *Nicomachean Ethics*). And against that, stoics notoriously claim that virtue "is" happiness. In an admirable and instructive article, Irwin ("Stoic and Aristotelian Conceptions of Happiness," 206) says that "The belief that virtue is identical to happiness separates [the stoics] from Aristotle; and the recognition of valuable indifferents separates them from the Cynics." He goes on to propose that the stoics argued for a distinctive middle position by adopting Aristotle's formal conditions for the highest good (roughly, that it be the ultimate end of all action, that it be complete, self-sufficient, and incapable of being increased by the addition of other goods), but then by rejecting Aristotle's contention that virtue alone cannot meet those conditions. This the stoics did by arguing that "Aristotle's inference from his formal conditions is unwarranted; a complete good need not include external goods, and is fully achieved by virtue" (208).

Readers will have to judge for themselves how well we succeed here in preserving this distinctive middle position. It is of course true that it is impossible to exercise agency at all when our stock of external goods falls below some minimum level. If that is all Aristotle meant by an adequate supply of them, then there is no difference between his position and ours. We assume, however, that for him, an adequate supply meant a good deal more than this minimum.

Affect, emotion, passion: stoics versus stoics, and stoics versus Aristotle. In our view, Posidonius is the sage among the ancient stoics on these topics. His views on emotion are known to us primarily through Galen's report of them in Galen, *On the Doctrines of Hippocrates and Plato* IV–V. Kidd, in "Posidonius on Emotions," and Cooper, in "Posidonius on Emotions," are of great help in drawing out the implications of this material, and in their hands it looks both different from Plato (to whom many have thought Posidonius was retreating by invoking a doctrine about the divisions of the soul) and strikingly modern. Inwood, in "Seneca and Psychological Dualism," carries the same sort of argument forward against claims that Seneca too was propounding a doctrine of a divided soul in which reason is pitted against passion.

No stoics ever held the view that the sage's life should be empty of affect, emotion, and passion. Inwood, in *Ethics and Human Action in Early Stoicism* (chap. 5), assembles a compelling case on this point even for the Early Stoa. The doctrine was not that we should be passionless (*apatheia*), but rather that "*apatheia* is *eupatheia* . . . [where] *eupatheia* is simply the impulse of a fully rational man" (173). The standardly cited stoic text on the nature of the good passions is the curious one from Diogenes Laertius, *Lives of the Eminent Philosophers* 7.116, quoted here in the translation by Long and Sedley, in *The Hellenistic Philosophers* (412):

> (1) They [the Stoics] say that there are three good feelings: joy, watchfulness, wishing. (2) Joy, they say, is the opposite of pleasure, consisting in well-reasoned swelling [elation]; and watchfulness is the opposite of fear, consisting in well-reasoned shrinking. For the wise man will not be afraid at all, but he will be watchful. (3) They say that wishing is the opposite of appetite, consisting in well-reasoned stretching [desire]. (4) Just as certain passions fall under the primary ones, so too with the primary good feelings. Under wishing: kindness, generosity, warmth, affection. Under watchfulness: respect, cleanliness. Under joy: delight, sociability, cheerfulness.

Sandbach, in *The Stoics* (59–68), while no better than anyone else at reducing the weirdness of that classification scheme, is nonetheless an effective antidote to the distortion of stoic doctrine on *eupatheia* in general, emphasizing that the passions the stoics were concerned to expunge were only those they regarded as excessive. Frede, in "The Stoic Doctrines of the Affections of the Soul," makes the important point, however, that what the stoics regarded as excessive must have been very different from what Platonists and Aristotelians so identified, else there would have been no dispute between them on this matter. (And there surely was such a dispute.) All hands rejected "excessive" affect, emotion, and passion; all insisted that well-modulated "good passions" remain in the sage. Frede's argument is that the stoic view is distinctive because it rejects the view that the "affections of the soul" come from some mental faculty other than reason, which reason must then subordinate and modulate. Rather, affections are certain manifestations of beliefs. In modern jargon: for the mature human agent, every attitude is a propositional attitude, in which the attitude supervenes on believing the proposition. (Things are different for animals and primal human agents.) Affects thus arise from our perceptual-intellectual apparatus, and are excessive just in case the beliefs that generate them are false. Since virtue (the perfection of reason; here the perfection of agency) eliminates false beliefs, it thereby eliminates all the affect generated by false beliefs. And since we are typically very far from being sages in every aspect of our lives, it is reasonable to think that our affective life (no matter how well modulated and appropriate it is by Aristotelian standards) is very different from a sage's. A sage's life would lack most of the affects (well modulated or not) that ordinary people have, because most of their affects are traceable to false beliefs.

Notice, though, that Posidonius raises a caution about a straightforward acceptance of such a belief-to-desire account, quoted in Galen, *On the Doctrines of Hippocrates and Plato* IV.5.26ff.:

Posidonius answers this objection in the following way: "On this interpretation of Chrysippus' words one might first raise the question how it is that wise men, who hold that all honorable things are good to the highest degree and unsurpassed, are not moved affectively by them, desiring the things they seek and taking excessive delight in these same things whenever they obtain them. For if the magnitude of apparent goods or evils moves one to believe that it is proper and in accordance with one's estimate of them to be moved affectively when they are present or approaching and to accept no reasoning that says one should be moved by them in another way, then the persons who think that the good they enjoy is unsurpassed ought to have been thus affected; but we observe that this does not happen. There is a similar difficulty in the case of those who are making progress and who suppose that their vice brings them great harm: they ought to have been carried away by fear and to have fallen victim to immoderate distress, but this too does not happen." After this Posidonius writes as follows: "And if they should say that in addition to the magnitude of the apparent good or evil, weakness of soul is also to blame, and for that reason the wise are completely rid of the affections, but inferior men, when their weakness is not a weakness of the ordinary kind but one that has gone to extremes, are not, even so the problem is not resolved. For all agree that men fall into affections because of sickness of soul; but the question asked is how the soul has been moved and what motion it causes, and that question is not answered." His next words are: "But not only those who have a vice that has gone to extremes and who fall easily into affections, but all unwise men, so long as they have their vice, fall into affections both great and small." And he continues, "To suppose that a person has been moved in this way in accordance with his estimate of events, so that the rejection of reason indicates a great affection, is to suppose wrongly; for this happens also through a moderate and a small (affection)." After this Posidonius writes the following: "When two persons have the same weakness and receive a like impression of good or evil, one is moved affectively, the other not; and one (is moved) more, the other less. And sometimes the weaker (of two persons), who supposes that what has befallen him is greater, is not moved. And the same person is sometimes moved affectively, sometimes not, at the same things, and sometimes more, sometimes less. Thus those who are unused (to a thing) are more greatly affected in situations of fear, distress, desire and pleasure; and the more vicious are quickly seized by their affections."

Posidonius next presents quotations from the poets and historical accounts of ancient exploits which testify to his statements. And after that he adds: "So what is evil is quickly seized by an unaccustomed thing, but what is given the opposite evaluation is seized only when its habituation is changed in the course of time; in these cases the suppositions held are often equal, and so is the degree of infirmity, but the affections do not arise equally and are not equal." Thereupon he poses questions such as the following; I shall quote them in his own words, even though the passages are rather long: "Why is it that some who believe that what is happening is of great import, even though they are infirm in judgment, nevertheless deliberate and call on others to advise them, as sleepless Agamemnon did? . . . For it is not convincing that the cause in this case lies in the supposition that what one is pushed toward is a great good; but the question must be asked." I can give Posidonius no answer to his question, and I believe that no one else will be able to do so, if I am to judge by the actual nature of the facts and by the Stoics of the present. In my time there have been no few (Stoics), and these not undistinguished; but I have heard none of them say anything convincing in answer to the question raised by Posidonius.

It is not entirely clear what Posidonius' positive position is on this matter. He rejects a direct and complete belief-to-desire account, but need not be interpreted as endorsing a Platonic tripartite soul. The most plausible view, we think, is that these texts are consistent with the line we take here: (1) Agency is a single faculty, but a permanently complex one. Its primal elements (impulses, reflexes, etc.) are not rooted out by reason and stoic training, and are thus present in the sage. (2) Under conditions agents face repeatedly throughout their lives, elements of primal agency generate false beliefs and thence disturbing emotions and passions. See Posidonius on "fresh" distress in Galen, *On the Doctrines of Hippocrates and Plato* IV.7. See also Inwood, *Ethics and Human Action in Early Stoicism* (175ff.), on "preliminary passions." (3) Stoic training (that is, the perfection of agency) allows us to cope with such disturbances successfully, much as we learn to cope with perceptual illusions. The thirsty traveler salivates in relief upon seeing an oasis mirage in the desert, but that "disturbance" dissipates quickly when he learns that there is no oasis. A sage will see mirages, too, whenever the perceptual conditions are right. He just won't fall for the illusion for long. His reason will correct his beliefs, and with that, his affect. Similarly for the somatic states (e.g., arousal reflexes of various sorts) that persistently generate false beliefs, which in turn generate disturbing passions. In the sage, such disturbances will dissipate quickly, when reason corrects the false beliefs.

But it does not follow at all from this that *true* beliefs do not generate passions—even passions an Aristotelian would find wildly immoderate. The poet says

Wild Nights—Wild Nights!
Were I with thee
Wild nights should be
Our luxury!

Futile—the Winds—
To a heart in port—
Done with the Compass—
Done with the Chart!

Rowing in Eden—
Ah, the Sea!
Might I but moor—Tonight—
In Thee!

Aristotelians will have to speak for themselves about whether, on their theory of virtue as moderation, they think Dickinson has come unhinged here. (Dickinson, *The Complete Poems of Emily Dickinson*, poem 249.) We certainly do not think so. We do not find *anything* unstoic—anything, that is, of infantile, immature, self-destructive, or unintegrated agency in such thoughts, or in the wild desires and actions they represent. She is, after all, talking about the luxury available to a heart moored safely in port. And frank as she may be, she is not, we suppose, talking about orgasms prolonged and intensified by brutal drugs and strangulation.

Historically, most of our efforts to talk about our views on the passions have been directed to dealing with its dangers rather than its safe luxuries. But nothing in our fundamental doctrine (as opposed to therapies and moral-training manuals drawn up for the benefit of those at risk) opposes passion as such. Infantile or bestial passion, yes, insofar as it lacks (or subordinates) propositional content. Immature, unintegrated, or incapacitating passion, yes, insofar as it is incompatible with the perfection of agency. But read the poem again. Then try to make an argument that such intensity is ruled out by the aim of perfecting one's agency. We think the try will fail.

It may be that this point was not adequately understood among our ancient brethren. Their standard line does seem to have been the one Martha Nussbaum characterizes as the "extirpation of the passions" and discusses with characteristic brio in Nussbaum, *The Therapy of Desire* (chap. 10). And they certainly appear to have assumed (as opposed to have argued) that the sage's *eupatheia* would be tranquil. Notice, however, the telling point Nussbaum later makes in discussing Seneca on anger (chap. 11). Seneca's description of the physical signs and incapacitating effects of anger (and the gruesome examples he gives of it) make it pretty clear that what he is discussing is infantile or incapacitating rage. And it is not at all clear to us that the striking example Nussbaum gives from Elie Wiesel (403) poses a problem for stoics.

> Wiesel was a child in one of the Nazi death camps. On the day the Allied forces arrived, the first member of the liberating army he saw was a very large black officer. Walking into the camp and seeing what was there to be seen, this man began to curse, shouting at the top of his voice. As the child Wiesel watched, he went on shouting and cursing for a very long time. And the child Wiesel thought, watching him, now humanity has come back. Now, with that anger, humanity has come back.

She continues:

> Wiesel's soldier was no Stoic. But it was just on account of the extremity of his justified rage that the child Wiesel saw him as a messenger of humanity. Seneca's treatise [De Ira] urges the extirpation of anger. It ends with the famous injunction "Let us cultivate humanity." Colamus humanitatem. . . . Can the Stoic have humanity while losing rage?

The question is beautifully posed. The answer, we think, lies in seeing that the soldier may well have been a perfectly good stoic. Time, place, duty, consequence, and words available to represent the truth are all factors in what counts as appropriate. Nothing in the event as described implies the least compromise with the stoic conception of virtue. No duty was breached. No one suffered or was incapacitated by the soldier's anger; on the contrary, a suffering child was comforted by it. And in that place even a sage might be forgiven for not finding elevated language accessible. Nothing in our doctrine entails that sages lack this sort of comforting passion.

Nonetheless, it may be that when ancient stoics (even Posidonius) tried to imagine what kind of affective life would follow from the sage's beliefs, they were too quick to think that it would be a tranquil one. For the standard array of relevant ancient texts, see Long and Sedley, The Hellenistic Philosophers (section 65). Striker, in "Following Nature: A Study in Stoic Ethics" (62–73), is sharply critical of us on this point. But as Posidonius himself suggests, if passions in the mature agent supervene upon beliefs, then sages ought to be the very people most passionately affected by virtue—and be surpassingly passionate about it because they perceive it to be surpassingly valuable.

How wild, though, or immoderate will the sage's passion be? We confess we have typically supposed that sages will be much cooler and calmer, emotionally, than the rest of us. Suppose that is so. Suppose (in line with the standard sort of abuse we have provoked) that the stoic sage cannot even contemplate having a wild night in a safe port with a wonderful poet. Even so, we should consider carefully why this is so. It may not be due to the absence of passion in the sage. It may rather be due to a complication in the causal link between the sage's beliefs about virtue and his passions. For example, the sage's coolness may be due to the way that the link is weakened by his awareness that he is fallible and possibly mistaken about what virtue requires in particular cases. It will not necessarily be weakened in every case, however, because (as in the case of Wiesel's soldier) general facts about human fallibility are not always a relevant consideration.

Virtue as an activity, the final end, and the only good. For the ancient doctrine on virtue as the final end, see Cicero, *De Finibus* III.v–vii, beginning at v.20. For the doctrine that virtue is the only good, and the notions of value and indifference, see Diogenes Laertius, *Lives of the Eminent Philosophers* 7.101–5. For other sources, and some differences between them, consult Long and Sedley, *The Hellenistic Philosophers*, section 63 on the final end, and section 61 on virtue generally, including the unity issue; sections 58 and 60 on value and indifference. Note especially the commentary to section 63. The ancient stoics were vigorously attacked on all these points for making silly or illogical arguments. Kidd, in "Stoic Intermediates and the End for Man," and Striker, in "Antipater, or the Art of Living," helpfully clear away some of the debris to reveal a logical way of understanding the traditional stoic "identification" of the final end with happiness, happiness with virtue, and virtue with an activity—a way that makes sense of their refusal to treat these assertions as either trivially or definitionally true.

Inwood, in "Goal and Target in Stoicism," and Striker, in "Following Nature: A Study in Stoic Ethics," section 3, helpfully explore the stoic notion that virtue is a special sort of craft—sometimes called a "stochastic" craft—like medicine or archery, in which the obvious aim of the enterprise must be distinguished from the issue of whether the craft is being practiced to perfection. In the case of medicine, the physician can have practiced his art perfectly even though he fails to restore the patient to health. Should he therefore have tried to practice imperfectly? Surely not. There is thus a sense in which the physician's goal or aim must be different from—more complicated than—simply restoring the patient to health. The latter is the "target" in every instance of practicing medicine, and in the long run success at hitting those targets determines what will count as safe and effective medicine, but the physician's *controlling goal* in each case is evidently as much to act appropriately *as* a physician—to practice the craft to its highest current standard—as it is to get a good result in that case. This is the point stoics want to make about perfecting the exercise of agency. The activity of acting appropriately is itself the controlling aim, even though it may not be the target. Just why this point about the complexity of stochastic crafts and virtue has generated so much dispute is hard to understand. Perhaps, as Striker argues, it is due to confusion about the variety of meanings that statements of the form 'X is Y' can have. In any case, modern readers should find the point so familiar as to be humdrum. It is made constantly in arguments for the importance of form and process in a democratic polity, or the importance of zealous advocacy in an adversarial legal system. And failure to appreciate the stochastic complexity of crafts, arts, and professions is precisely the point at issue in complaints about managers, legislators, and administrators who see nothing but the bottom line about outcomes.

Striker, in "Following Nature: A Study in Stoic Ethics" (2) makes the point that when ancient stoics spoke about eudaimonia, or the final end, they defined it as "something that everyone should or ought to pursue, rather than as an aim that everyone does in fact pursue." This much is consistent with our view here as well, though we no longer endorse the idea that the "ought" comes from cosmic *telos*.

The task of agency is to implement our endeavors successfully. In that respect it appears to be a means to various ends—and perhaps the perfection of agency is *the* means to *the* optimal integration and realization of our ends. But that may seem to fall short of a warrant for thinking it is an end in itself at all, let alone for thinking it has the incomparable value the ancient stoics assigned to virtue. In particular, people who find some affinity between the stoics and Kant on this point are likely to be dissatisfied with the rough handling this doctrine gets in the text of this chapter. Ideal agency as described here may seem to some to be entirely too instrumental and intermediate to be a plausible candidate for the final end, or a candidate at all for something so precious that it cannot even be put on the same scale as ordinary goods.

The Kantian interpretation of stoic doctrine is fascinating, and is perhaps most striking on the subject of natural law and justice (see Annas, *The Morality of Happiness*, 304ff.). But we think it is dangerous. The danger comes from the fact that stoic ethical theory is a relentlessly naturalistic and particularistic one, and Kantian ethical theory is decidedly not. Doctrines that look alike in slogan form may look very different when each is fully explained. When stoics give an account of what can plausibly be regarded as the final end, we do it by giving an account of human psychological development. We give a cradle argument that shows how healthy agents just *do*, in the course of becoming fit, come to have an independent affection for acting appropriately—that is, for "getting it right," where "it" is a universally quantified variable. This soon includes an affection for the *ability* to act appropriately—that is, for the perfected powers of agency itself. And our account of the way in which sages come to identify the exercise of ideal agency powers with virtue, and to prize it above all else (indeed, beyond comparison with anything else) is also a developmental one, which is in outline quite mundane. Our *arguments* for pursuing virtue are arguments from the inside, as it were. They are the arguments healthy agents construct and have the motivation to act upon, *given the nature of their agency*.

The difficulty (and we suppose the fascination for rationalists) is that reasoning about the nature and worth of virtue itself plays a central role in this developmental story. Reason itself leads agents to the conclusion that virtue is their final end and the sole good. If we are not thinking carefully, the abstract, formal properties of reason may appear to make ethical doctrines grounded in "pure" reason somehow independent of the existence and subjective states of particular agents, and thus truly "objective"—in contrast to the sort of theory we have presented here. But we reject the idea that *pure* practical reason is sufficient to lead us to stoic doctrines about virtue. We think that pure practical reason, operating in unhealthy agents, or in healthy agents in unfavorable circumstances, will often lead them very far away from our doctrines. And we reject the idea that our particularism—our insistence that all norms are facts about the endeavors of particular agents—makes our ethical theory "subjectivist."

Engberg-Pedersen, in "Stoic Philosophy and the Concept of Person," is very helpful on this point in contrasting ancient stoic doctrine with recent discussions about subjective versus objective points of view, especially ones found in Williams, *Ethics and the Limits of Philosophy*, and in Nagel, *The View from Nowhere*. He criticizes ("Stoic Philosophy," 124) the assumption that "if practical rationality remains *somebody's*, then it will necessarily lose its rational and objective character." He asks us to contrast that assumption with the stoic view in which practical rationality is consistently regarded as belonging to *somebody* and to somebody who has, and retains, an individual self throughout the development of the objective view. The objective view is a view *on oneself*, and this fact has a number of welcome consequences. One is that we can avoid the idea, which when taken literally is in fact absurd, of a "point of view of the universe." Another . . . is that there is now no difficulty in understanding how one should come to *act* on the insights gained in applying the objective view. Most importantly, . . . there is no suggestion that the connection of the objective view to the individual makes it any less objective or rational.

Our differences with Kant show up also in matters concerning the value of rational agency. Kant admired stoicism in several respects. But his rejection of our (highly conditional) endorsement of suicide shows nicely the contrast between our mundane views about virtue and the value of human life and his decidedly nonmundane ones. Seidler, in "Kant and the Stoics on Suicide," lays out the contrast in a particularly clear way.

Sages as humans. Among the fairest and most elegant descriptions of the stoic sage that have been culled from the ancient sources is the one given by Amélie Rorty, in Rorty, "The Two Faces of Stoicism: Rousseau and Freud" (12–15). Here is a portion of it, with her copious citations omitted.

> Although they may differ in important details, the physical constitutions of the [common man] and the sage are alike. Both are subject to disease and injury. . . . Both have cognitively-based reflex motions, and the sage may even find himself making the first minute reflex actions of shocked fearful flight at a sudden onslaught in battle. . . . Both have perceptual illusions; and when they are severely dehydrated, both are subject to hallucinations. . . . Under such conditions, even a sage might briefly treat a perceptual illusion as an indication of an oasis and find himself with what appears to be an inclination to move towards it. Unlike the common man, the sage knows that his physical constitution can expose him to epistemological danger. Because he knows that dehydration tends to induce hormai-inducing *phantasmata* and that shock and deprivation produce certain sorts of impulses, he will not automatically act from them. Sage that he is, he also knows that under certain conditions, even a rational person—physically constituted as he is—can find himself with what would, in an ordinary man, be weak opinions and excessive impulses. . . . He does not act from those opinions and impulses—his reason is not affected by them—because he forthwith understands them to be incomplete and partial. Properly and fully understood, they indicate a therapeutic regimen, much as fever and shivering are signs of an illness that mandates a specific therapy. Where the [common man] might impulsively act on his passions—unwisely drinking to quench a feverish thirst—, the sage stands as an internalized physician to his own psychological conditions. Rather than straightway affirming or denying the *phantasiai* and *phantasmata* that the common man impulsively follow, the sage does not take them at face value. In him, they function rationally, set in their proper full context. This does not mean that the mind of the sage is divided, or that his rationality controls his psychology as a master directs a slave. While he shares at least some of his psychology with the common man, his conditions are

distinguished by their functional roles, by the ways that they are integrated within the whole system of his thought.

Since many of his hormetic motions—cringing, fleeing, weeping—are conceptually based and conceptually laden, the sage may find himself having cringing, fleeing and weeping thoughts and impulses. But he is not *just* the body that cringes or flees, even when he finds himself with the thoughts that attend such motions. As a part of his body, his *hegemonikon* traces the etiology and functions of those "passive" conditions: his actions directed by the all-things-considered judgments that encompass and explain them. He regards those psycho-physical states as no more—and no less—essentially his than the pain of the wound that *he* attends or the shiver of a fever that *he* must cure. Instead of treating himself as a disembodied *hegemonikon* that bears no effective relation to that body, he also understands that his psychophysical states are conditions of his body, towards which he happens to have a special relation. It is, after all, the body that *he* feeds and exercises. While he does not act from what he regards as pre-rational passion-based proto-impulses, he takes those conditions as providential signs that—barring better judgment—might reasonably direct his actions. The sage integrates his immediate conditions—hunger, fever or sexual arousal—within a larger psycho-physical context. This process does not divide the mind of the sage into two parts or layers: it rather places his initial proto-passions *(propatheiai)* and impulses in a larger, properly evaluated context, one in which his essential nature is given its proper weight. When their psychological conditions are abstractly compared in isolation, out of context, the sage and the common man share at least some thinly-described *pathe*. The difference lies in the way that the sage's integration of his conditions affects their functional roles, and affects the way he acts.

The sage's virtue just consists in his forming, and acting from "all things considered judgments." The dehydrated man and the injured soldier are sages just insofar as their proto-passions are not merely fragmentary and partial, but reflect their place in the cosmic order. They are actively rational insofar as they see their initial tendencies as expressions of the laws of optics and the constitution of human bodies. Both the condition of the rational unity of mind and of the unity of the virtues are satisfied. Even in those cases where the motions of the sage seem to be extensionally identical with those of an ordinary man, his reigning impulsive intentions are formed by his integrative understanding. The *phantasiai*-ridden *hormai* that would, in a [common man], be passive passions, actively express not only his knowledge of what is genuinely valuable, but also of the hierarchical structure of instrumental goods.

There is much more in this vein, but that should be enough to make the point that there is ample warrant in the stoic tradition for correcting the picture of the sage painted by critics. Baron, *Kantian Ethics Almost without Apology* (chap. 6), considers in a helpful way Kant's endorsement of the stoic sage as having a "sublime" way of dealing with loss and futility. In defending Kant she makes points about control of emotion, futility and agency that are similar to some of the things we say on those topics.

Acknowledgments

I am indebted to correspondence from David Jones that helped me to clarify important matters in metaphysics and philosophy of mind, to correspondence with Asli Gocer on naturalism in ethics, to conversations with George Harris on the differences between Aristotle and the stoics, to bibliographic advice and conversations on psychology with George Ledger (who kindly read the relevant passages on the development of agency), and to correspondence from Julia Annas, Stephen Darwall, and John Marshall that pressed me to revise an earlier version of what is now the section called "Exalted Virtue." The section on the argument for virtue owes its existence to queries from two readers for the Princeton University Press— and to the skepticism some contemporary philosophers have expressed about whether there is an argument at all (as opposed to a description) to be found in ancient versions of the cradle argument. Rachels and Ruddick's chapter, "Lives and Liberty," in *The Inner Citadel: Essays on Individual Autonomy*, has for some years been very useful to me in thinking through matters related to a distinction they make between one's biological and biographical lives. Gould, in *Rethinking Democracy* (chap. 2), has been similarly fruitful in casting some features of the self-other distinction in terms of internal relations. Searle's articles, "The Mystery of Consciousness: Part I" and "The Mystery of Consciousness: Part II," were especially useful in sorting through some recent literature on the nature of consciousness.

7

Happiness

STOICS put the discussion of happiness at the end of their ethical concerns, and are impatient with protracted discussions of it. Even children rarely seek happiness directly, in the sense of directly seeking pleasant mental states. And when that narrow sense of happiness (as pleasant affect) is replaced with one constructed by fit or virtuosic agents, stoic doctrines about it seem obvious consequences of our account of virtue. We hold that happiness as understood by mature and fit agents is a property of whole lives, not of transient mental states. We hold that it is achievable only through a proper balance of stability and control in the exercise of agency. We hold that virtue is necessary for happiness, and sufficient for it too, even in adversity, as long as ideal agency can be exercised. Happiness in this broad sense—*eudaimonia*, a good life—is the polestar of our ethical theory. It is a reference point for navigation rather than an announced destination, but when sages reach virtue they coincidentally reach happiness in the most exalted sense imaginable; and that is inspiring. The rest of us, who only more or less approach virtue, seem able only to orbit happiness like comets, swinging in great ellipses in which near-virtue intersects only rarely, briefly and dangerously, with near-happiness. This misfortune of orbital mechanics, however, constitutes no objection to the argument that virtue, and not happiness, should be our aim.

A Complete Life

We learn very early that things look different in retrospect. We get through some fearful, painful thing and find not only that it was bearable but that it seems insignificant in relation to everything else we have experienced, and in relation to the future (good or bad) that stretches in front of us. We reach some much anticipated goal and find ourselves disappointed by how transient the pleasure of it is, and how trivial the achievement. It soon becomes clear to any healthy agent that a restricted frame of reference distorts rational assessment of any endeavor or experience. This is reinforced by the agent's efforts to integrate and optimize the success of her various endeavors—a process that often requires sequencing, modulating, and subordinating them in surprising (but satisfying)

ways. The combination of surprise and satisfaction—in the postpone-
ment of projects and in the modulation of motivation to pursue them—
immediately suggests to the agent that the scope of her efforts to integrate
and optimize her endeavors is crucial to her success in doing so. A restricted frame of reference is systematically misleading. But what is an
unrestricted frame of reference in this context? The developmental project
of agency is to move from health to fitness and then to virtue, which is
ideal agency. Ideal agency is comprehensive; it aims to integrate and optimize the success of every single thing we do, in relation to everything else
we do or might do, over our entire lives. The ideal agent's frame of reference is thus her whole life, represented as accurately as a human being can
remember its history and imagine its future, and lived as intelligently as a
human being can exploit its possibilities.

The picture of a complete life, then, is the picture of a life that is an
organized whole, with no unconnected parts. It is also the picture of a life
replete with successful ventures, opportunities taken, lessons learned—in
short, replete with intelligent activity carried out with the benefit of an
impressive array of developed endowments and constructed traits, operating in a challenging environment. But we have at least three other concerns about completeness that are the product of reflecting on ideal
agency.

Two of them have to do with how a life can be completed, as opposed
to simply being ended. On the one hand the notion of a completed life—
one that has run its full course—is the notion of a life that completes its
particular biological arc, from infancy to death, *in terms of the physiological possibilities available to it*, and is not prematurely ended by disease,
natural disaster, accident, or murder. (We say "its particular" arc to indicate that even among ideal agents there is not uniformity in what constitutes a completed life in this sense. Ideal agency requires the endowments
necessary for psychological health, of course, as well as the length and
breadth of experience required to develop health to virtuosity, but it does
not require ideal human endowments. Not all sages live past their prime,
for example, or have good teeth.) Another notion of a completed life is of
a life that is finished in a biographical sense—one whose "story" is essentially complete, even if its biological arc is not. Ideal agents, we suppose,
will want the two sorts of endings to coincide in their lives. They will
want to finish what they start in a biographical sense, and thus not die
prematurely, but they will not want to linger pointlessly.

Finally, ideal agents have practical concerns about how their completed lives will fit into, and can be rationally assessed in terms of, the
larger things in which they are embedded, from local legend to cosmic
history. You do not have to have world-historical ambitions, or even be
a sage, to ask questions about the meaning of your life. But when a sage

asks those questions, what matters to her is not whether her life has cosmic significance or a useful place in family legend. What matters is its virtue—the extent to which it is the product of the exercise of ideal agency. That means, in part, the exercise of agency assessed in terms of all of its circumstances, from local to cosmic. In sum, then, a good life for the sage (happiness, or *eudaimonia* in the sense constructed by the exercise of her agency) is a life that is unified, replete with activity that exemplifies the virtuosic exercise of practical intelligence in every context, from local to global.

Good times. Stoics have occasionally claimed that, for the sage, *eudaimonia* somehow replaces ordinary happiness. This has been the source of much confusion, both among stoics and their critics, and is partly responsible for the false notion that the stoic ideal is a life devoid of the ordinary pleasures of sex, food, drink, music, wealth, fame, friends, and so on (let us call them nonagency pleasures or, more generally, nonagency goods) that are either not necessary for, or do not come merely from the exercise of, agency itself. To avoid the confusion, we make the following observation: If we consider what is necessary and sufficient for a good life as conceived and lived by an ideal agent, we will not be able to put any particular set of the nonagency goods on the list. This is so because it is clear that healthy agents regularly sacrifice one or another of all such goods in order to integrate and optimize their lives, and because it is clear that sages have the ability to thrive as sages in extremely reduced circumstances—circumstances in which their only pleasure (though a very considerable one it is) comes from the virtuosic exercise of their agency. The joy that comes from that is the joy that comes from virtue itself, and since virtue is what ultimately matters to the sage, that joy is (for the sage) sufficient for a good life (happiness), even in the ordinary sense of the term. It is true, then, that stoic happiness does not *necessarily* include nonagency pleasures—all the other possibilities for what we ordinarily call having a good time. But it is highly misleading to go on to say that such pleasures are superfluous, or that they "add" nothing to virtue. They do not add *virtue* to a virtuous life, but they add something else to it. They add ordinary pleasures to it—something stoics decidedly do not reject. (Think of this in terms of Galileo's paradox: The set of all even integers is an infinite set whose cardinal number is $\aleph_0$. When we add to that the set of all odd integers we get an infinite set with the same cardinal number. We have not added to the infinity, but we have certainly added to the set.) If, then, we go on to consider (as the ancient stoics certainly did) whether a life with both agency and nonagency pleasures is to be preferred to a life with only agency ones, we will get a series of obvious and uncontroversial conclusions that do a great deal to correct the caricature of stoicism. The pleasures of virtue are never to be traded for nonagency ones, but among virtuous lives, those with nonagency pleasures, and nonagency goods generally, are preferred to those without them. Further, with virtue held constant, the more nonagency goods the better.

There is a serious theoretical problem here, but it is not the one stoics are usually taxed with. The problem is that below the level of ideal agency there appears to be no helpful rule for deciding *a priori* in a given case what mix of agency and nonagency goods is to be preferred. Fit agents for whom virtuosity is directly possible will presumably be motivated, finally, by the endeavor to achieve it. Agents for whom virtuosity is only an indirect possibility—that is, agents who can achieve it, if at all, only by first trying to make it possible where success is uncertain—will presumably be motivated to try to do that. But we know from experience that below the level of ideal agency, there is no simple correlation between the degree to which we approximate the ideal and the degree to which we experience its goods, or achieve the good life defined by it. One misstep can wreck everything. (Count no man happy until he is dead.) Moreover, some nonagency goods may reinforce, while others inhibit, progress toward the ideal. But which goods do which, and in what mixtures and amounts, appears to vary widely from person to person. Thus it is highly unlikely that we can construct a unitary account of the good life for nonideal agents, even a sketchy account that changes in a regular way as agents approximate the ideal. The best we can do, as Chapter 3 suggests, is to characterize some general arrangements that seem successful, and construct norms for stoic moral education accordingly.

Plans and narratives. There is also the question of how much and what kind of additional structure a complete life will have—for sages and for the rest of us. Must sages have a rational life-plan? Must their lives have narrative unity? To have virtue as our final end, and to organize the exercise of our agency in terms of it, is surely to have some sort of life-plan. And our development as agents—from infancy to death, primal agency to virtue—is an archetypical narrative. The details of this chapter and the previous one add some sketchy content to these notions. But these discussions also make clear that commitment to detailed long-range plans and thick narratives can be dangerous even for healthy agency, let alone for progress toward fitness or virtuosity. It can block or distort perceptions, reduce our adaptability, fill our lives with indefensible attachments, and so forth. Thoughtful treatments of these matters by nonstoics always include cautions of this sort, and we certainly endorse them. We also recognize that plans and narratives are ubiquitous in human lives, and that detailed long-range plans and thick narratives often play an effective role for particular people in perfecting their agency. What we do not yet endorse is the notion that the psychology of our development as agents (toward virtue and happiness) *requires* that we live in terms of such enabling plans or narratives—for example, because doing so is necessary for psychological health. That is at best an unproved empirical hypothesis. We suspect it can be defeated by thickly described counterexamples, but we leave that task for another time.

A Controlled Life

Consider an instructive analogy between stability in an airplane and stability in the traits of character that agents develop. A fixed-wing aircraft is said to have positive stability if it stays in, or returns to, straight and level flight unless pressure is continuously applied to the controls. It has neutral stability when it holds any given attitude (roll, pitch, yaw) in which it is placed, tending neither to exaggerate that attitude nor to return to straight and level flight. It has negative stability when it deviates from any given flight attitude unless corrective control is continuously applied. At the theoretical limit of either positive or negative stability, an aircraft is virtually uncontrollable. On the one hand, perfect positive stability means that any attempt to maneuver using the control surfaces will be defeated by the airplane's tendency to stay straight and level. Advancing and decreasing the throttle would allow the pilot to take off, gain altitude, fly in a straight line, lose altitude, and land (very carefully, on a runway lined up with the original). But course corrections would not be possible. On the other hand, perfect negative stability means that an attempt to maneuver would be defeated by the airplane's tendency to deviate from any given attitude. Each such deviation would require correction, and the perpetual oscillation of correction and countercorrection would quickly increase in frequency, amplitude, or both, soon either exhausting the pilot or putting the aircraft beyond control altogether. It is clear that for practical purposes we need a reasonable balance between stability and control.

Agency is a balance of control and stability in an analogous way. That is, it is a balance between our dispositional ability to maneuver effectively toward our goals, responding with practical intelligence to salient events along the way, and our dispositional resistance to being deflected by the shifting winds of impulse and circumstance. When we have perfect control over our conduct, we no longer have anything worth calling character; we are simply untethered actors in an atmosphere of possibilities. When we have perfectly stable dispositions, we no longer have anything worth calling control; we simply follow the trajectory determined by our fixed traits, unable to maneuver at all in response to new information about our endeavors or circumstances. Neither state makes the effective exercise of agency a practical possibility. In aircraft, the ideal level of control and stability is determined by the purpose of the machine and the range of technological possibilities for flying it. If the airplane is designed as a trainer for novice pilots, a significant amount of positive stability is a desirable trait. If it is a high-performance fighter with computer-assisted controls, even some negative stability may be a tolerable trade-off for other characteristics. In the case of agency, the ideal level of control and stability is determined by the task of virtuosic practical intelligence operating in the range of practical possibilities available to human beings.

Fixed and malleable traits. The details of stability and control for agency are mostly matters for psychological theory rather than ethics, but several general observations of a normative sort follow from the account of virtue we have given. All of them, however, depend on noticing that the notion of stability, as applied to the traits of agency, has several dimensions. One is what we will call the fixity, or conversely the transformability, of a trait. In general, endowments can be damaged or deformed, developments can be reversed, constructed traits can be demolished or remodeled. What is acquired through learning can be transformed through additional learning, and it is obvious that making progress toward ideal agency often requires that a given trait be transformable. But the possibility of such transformation varies, and while it is clear that once ideal traits are achieved we want them to be maximally fixed—that is, insofar as is humanly possible, invulnerable to further change—it is not entirely clear how much stability of this sort we want in the traits we develop at intermediate stages between healthy and virtuosic agency. A great deal of challenging empirical and conceptual work on these matters remains to be done. Here we will have to be content with this general suggestion for such work. Health is preferred to ill health, fitness to mere health, and virtuosity to fitness. It seems plausible to conclude, both from ordinary observation and the relevant psychological literature, that we do not need perfect or perfectly stable health in order to pursue fit and virtuosic agency effectively. Deafness in one ear or periodic upper-respiratory infections may present obstacles, but do not by themselves prevent the development of ideal agency. It is also plausible to conclude, however, that there is an identifiable kernel of bodily and psychological health that is a necessary condition of all further development. If this kernel is damaged, so is the capacity to develop agency. Brain damage of various sorts will certainly do this on the bodily side, and autism will do it on the psychological side. Moreover, there is a set of traits that jointly constitute a sort of boot sector for agency—a mechanism for recovering from various sorts of failure and loss. For example, people whose default positions with respect to their basic psychological tenor and primal dispositions are characterized by optimism, a sense of security or trust, and primal curiosity, courage, perseverance, benevolence, and reciprocity will be in a position to rebuild productive social relationships even out of the ashes of total war. For when the horrors cease, such people will by default be ready to undertake new cooperative ventures of the sort that can rebuild conditions favorable to human health and development. People whose defaults are pessimism, anxiety, suspicion, and malevolence will continue, and continue to elicit from others, warlike behavior that compromises the health and development of agency. This suggests that we will prefer to have maximal fixity in the boot sector of agency—in those primal traits necessary to recovering and developing psychological health—throughout the whole process of development, and not just when we have reached the ideal. We will want control of (healthy) primal traits only in the form of having the ability to refine them, or to suspend their operation in certain situations. We will not want to be vulnerable to having these primal traits erased. Since there is a good deal of evidence to the effect that both healthy and unhealthy primal traits can become fixed in childhood, some important norms for moral education follow rather directly.

Gravitational force. Another dimension of stability in the traits of agency is the degree to which they resist our efforts to maneuver away from the paths they define, and generally attract our endeavors into those paths. Perfect gravitational stability is, we suppose, what the sage achieves for virtuosic agency in making it comprehensively controlling. But notice that maximal stability of this sort is extensionally equivalent to maximal control. Of course this control is dispositional. It need not always be exercised at the level of conscious deliberation and choice, and it need not be exercised at all if practical intelligence has no work to do. Still, this remark about ideal agency implies very little of interest about how much gravitational force various traits short of the ideal ought to have. Obviously, insofar as we need to maneuver outside of a given trait in order to improve our agency, we will want that trait to be weak enough to permit the maneuvers. And just as we prefer not to have neutral or negative stability in an aircraft, we will want enough gravitational pull from our settled traits to make it easy to be drawn back into the paths they define, and to stay there without exercising constant control. But such observations are mere metaphors. Serious hypotheses about these matters are, we suppose, empirical ones about what sorts of gravitational stability are best for the development and exercise of agency, either in a particular case or in various sorts of cases.

Release and recapture. With apologies for the violence it will do to the gravity metaphor, let us say that yet another dimension of stability relevant here is the extent to which (and speed with which) a trait will release or suspend its gravitational pull on our behavior temporarily, and then subsequently recapture it. There are cases in which having control means having the ability merely to turn the operation of a trait off or on, rather than having the ability to transform it or effectively resist its pull. Emotions make a good example here, but there are many others. (The "willing suspension of disbelief"we need in many situations, for example, gives us another large inventory of cases.) Think of a woman alone in a darkened room—weeping, as we incautiously say, uncontrollably. Now imagine that she is in some sort of uniform; that the room is a staff lounge; that colleagues occasionally enter, comfort her briefly, and quietly leave. She is not consoled. Now imagine a sudden emergency. Imagine that she suddenly, and effectively, resumes her role and takes charge with ease, dry-eyed. That is the sort of quick release from emotion that stoics admire. It is not something that is only available to sages. On the contrary, it is an ordinary phenomenon of healthy agency; and a good thing for us all that it is. Getting such release does not mean that she has transformed her emotional dispositions; nor does it mean (we believe) that she is successfully resisting their power, or suppressing them with iron control. Rather, from all appearances, it means that she simply stopped weeping—stopped feeling that way in order to undertake another endeavor. Such an abrupt stop often has the consequence, in the case of emotions and passions, that they seem gone when the emergency is over. But not always. We can plausibly imagine the woman soon resuming her weeping, unexpectedly, in a church, just as suddenly as she stopped. The ability to stop feelings (or break attachments) suddenly, when practical intelligence calls for it, is a survival trait. The fact that it is a leading property of some sorts of unhealthy agency should not be allowed to obscure the fact that it is also a property of fitness in agency. Stoic admiration for it, however brutally and provocatively the ancients expressed it, is no more than admiration for ordinary varieties of fitness.

It does not follow from the fact that we prefer to have optimal abilities to control our lives that we think we ought always to exercise such control. This is a point that many modern critics of stoicism appear to misunderstand. Good and bad fortune in endowments and circumstances play a very large role in how much control needs to be exercised. Being overcome by emotion is no more problematic for a stoic than being overcome by sleep. Sometimes sleep is dangerous (think of trying to avoid hypothermia), or a dereliction of duty, even when it is desperately needed. So too for all-consuming grief, or lust. But at other times luxuriating in sleep or passion is a harmless pleasure, much preferred to the tightly controlled variety. Stoic norms about a controlled life are all conditional. What we endorse is the ability to exercise control whenever practical intelligence calls for it. When the world is safe enough, and slack enough, for us to live recklessly or be wildly passionate or refuse even to monitor our emotions, then as long as we can and do recapture control when it is needed, and as long as the wildness does not inhibit our progress toward virtue, we can take as much delight in it as a libertine. (More, perhaps, since it often has a rareness for us that it lacks for libertines.) There is nothing in stoic doctrine that means a sage is limited to faint smiles and frowns.

Life on the Rack

Consider the hapless pilgrim, stripped and strangled by Thugs, and left for dead. He is resuscitated, only to be enslaved by traders. They use him as a beast of burden. Years later, the traders are slaughtered by brigands. The pilgrim's burden is doubled, and eventually he breaks down. He is tormented, used for vicious games, and finally dragged out into the desert night to be blinded and buried alive. The brigands will leave his head out, they say, and a straw in a jar of water within reach. Would he like to face the moon? Or perhaps he would rather not be buried at all but left waterless, broken-legged on the sand? He may choose, or let them choose. In a brief essay, explain the role stoic ethics can or should play in bringing happiness to the pilgrim. 30 minutes. 25 points.

It is not amusing to be asked for a serious response to a less-than-serious question, no matter how vividly put. But we concede that our ancient brethren have done a good deal to invite the sarcasm implicit in the question, and so it must be answered. First, we merely note that nothing in stoic ethics has ever suggested that we think humans are immortal, or invulnerable to having their agency damaged or destroyed by disease or injury. Even the exercise of ideal agency can be stopped in its tracks by excruciating pain, and there is no stoic anesthetic for that, only the prospect of recovery if and when the pain subsides enough to permit sustained thought. If it does, then we recommend the same thing here that we recommend in every other case: the exercise of practical intelligence all-things-considered. A sage will wring as much out of that as the situation allows, but it is foolish to pretend that it will be much in this case. The pilgrim has his allotment of fears, courage, physical strength; his attitude toward the brigands; his subsidiary duties, desires, plans; his pilgrimage. And he has very little room or time to maneuver. If the pilgrimage is still his ultimate commitment, his reason-for-being, and if he somehow has the fortitude to continue, then he might wonder about whether he can last longer buried or broken-legged; about the likelihood that help will come; about the likelihood that if help comes, he will be able to complete the pilgrimage. If, however, there is no practical possibility of rescue, and he now wants a release from his suffering, and there is no countervailing reason for prolonging it, then the issue for him will be to get the death he prefers, and to take what solace he can in the little control he can exercise.

His happiness in the larger sense will come from his virtuous life, just as it does for sages who have had more fortunate circumstances. If this answer is less than satisfying, it may be because this is not a very instructive case.

Here is a better one. A man lies naked, under a sheet, on a hard table in the bowels of a research hospital. The room is small, dimly lit, cluttered with electronic equipment. The only other person in the room is a woman (a sage) in a lab coat, patiently probing the man's muscles with needle electrodes. The task is a demanding and tedious one—to assess the enervation of small groups of muscle fibers in the man's limbs and trunk by carefully inserting an electrode into a fiber (into the nerve itself, it seems to the man) and then recording the activity of the nerve, both in response to electrical stimulation and in response to his efforts to tense the pinned muscle. Each probe is protracted and unpleasant enough to cause the man to wince, or in the case of needles next to the bone, to gasp. There is no conversation for an hour, just the relentless probing—now three or four in a lower leg, then a few in an arm, then back to the leg, then to a shoulder. At first the man tries to take a clinical interest in what the woman is doing—observing the length of the needles, the depth and angle of each probe, the numbers that come up on the display she watches. That is good enough for a few minutes, but he soon begins to be obsessed with his sensations—the sweat on his forehead, the heat and soreness at each site after the needle has been removed, the cramps he begins to get when he tenses a pinned muscle. No single stick is difficult to endure, or even very much more than uncomfortable, even near the bone. But after an hour of this, with no end in sight, the relentless succession of small, sharp, insistent pains is maddening. The woman is engrossed in her work. This is research. The man is a patient in another wing of the hospital, but here he is an experimental subject. He becomes irritable, but says nothing. Then suddenly he has a pleasing thought, mixed with a little malice. "Doctor," he says. She looks up from his left ankle, where she is just about to get near another bone. "The difference between this and torture . . . is only the intention." She grunts and says, "We're almost finished." His pleasure in the thought, and in needling his tormentor, spreads over his limbs like a warm balm. It is good for two minutes.

The instructive thing about this case is its ordinariness. For purposes they endorse and join, ordinary agents can bear much more suffering than this, for much longer periods, from much less pleasant people, and not for a moment think their happiness has been compromised. The damage torture does to happiness comes from the malice of the torturer and her defeat of the victim's agency, not from the pain she causes. Sages suffer on the rack. They differ from the rest of us only in having virtuosic human abilities to resist the defeat of their agency, and to act with practical intelligence under conditions that would defeat the merely fit. When they succeed in that, they suffer less than ordinary agents, both in hospitals and under torture. But virtuosic abilities are not inhuman ones. Pushed beyond human endurance, sages break down. Their lives are nonetheless virtuous for that, even in defeat. For if a sage's life can end in death without compromising virtue (that is, end in a way that preserves happiness in the grand sense), then it can end happily (or be interrupted without consequence to happiness) even when the sage's agency is destroyed by suffering. When that happens, the joke, such as it may be, is on the torturer. Next question.

Joy

In fortunate circumstances, when life is a costless feast, a sage has as much fun as anyone else—more, perhaps, because she is better at exploiting the whole range of available delights. Her palette does not get dull. Socrates, we should remember, could make himself at home at a rowdy banquet, and not by declining the wine. But he did not suppose that such transient joys amounted to anything much in the long run. Filling his life with them was not his aim, though he surely would have thought it foolish to spurn them for that reason.

It is equally foolish, we think, to ignore two prominent and permanent features of ordinary experience: One is that for most of us, a life full of pleasures but empty of purpose would not be a happy one. In fact, in the end, if that is all there was to it, we would think it was an empty life. Without the vessel of purpose, pleasures drain away without residue. This appears to be a psychological consequence of ordinary, garden-variety healthy agency, because it always subordinates the pursuit of pleasure to the task of optimizing the success of our endeavors generally, and healthy agents always have a much more complex agenda than merely getting and sustaining pleasant mental states. (*Pace*, Epicurus.) It follows that if you endeavor to become or remain a healthy agent, and expect to succeed at that, it will be futile for you to try to build a happy life by accumulating pleasures. The coffers will be empty every morning.

The other feature of ordinary life to notice is the unreliability of good fortune, and hence of its joys. It is sensible to be prepared for famines as well as feasts. And there is this considerable consolation for agents who are fit for adversity: the effective exercise of agency always brings joy, even in the midst of misery. Its sustained exercise in difficult, complex, richly varied endeavors is deeply engrossing and profoundly pleasurable. Sustained over a whole life, it is, in the end, satisfying for most of us— nonempty, surely, even if trivial on a cosmic scale. This sort of happiness with one's life also appears to be a psychological consequence of healthy agency—at least when the exercise of it has come to be the determining factor in most of our waking experience. The life of a stoic sage is filled with such happiness, as a consequence of her virtue. We imperfect ones, who see this prize and sometimes, in favorable circumstances, fleetingly possess it, cannot wish less for those we love.

Commentary

Ancient doctrine. Julia Annas (*The Morality of Happiness*, 329–35) rightly insists that we must take eudaimonists at their word—that they are, in fact, ultimately giving an account of a happy life, not just a virtuous one, and that these things are conceptually distinct. We agree. It matters, theoretically, whether we stoics can make good on our claim (against Aristotelians, among others) that virtue is both necessary and sufficient for happiness, because unless that is true we will not be able to reconcile our eudaimonist theoretical project at all with our claim that virtue is the final end.

The ancient fragments (as opposed to the work of Cicero; see below) are very skimpy on the subject of stoic happiness—not on what the theses about it were, but on the arguments for those theses. Striker ("Ataraxia: Happiness as Tranquility") discusses the way in which tranquility characterized, for ancient stoics, the mental state associated with happiness—though that mental state did not constitute happiness; Annas (*The Morality of Happiness*, chap. 19) reconstructs arguments on the sufficiency thesis. The range of fragments can be seen nicely in Long and Sedley, *The Hellenistic Philosophers* (section 63); and it is especially worthwhile to read their commentary on these matters. Here is part of it, reproduced with the permission of the publisher. Parenthetical references refer to sections and items in their book; "SVF" refers to a collection of fragmentary texts done early in the twentieth century: Hans von Arnim, *Stoicorum Veterum Fragmenta* (4 vols.).

> In Hellenistic philosophy the different schools were regularly characterized by their different specifications of the end, a concept on whose formal definition they could all agree: 'that for the sake of which everything is done, but which is not itself done for the sake of anything', or 'the ultimate object of all desires'. Such agreement, which may seem curious within the non-teleological context of modern ethics, was made possible by the scarcely questioned assumption . . . that human life must be purposive by nature, and by the identification of the end with 'happiness' (eudaimonia) or 'living well'. . . . Hence investigation of the end is a functionalist inquiry, a specification of the kind of life which will enable a person to fulfil his or her nature, to act in the way that human nature requires. Agreement on these points imposes important constraints on Greek ethics, which may seem to cause particular difficulty for the Stoics. They accepted the then traditional conception of the end as 'living well', 'being happy', 'the fulfilment of all desires'. Yet they made moral goodness the sole constituent of 'being happy', going as far as to claim that the sufferings of Priam will not disturb the virtuous man's happiness (SVF 3.585). Thus they rejected the Aristotelian doctrine that happiness requires some good fortune in addition to virtue. If the Stoics had conceded this point (a fundamental objection to their ethics), they would have had to drop their grand claims concerning the wise man's supreme and impregnable happiness (L), and their insistence that happiness is always in his power (M).

The paradox would be toned down if we took the Stoics to be redefining 'happiness', severing its connexions with any accepted sense of 'self-fulfilment' or satisfaction of desires. Their ethics is often represented along these lines—a move away from teleology towards the conception of doing what is right because it is right, with 'self-satisfaction' totally excluded from all consideration. Yet this Kantian reading of Stoicism is a serious misrepresentation. The Stoics preferred being charged with paradox (cf. 66A) to dropping their teleology and eudaemonism. The material here (A, B I, C 4, F, H. I) shows that virtue and vice respectively are taken to constitute happiness and unhappiness as these latter terms were understood within the mainstream tradition. What 'happiness' means, in this regard, is summed up in a definition falsely attributed to Plato (Definitions 412d): 'the sum of all goods; a potency sufficient for living well; fulfilment in accordance with virtue; a living being's sufficient benefit'. The Stoics claim that a virtuous man does possess all that he needs to fulfill himself, to live well, to have his desires satisfied (cf. L, M). They challenge us to suppose that a life so constituted (not of course the intermittent satisfaction of momentary wants) is what we all naturally desire, or would desire, if we were capable of fully grasping its benefits to ourselves as well as to those who benefit from being the recipients of virtuous actions.

Detailed arguments for the Stoic conception of happiness, if there were any, have not survived. But plainly happiness is neither synonymous with virtue nor arbitrarily constituted by virtue. Zeno defined happiness as 'a good flow of life' (A2), and this is expressed by Seneca (F 1) as 'peacefulness and constant tranquillity'. The benefits of such a state, which recalls Epicurean 'freedom from disturbance' (see 21), may have been regarded as intuitively obvious. Zeno at any rate appealed to the unhappiness of 'those who live in conflict' (i.e. with themselves) as the ground for his account of the end: 'living in agreement', amplified in keeping with the etymology of *homologoumenos* by 'living in accordance with one concordant reason' (*logos*, B I). If, as the Stoics argued independently (61 B 8), rational consistency defines virtue, the benefits of happiness must be constituted by virtue (cf. Seneca's procedure in F). Like virtue, happiness is an all-or-nothing affair, and it is complete at any moment (I), a striking difference from Aristotle's insistence on a whole lifetime. Since happiness has no requirements except moral goodness, the Stoics could disregard the ordinary vicissitudes of life in defending its momentary completeness.

Does the Stoics' eudaemonism sully the purity of their morals? Only for the purest of Kantians. Panaetius was prepared to say that the virtues have our own good or happiness as their objective (G), and that each virtue is targeted at a different 'colour' of this single objective—an image which explains the 'different perspectives' of the inseparable virtues (61 D I). But the virtues are 'final' as well as 'instrumental' goods (60M): they are both the means of attaining happiness and the excellences of which it consists. Therefore someone who desires happiness, in the Stoics' sense, must desire virtue for its own sake since the former consists in the latter. Like Plato and Aristotle, the Stoics held that the intrinsic desirability of the moral life is identical to a person's self-fulfilment. There is thus a continuity between the primary impulse to self-preservation, directed at physical well-being, and the self-satisfaction of the moral life. But 'self', in the case of the latter, is extended to something analogous to Kant's universalized imperative—the good of all rational beings: harmony of one's own nature and that of the whole (C 2–4) or 'community' (K).

Cicero, in *Tusculan Disputations*, devotes the whole of book V to a defense of the sufficiency thesis, with special attention to whether the sage can be happy even under torture. The argument ostensibly gets going in V.v, but after numerous starts begins to make progress beginning at V.xiii.40. The argument winds its way in a leisurely fashion to V.xli.121, but its crucial premises are these:

1. "No one can be happy except when good is secure and certain and lasting" (V.xiv.40).
2. The good of virtue is secure and certain and lasting because (a) once achieved, its maintenance is within the agent's control (V.xiv.42), and (b) it is free from the disturbances of the soul that produce wretchedness (V.xv.43).
3. Moreover, in its affective dimension, a virtuous life is characterized by tranquility and joy, and thus may unproblematically be described as a happy life (V.xv.43).
4. No form of happiness can be good unless it includes, or is founded upon, virtue, or what is right (V.xv.44–45).

Virtue is thus necessary and sufficient for happiness. It remains, then, to be shown (as against the Peripatetics) that nothing needs to be added to a virtuous life to make it a supremely happy one, even on the rack. Here Cicero's argument depends on imagining the life of a sage (despite what he says about this being motivational rhetoric).

XXIV. . . . . Let us assume a man pre-eminently endowed with the highest qualities and let our imagination play for a moment with the picture. In the first place he must be of outstanding intelligence; for virtue is not easily found to go with sluggish minds; secondly he must have an eager enthusiasm in the quest of truth; and from this springs the famous threefold progeny of the soul [physics, ethics, logic]: one centred in the knowledge of the universe and the disentanglement of the secrets of nature; the second in distinguishing the things that should lie sought out or avoided and in framing a rule of life; the third in judging what is the consequence to every premise, what is incompatible with it, and in this lies all refinement of argument and truth of judgment. With what joy, pray, must then the soul of the wise man be thrilled when in such company he spends his life and passes his nights in their study! When for instance he discovers the movements and revolutions of the whole heaven and sees the countless stars fixed in the sky in unison with the movement of the vault itself as they keep their appointed place, seven others preserving their several courses, though far remote from one another in the height or lowliness of their position, and yet their wandering movements mark the settled and regulated spaces of their course— no wonder the spectacle of all this stimulated those men of old and encouraged them to further search. . . .

XXV. To the soul occupied night and day in these meditations there comes the knowledge enjoined by the god at Delphi, that the mind should know its own self and feel its union with the divine mind, the source of the fulness of joy unquenchable. For meditation upon the power and nature of the gods of itself kindles the desire of attaining an immortality that resembles theirs, nor does the soul think that it is limited to this short span of life, when it sees that the causes of things are linked one to another in an inevitable chain, and nevertheless their succession from eternity to eternity is governed by reason and intelligence. As the wise man gazes upon this spectacle and looks upward or rather looks round upon all the parts and regions of the universe, with what calmness of soul he turns again to reflect upon what is in man and touches him more nearly! Hence comes his knowledge of virtue; the kinds and species of the virtues break into blossom, discovery is made of what nature regards as the end in what is good and the last extremity in what is evil, the object of our duties and the rule for the conduct of life that must be chosen. And by the exploration of these and similar problems the chief conclusion of all attained is the aim of this discussion of ours, that virtue is self-sufficient for leading a happy life. In the third place follows that which spreads freely over all parts of the field of wisdom, which gives the definition of a thing, distinguishes kinds, links up sequences, draws just conclusions, discerns true and false,—the art and science of reasoning; and this, besides its supreme usefulness in weighing judgments, affords particularly a noble delight which is worthy of wisdom. But this is the occupation of leisure: let the wise man we have imagined also pass to the maintenance of the public weal. What course more excellent could he take, since his prudence shows him the true advantage of his fellow citizens, his justice lets him divert nothing of theirs to his own family, and he is strong in the exercise of so many different remaining virtues? Add to this the fruit which springs from friendships in which learned men find the counsel which shares their thoughts and almost breathes the same breath throughout the course of life, as well as the supreme charm of daily social intercourse. What, pray, does such a life require to make it happier? And to a life filled with joys so abundant and intense, fortune itself is bound to yield its place. If then it is happiness to rejoice in such goods of the soul, that is virtues, and all wise men have full experience of such joys, we are bound to admit that they are all happy.

XXVI. A. Even in torture and upon the rack?—M. Do you think I meant on beds of violets and roses? Or is Epicurus, who merely puts on the mask of a philosopher and has bestowed the title on himself, to be allowed to say (and say it indeed he does, really and truly, with my pronounced approval, [in] spite of his inconsistency) that there is no time when the wise man, even if burnt, racked, cut in pieces, cannot cry out: "I count it all as nothing," particularly as Epicurus restricts evil to pain and good to pleasure, makes a mock of this "right and base" of ours and says we are busied with words and uttering sounds empty of meaning, and that nothing interests us except the bodily sensation of either rough or smooth? Shall we allow this man, whose judgment differs but little from the instinct of the beasts, to be forgetful of himself and be disdainful of fortune at the moment when all that he holds good and evil is at fortune's disposal; to say that he is happy in the extremity of torture and upon the rack at the moment when he has laid down that not only is pain the worst of evils but is the only one as well? And he has in no way provided for himself those healing aids to the endurance of pain to be found in strength of soul, shame of baseness, the habitual practice of patience, the lessons of fortitude, a manly hardness, but says that he finds peace in the recollection of past pleasures and in that alone, just as if a man sweltering in uneasy endurance of violent summer heat should choose to recollect a dip in the cool freshness of the streams in my Arpinum; for I do not see how past pleasures can allay present evils. But as this man, who would have no right to say it if he chose to be self-consistent, says that the wise man is always happy, what ought to be expected of those who consider nothing desirable, nothing worth reckoning as a good where rectitude is not found?

For my part, I should say, let the Peripatetics also and the Old Academy make an end some time or other of their stuttering and have the courage to say openly and loudly that happy life will step down into the bull of Phalaris [a metal device in which prisoners were slowly burned to death]. XXVII. For grant that there are three kinds of good things (to make a final escape from the meshes of Stoic subtleties of which I realize I have made more use than I generally do), grant if you will the existence of these kinds of good, provided only that goods of the body and external goods lie groveling on the ground and are merely termed good because they are to be "preferred," whilst those other divine goods extend their influence far and wide and reach to the heavens: why should I pronounce anyone who has secured them to be happy only, and not supremely happy as well?

But will the wise man be terribly afraid of pain? For pain is the chief obstacle to our view: for against death, our own and that of our relatives, and against distress and all other disorders of the soul we have, I think, been sufficiently armed and provided by the previous days' discussions: pain seems to be the most active antagonist of virtue; it points its fiery darts, it threatens to undermine fortitude, greatness of soul and patience. Will virtue then have to give way to pain, will the happy life of the wise and steadfast man yield to it? What degradation, great gods of heaven! Spartan boys utter no cry when their bodies are mangled with painful blows; I have seen with my own eyes troops of youngsters in Lacedaemon fighting with inconceivable obstinacy, using fists and feet and nails and even teeth to the point of losing their lives rather than admit defeat. What barbarous country more rude and wild than India? Yet amongst its people those, to begin with, who are reckoned sages pass their lives unclad and endure without show of pain the snows of the Hindu Kush and the rigour of winter, and when they throw themselves voluntarily into the flames they let themselves be burnt without a moan; whilst the women in India, if the husband of any of them dies, compete with one another to decide whom the husband loved best (for each man usually has more than one wife): and she who is victorious, accompanied by her relatives, goes joyfully to join her husband on the funeral pyre; the conquered rival sadly quits the field. Never could custom conquer nature; for nature is always unconquered; but as for us we have corrupted our souls with bowered seclusion, luxury, ease, indolence and sloth, we have enervated and weakened them by false beliefs and evil habits. Who does not know of the custom of the Egyptians? Their minds are infected with degraded superstitions and they would sooner submit to any torment than injure an ibis or asp or cat or dog or crocodile, and even if they have unwittingly done anything of the kind there is no penalty from which they would recoil. I am speaking of human beings: what of the beasts? Do they not go through cold, through hunger, ranging the mountains and traversing the forests in their wanderings? Do they not fight for their young so fiercely that they sustain wounds and shrink from no assaults, no blows? I pass by all that ambitious men go through submissively to win distinction, men covetous of fame to win glory, men inflamed with love to gratify passion. Life is full of such examples.

XXVIII. But let us check our eloquence and return to the point at which we digressed. Happy life will give itself, I say, to torture, and following in the train of justice, temperance and above all of fortitude, of greatness of soul and patience will not halt at the sight of the face of the executioner, and, when all the virtues, while the soul remains undaunted, pass on to face torment, it will not stay behind outside the doors, as I have said, and threshold of the prison. For what could be more abominable, more hideous than to be left desolate, severed from its glorious companions? And yet this is by no means possible; for neither can the virtues subsist without happy life, nor happy life without the virtues. And so they will not suffer it to make evasions and will hurry it along with them to whatsoever pain and torment they shall themselves be led. For it is characteristic of the wise man to do nothing of which he can repent, nothing against his will, to do everything nobly, consistently, soberly, rightly, not to look forward to anything as if it were bound to come, to be astonished at no occurrence under the impression that its occurrence is unexpected and strange, to bring all things to the standard of his own judgment, to abide by his own decisions. And what can be happier than this I certainly cannot conceive.

For the Stoics indeed the conclusion is easy, since they hold it the sovereign good to live according to nature and in harmony with nature, seeing that not only is this the wise man's settled duty but also it lies in his power, and so for them it follows necessarily that where a man has the chief good in his power, he also has the power of happy life: thus the life of the wise is rendered happy always. Now you know the utterances I think the most courageous about happy life and, at the point we now are—unless you have something better to suggest—the truest as well.

Connectedness. In a sage's life, there are no "unconnected" parts. This is so because the sage's agency is comprehensive. Every endeavor is undertaken all-things-considered, and integrated with all others. Yet, especially in fortunate circumstances, the life of a sage can be filled with spontaneous fun. The question is how robustly all these joyous and spontaneous endeavors must be connected or integrated into one's life as a whole. A very robust form of connectedness would require that sages be able (after the fact) to give a "positive" justification for everything they do—in the sense of being able to show that even their spontaneous fun was somehow something they ought to have had, or were required to have, all-things-considered, by the endeavor of perfecting their agency. Insisting on such a robust connection, however, makes stoicism repugnant in much the way that applying the principle of utility to every activity makes utilitarianism repugnant. Moreover, such a robust connection is inconsistent with the claims (in Chapters 4 and 5) about the way stoics use norms of indifference in their practical reasoning.

Stoics do not think connectedness is robust in the way just described. Sages can shout for no reason at all, and have harmless, indefensible hobbies—indefensible in the sense that they are matters of moral indifference. Is this a problem? Does it trivialize the notion of connectedness? We do not think so. Norms of indifference are "remainders," and being able to show that one's bizarre hobby is a matter of moral indifference is a challenging task that establishes a significant logical connection between the hobby and the rest of one's endeavors. Specifically, it establishes that there is *no* superordinate norm, from *any* other endeavor of the agent, to the effect that the hobby (or perhaps the hobbyhorse) is prohibited or ought not to be pursued. That is very far from being a trivial form of connectedness.

Virtue not in isolation. It is perhaps worth underlining something the text mentions only in a glancing way; namely, that the sort of integrated life that stoics pursue should not be thought of as an encapsulated one, having solved only its internal integration problems. Agents live in environments, in local to cosmic contexts, and virtue consists as much in integrating one's endeavors with those contexts as it does in integrating them with each other. Most agents live in social environments, facts about which (together with the agents' purposes) generate normative propositions about participating in social and political life. The stoics of antiquity differed dramatically from one another in the extent to which they participated in families, social and political affairs, and public life. And nothing in our account of healthy, fit, or virtuoso agency—then or now—entails that a virtuous life must be an abundantly social or political one. Such conclusions may (or may not) come out of an Aristotelian ethical theory, but they do not come out of a stoic one. For some people, in some life circumstances, virtue may require or be consistent with ultimate entry into a cloistered, contemplative life. For others it may require or commend lifelong immersion in familial, community, national, or international activity. What is ruled out is merely the truncated or stunted development of agency. Thus, while we may safely say that early withdrawal into a cloister is a bad choice because it deprives the agent of the range of worldly experience that she needs to develop wisdom, we may also safely say that permanent immersion in social life that leaves her no time or energy for reflection is also a bad choice. The overall point, however, is that virtue is as much a matter of achieving proper integration into the world as it is a matter of achieving an encapsulated form of inner harmony.

This result may seem at odds with several aspects of standard expositions of stoic themes: the notion that virtue is self-sufficient, for example, in the sense that the sage needs nothing else to make her life a good one and to sustain her happiness; the notion that stoics are indifferent to worldly goods; the notion that we cultivate emotional detachment. But I have argued throughout this book that these aspects of stoic doctrine have to do with our efforts to immunize ourselves against bad fortune. We do not want to *be* detached; we want to be *able* to detach ourselves when that is necessary to preserve our agency. Our discussions of encapsulation and detachment from the world do not, then, describe our *preferences* about the way our lives should go in fortunate circumstances. Inwood (*Ethics and*

Human Action in Early Stoicism, 122ff.) makes related points about the ancient doctrines—even the harshest sayings of Epictetus. Among the ways of life that humans can live, we do not have a theoretical preference for the ones that are solitary, grim, emotionally detached, contemplative, or free of social baggage. Rather, we say that sages are attentive to and act on the norms generated in all the contexts in which their lives are embedded, from local to cosmic ones.

Plans and narratives. A young man and woman sit in a parked car, hunched in their overcoats, hands in their pockets. They twist and lean toward each other, arms at their sides. They kiss, surprised by each other's soft lips, their sudden fierce heat, the length of the lingering kiss, the perfection of it.

"I will go with you," she says afterwards. Meaning I will marry you and kiss you always with just this softness and surprise. I will care for you, and get you through this desolation by anchoring you again in the life of a family, by holding fast to you just so, by satisfying your hungers. I will love you, use you, direct you, teach you our story—the story that began with this kiss, with its perfection, with the knowledge that we are perfect for the parts this kiss sketched for us. You will love your life and love me for it. I will love my life and love you for it. An old, wonderful, well-known story. The best story. And we will live it happily, wisely, and well if we inhabit it wholly—if we enter it once and for all, and now. "I will go with you," she says again, burning with desire to play out this story with him, to commit herself ferociously to it, and thus to him.

The young man says nothing. Meaning no. Meaning he will not commit himself now. Meaning this perfect kiss, this electrifying proffer, is not a plan, not something he is ready for, or equipped for. Meaning he thinks there is much he must learn to do *first*, much he must acquire and become *before* he is ready to start this story, if *ever* he starts it, or starts any other. He is suspicious of stories, especially the old, wonderful, well-known ones that so many people inhabit so miserably. He is suspicious of his passions, here, so sudden, muddled, uncontrolled. He thinks he lacks adequate control, adequate knowledge of himself, goals worthy of his possibilities.

"The timing is all wrong," he says finally.

"Oh, I think the timing is exactly right." She looks for his eyes, for him to see her eyes, spilling tears.

"And to tell you the truth," he says, gathering himself to look at her and break the exalted tension, "I'm tired of being led around by my . . ."

He stops in dismay at her tears just as she stops his mouth with her hand, and with her sudden, hopeless laughter. And in the long, fierce embrace that follows, in the midst of the tears and laughter she evokes in him, they come to terms.

From this distance we cannot say what those terms ought to have been—whether more in her direction or in his. But stoicism does not license stupidity. As much as we counsel self-mastery rather than submission to desire (or to an old script), and as little as we value a perfect kiss (or a perfect part) compared to the perfection of agency, we do not counsel timidity and priggish dithering. Nor do we have an *a priori* preference for living out a plan (complete with mission statements, benefit-cost analyses, and Gantt charts) over living out a rousing story in which the parts are largely improvised by the players.

Acknowledgments

Helpful critics have raised several issues about this chapter that called for some clarification. In particular, my thanks go to Julia Annas, Marvin Kohl, John Marshall, and Amélie Rorty in this regard. Rachels and Ruddick's article "Lives and Liberty," and objections from Marshall and Rorty, were of particular use in the section on a complete life. The aeronautical analogy in the section on control is a reworked version of one in Becker, "Trust as Noncognitive Security about Motives." I am grateful to my Hollins colleague (and pilot) Robert Hansen for discussion of its usefulness and limitations, as well as its details.

Appendix

A Calculus for Normative Logic

FOR CLARITY and economy, the exposition here is roughly that of an interpreted axiomatic system. It is, however, replete with rules of inference characteristic of a system of natural deduction, and by the standards of pure logic it is an inelegant contraption in many other respects. The aim here is to apply existing logic to ethics, not to extend logic in a significant way.

Nonetheless, in order to represent moral reasoning adequately, it is necessary to do several things that diverge from mainstream accounts of deontic logic. We employ three normative operators, for example, to mark the distinction between things that are mandatory, advisable but not mandatory, and completely optional. We insist that normative propositions always be constructed from facts about the endeavors of individual agents. And we propose to preserve the truth of conflicting normative propositions—that is, to preserve them as accurate representations of persisting conflicts within and between agents—by resolving inconsistencies with a combination of two basic strategies, rank-ordering and forced choice. The complexities these things introduce are not the sort that will please a pure logician, since they are likely to limit rather than enlarge the range of interesting formal operations. We are concerned here, however, only with producing an adequate formal and systematic representation of the normative inferences we make in our ethics.

Notation and Interpretation

For practical purposes we can avoid most of the complexities of predicate logic. In effect, we can deal with atomic propositions, manipulated by truth functional, normative, and modal operators, where first-order predicate language is used merely to indicate some important content distinctions in a perspicuous way. These distinctions could in principle be made with an array of propositional constants. All propositional and predicate variables are understood to be descriptive rather than prescriptive or normative. We will insist that any predicate or atomic proposition with buried modal or normative content be stated in a normal form in which modal or normative operators are never placed inside the scope of quantifiers. For example, we will insist that the normative implications of statements of institutional fact ("Here is a dollar") be extracted, as it were, and restated as normative operations over statements of brute fact (e.g., about what can or ought to be done with certain pieces of paper). (See Searle, "How to Derive Ought from Is".)

Notation

The notation is as follows. *Propositional* variables p, q, r, . . . ; *Predicate* constants A, B, . . . U, and variables X, Y, Z, . . . ; *Individual* constants a, b, . . . u, and variables x, y, z; existential and universal *Quantifiers* ($\exists$x), (x); *Truth functional* operators: $\sim$ for negation, $\vee$ for the inclusive disjunction "either p or q or both," $\underline{\vee}$ for the exclusive disjunction "either p or q but not both," & for the conjunction "and," $\supset$ for the material conditional "if p then q," $\equiv$ for the material biconditional "p if and only if q"; *Punctuation*: (,), [,], {, } . . . *Modal* operators, $\square$, $\diamond$, read respectively as "It is necessary that . . . It is possible that . . ." *Normative* operators **R, O, I**, read respectively as "It is required that . . . , It ought to be that . . . , It is a matter of indifference that . . ." *Ordinal* operators <, < >, >, $\leq$, $\geq$, read respectively as "that . . . is subordinate to that . . . ," "that . . . is coordinate with that . . . ," etc.

Some additional twists are needed in the modal and normative vocabulary, due to the fact that possibilities and norms of different sorts have to be ordered (e.g., logical, theoretical, practical possibilities; moral, legal, social norms). Thus subscripts $_l$ for logical, $_t$ for theoretical, and $_p$ for practical will sometimes be added to modal operators. N.B.: When an alphabetic subscript is not given, the operator is shorthand for the disjunction of all the subscripts. Thus $\sim\diamond$p stands for ($\sim\diamond_l$p $\vee$ $\sim\diamond_t$p $\vee$ $\sim\diamond_p$p). For normative operators, numerical subscripts (e.g., R_1, O_2, I_n) indicate that the norm referred to is drawn from restricted, submoral considerations (etiquette, role obligations, etc.). The subscripts indicate the ordinal status of that *type* of norm relative to other submoral considerations. Priorities among norms of the same type or rank will be indicated with ordinal operators—e.g., R_2p > R_2q.) The subscript letter $_t$ will be used to identify norms that arise from transactions between individuals. Normative operators without numerical subscripts are understood to refer to moral (ethical) norms. Thus, given the stoic account of the moral point of view as the most inclusive possible sort of practical reasoning, we will read unsubscripted normative operators as "All-things-considered, it is required that . . . ," etc.

Interpretation

This logic diverges sharply from standard presentations of deontic logic in which the normative operators are obligation, permission, and prohibition—all interpreted in terms of the alethic modal notions of necessity, possibility, and impossibility. Instead we use normative operators of requirement, ought, and indifference, and it seems unlikely that the (informal) interpretation of them can be represented more formally in the noble semantics of alethic modal logic. Further discussion of this matter, and for the choice of these operators, is given in the commentary to this chapter, and (implicitly) throughout Chapter 5.

Ought. To say that it ought to be the case that s does (or is) c in e is to say that s's doing (or being) c in e is *advisable*—that is, is an element in the process of pursuing the endeavor e that advances the enterprise along a defined trajectory toward its goals. Endeavors are intentional, goal-directed activities. Some things we do in pursuit of them are, as we say, steps in the right direction—on track, on course, on target, in accord with what we are trying to do, true to our purposes, right, correct—in a word, advisable. Other things are *in*advisable, in the sense that they are deviations from the defined trajectory. Still others are neither advisable nor inadvisable with respect to e, in the sense that they have no effect on our progress along the trajectory. Note that, as in navigation, deviations from a defined course do not necessarily prevent reaching one's destination. One can make course corrections to get back on the original path, or one can chart a new course. Moreover, to say that an act is correct is not to say that it is unique in that regard (there may be several correct solutions to a given navigational problem), or that it is the optimal choice (one correct solution may be preferable to another).

Requirement. To say that it is required that s do (or be) c in e is to say that doing or being c is a necessary condition for pursuing e, or that ~c is a nullity in e, or that it is correct, in e, to sanction s for doing or being ~c. (We include nullity as an alternative to make note of the cases in which the failure or "sanction" attendant to ~c comes from the fact that it does not count for anything in e. Legal requirements that a will be witnessed are of this sort. Failing to meet them is just failing to make a valid will. This is a special case of the "necessary condition" alternative, but one that is frequently forgotten.) For present purposes we do not think this triple disjunction needs to be broken apart to identify two or three different sorts of requirement. (It is clear that it could be parsed if need be, however, and that the types of requirement could be rank-ordered.) Note that its being *required* that s do c in e is quite distinct from its being the case that s *ought* to do c. Requirements often constrain or even frustrate the pursuit of a goal.

Indifference. The indifference operator is interpreted as a logical remainder. To say that it is a matter of indifference that s does c in e is to say that s's doing c is neither required, prohibited, advisable, or inadvisable in e. Note that it is not otherwise interdefinable with requirement and ought, however. See "Definitional Equivalence" below.

There are important and interesting logical relationships between these normative operators and the various sorts of imperatives, endorsements, recommendations, exclamations, and other speech acts typical of ethical discourse. Imperatives, for example, often elide the distinction between requirement and ought. ("Just do it" is ambiguous in that way.) And it is not clear that the distinction between categorical and hypothetical imperatives resolves the matter. See "Normative Constructs" below. It is also challenging to try to think through the extent to which the meaning of prescriptive language in general overlaps that of the normative propositions used here. We leave all such matters for another time.

The logic of the descriptive bases for normative propositions, both modal and nonmodal, is straightforwardly two-valued here. Such propositions are interpreted as either true or false. That means that modal logic will be treated as merely an extension of propositional logic, in which the modal propositions are interpreted by means of quantifers (Feys, *Modal Logics*, 27–30). The logic of normative propositions, however, will be treated as three-valued in the following sense. We will say that a normative proposition is *sound* if it is either an axiom, a theorem, or a construct from a true descriptive basis. (A construct is a normative proposition whose normative form is derived from a descriptive basis by rules of inference. See "Normative Constructs" below.) We will say that a normative proposition is *un*sound if it is constructed from a false basis, or if its negation is a theorem or a construct from a true basis. The need for a third value arises from the fact that people frequently must come to conclusions about what they ought to do without being able to determine the truth or falsity of the relevant descriptive bases and therefore cannot extract or construct norms at all, or in situations where normative propositions conflict. Normative logic must be able to represent inferences for those sorts of situations. We will say that a proposition is normatively *open* if no normative operators range over it, or if its normative elements are either incoherent (conflict at the same ordinal level) or are indeterminate (e.g., a requirement that one choose between unranked options).

A proposition $\Box_1 w$ asserts a logical necessity—that is, it asserts that w is a tautology. $\sim\Diamond_1 w$ asserts that w is self-contradictory. All the space between those poles is the area of logical possibility. What is logically possible, however, may not be possible in terms of our theories of the way things work. Einsteinian physics holds that travel at speeds greater than that of light is not possible; Kohlberg's theory of moral development holds that people cannot reach stage 6 without going through stages 1–5 in order. So a proposition $\sim\Diamond_t w$ asserts a theoretical impossibility—that is, it asserts that w is logically inconsistent with the laws, postulates, predictions, or explanations of a given theory. The range of practical possibility is defined by the abilities of given individuals in given circumstances. So a proposition $\Diamond_p w$ asserts that w is logically consistent with the abilities of the people in some referenced class. Note that theoretical and practical possibility are merely context-restricted forms of logical possibility.

Basic Definitions, Rules, and Axioms

This section assembles, and modifies as necessary, some basic elements of propositional, predicate, and modal calculi. Most of the specifically stoic elements are given in the separate sections "Normative Constructs" and "Axioms of Stoic Normative Logic" below. There are, however, some adjustments in the materials of this section that should be noted.

Well-Formed Formulas

Our otherwise standard definition of a well-formed formula (wff) has only two unusual elements. One is the restriction on the scope of quantifiers introduced in rules 3, 4, and 5. This restriction is merely meant to avoid some well-known technical complications, and its use here is philosophically innocent. The restriction on normative operators introduced in rule 4 is a different matter, however. It is as far from innocence as it is from elegance. Rather, it is meant to capture same matters about norms argued for at length in Chapter 5—namely, that they are all facts about the purposive activities of individual agents. As the commentary to this chapter points out, however, rule 4 may be too restrictive. An alternative is proposed there.

    1. Any individual propositional variable or constant is a well-formed formula (wff).

    2. Any predicate constant or variable that is bound with individual constants or quantified variables is a wff.

    3. If anything w is a wff, then $\sim w$, $\Box w$, or $\Diamond w$ is a wff, provided no quantifiers in it range over $\Box$, $\Diamond$, **R**, **O**, or **I**.

4. If anything *w* is a wff, and if R*w*, O*w*, or I*w* is a construct as defined in the section "Normative Constructs" below, then R*w*, O*w*, or I*w* is a wff, provided no quantifiers in it range over □, ◇, R, O, or I.

5. If anything *w* is a wff, and if anything *y* is a wff, then *w*∨*y*, *w*⊻*y*, *w*&*y*, *w*⊃*y*, *w*≡*y*, *w*<*y*, *w*< >*y*, *w*>*y*, *w*≤*y*, or *w*≥*y* is a wff, provided no quantifiers range over any □, ◇, R, O, or I within *w* or *y*.

6. Nothing is a wff unless its being so follows from rules 1–5.

Rules of Inference for Propositional, Quantificational, and Modal Logic

We use rules adapted from the Russell-Bernays system for the propositional calculus as found in Hilbert and Ackerman, *Principles of Mathematical Logic*, and Quine's approach to first-order quantification as found in Feys, *Modal Logics* (p. 22).

Definitional Replacement. Definitionally equivalent expressions may replace one another without restriction.

Substitution. In a given formula, any wff whatsoever may be substituted for a given propositional variable, provided the substitution is made for every occurrence of the variable in the formula, and does not introduce quantifiers that range over modal or normative operators.

Detachment. If any wff of the form *w* ⊃ *y* is an axiom, theorem, or construct, and if *w* standing alone is an axiom, theorem, or construct, then *y* standing alone is a theorem or construct.

Generalization. If any wff of the form *w* is an axiom, theorem, or construct, then (x)*w* standing alone is a theorem or construct, provided it does not range over modal or normative operators.

Modality. If any wff of the form *w* is an axiom or theorem, then □*w* standing alone is a theorem.

Axioms of Propositional and Quantificational Logic

For the standard propositional calculus, we will adopt the axioms of the Russell-Bernays system, as found in Hilbert and Ackerman, *Principles of Mathematical Logic*.

I.   ⊢ (p ∨ p) ⊃ p

II.   ⊢ p ⊃ (p ∨ q)

III. ⊢ (p ∨ q) ⊃ (q ∨ p)

IV.   ⊢ (p ⊃ q) ⊃ [(r ∨ p) ⊃ (r ∨ q)]

For the first-order predicate calculus we will use Quine's axioms, as found in Feys, *Modal Logics* (p. 22). Expressing them as metalogical schemata eliminates the need to elaborate the rule of **Substitution** above.

V.   ⊢ (x) (P ⊃ Q) ⊃ [(x)P ⊃ (x)Q]

VI.   ⊢ (x) [(y)P] ⊃ (y) [(x)P]

Axioms of Modal Logic

Since we will not venture into the project of constructing an account of entailment (strict implication), we will not need any of the special axioms of the various systems of modal logic devoted to it. We will, however, follow Feys, *Modal Logics* (at p. 32) in adopting two axioms to make this variant of modal logic deductively equivalent to its analog in the propositional calculus.

VII.   ⊢ □(p ⊃ q) ⊃ (□p ⊃ □q)

VIII. ⊢ □p ⊃ p

Moreover, we will firmly decline analogous axioms for normative logic. Axiom VIII is clearly false when a normative operator replaces □, since it surely does not follow from the proposition that "it is required that s undertakes c in e," that "s undertakes c in e." The normative counterpart to Axiom VII is no better.

Definitional Equivalence

Standard rules for the interdefinability of truth functional and modal operators hold here: $w{\supset}y$ may be written as $\sim w \vee y$, □w may be written as $\sim\Diamond\sim w$, etc. Quantifiers are interdefinable in the usual way: (∃x)Fx may be written as $\sim$(x)$\sim$(Fx), (∃x)$\sim$(Fx) may be written as $\sim$(x)(Fx), and so on. For ordinal operators, the translations are also routine. If w is superordinate to y, then it is not the case that it is either coordinate with it or subordinate to it. So $w{>}y$ may be written as $\sim(w{\leq}y)$, $w{<}{>}y$ may be written as $\sim[(w{<}y) \vee (w{>}y)]$, and so on.

   For normative operators, the situation is more complex. For one thing, interdefinability operates only within a given ordinal level. Being required to do p by the rules and customs of chess (**R**p) is identical to being forbidden to do $\sim$p by those rules (**R**$\sim$p), but it is not identical to being forbidden, *all-things-considered*, to do $\sim$p. Rewriting across ordinal levels can only be done by inference, not by translation rules for the operators.

Moreover, even within a given level there is an implicit rank order that blocks simple interdefinability of the operators. There is an obvious conceptual connection between Rp and Op, but the latter is a weaker normative statement than the former. It might, for example, express an ideal rather than a requirement. ("You really ought to take Greek, even though it isn't required.") So the two are not interchangeable. Moreover, though ~Op (it is not the case that one ought to do p) is quite distinct from O~p (one ought to do ~p), and both deny Op, neither can be rewritten as forbidding or requiring either p or ~p.

It is tempting to suppose that each normative operator has an "eliminative" equivalent within a given ordinal level, however, since the three of them jointly exhaust the normative possibilities within that level. For example, to say that p is a matter of indifference is to say that it is neither required nor forbidden, neither something one ought to do or ought not to do. It is interpreted as a normative remainder. See "Interpretation" above. Thus we might be tempted to think that Ip is definitionally equivalent to ~(Rp ∨ Op ∨ O~p). What this misses, however, is the possibility that the normative status of p might be open—that is, that no normative operator might be attached to it at all. In this logic, normative propositions are "constructed" from descriptive ones by way of rules of inference, so all we have asserted with ~(Rp ∨ Op ∨ O~p) is that *if* p is a normative construct, it is Ip. Thus the relationship between Ip and ~(Rp ∨ Op ∨ O~p) is an inferential one, not a matter of definitional equivalence. From Ip, one can infer ~(Rp ∨ Op ∨ O~p), but not the other way around. (See "Immediate Inferences" below.) Some analogous inferences hold for R and O.

There is, however, one definitional equivalence worth noting in the normative domain. To say that p is a matter of indifference is to say that neither p nor ~p is either required, forbidden, or something one ought or ought not to do. Thus I*w* may be written as I~*w*, and vice versa.

Proof, Consistency, and Completeness

A theorem is a proposition derived from axioms by rules of inference. A construct is a normative proposition whose normative form is derived from a descriptive basis or modal proposition by rules of inference. A proof of a normative proposition is a finite series of wffs, the first of which is an axiom, theorem, or descriptive basis, each successive wff of which is derived by the rules of inference from its immediate predecessor, and the last wff of which is a nonopen normative proposition.

Proof of the consistency of this system of normative logic can be accomplished by showing (1) that for any descriptive or modal proposition

w, it is not possible to prove both w and $\sim w$, and (2) that any pair of normative propositions w and $\sim w$ will yield a superordinate normative proposition without conflicting elements. The first step is not problematic, since the consistency of the standard bivalent propositional and quantificational logic used here is well known. The second step is also unproblematic, given the rules of Escalation and Transcendence and the Axiom of Closure. (See the sections "Normative Constructs" and "Axioms of Stoic Normative Logic" below.)

We happily leave the question of the completeness of the system to logicians. The completeness of standard bivalent propositional and first-order quantificational logic, and the seemingly innocuous way in which this logic of norms attaches to them, gives us hope for a proof, but we do not have one.

Normative Constructs

The rules for constructing well-formed normative propositions are of four sorts: (1) rules governing the construction of first-order normative propositions from descriptive bases, (2) rules governing the ranking of normative propositions within a given ordinal level, (3) rules governing the construction of normative propositions of ordinal level n + 1 from normative propositions of level n, and (4) rules governing the construction of normative propositions without ordinal subscripts (moral ones) from normative propositions of any level n.

(1) First-Order Constructs

Certain constellations of facts, necessities, and possibilities license the construction of normative propositions. There is no sleight of hand in this process. Given facts about the rules of a game, for example, and facts about the possibilities open to players, it is plain how we can legitimately construct normative propositions about what the players ought to do *strictly in terms of the game they are playing*. And it is equally plain how we can then reconstruct such normative propositions in terms of the players' more comprehensive activities—by enlarging the frame of reference to include facts about the various aims and preferences that have brought them to play the game, and the terms under which they are willing to stay in it. The normative power of such propositions is conditional: *If* we restrict ourselves simply to the rules of the "game" we are playing and the possibilities open to us, *then* we ought to . . .

All the licit normative constructs in this logic are conditional in that sense—they are all constructed from (and thus logically tethered to) antecedents that define an ongoing activity, its participants, and their possibilities. If the antecedent conditions are all-things-considered ones—that is, if the antecedent ongoing activity in terms of which the normative judgment is constructed is simply all-things-considered practical reasoning applied to a given situation—then such constructs have some similarity to categorical imperatives. This is so because, by definition, there is no way to reconstruct all-things-considered judgments in terms of antecedents that have not been considered. Thus in effect they have the sort of finality claimed for categorical imperatives (see Becker, "The Finality of Moral Judgments").

The classic stoic injunction to "follow nature" is thus realized here as following the facts. We begin with the rules for transforming descriptive propositions about the aims, rules of play, and practical possibilities within a given ongoing activity into normative propositions about those activities. This is the process of extracting the normative content of "institutional facts" mentioned earlier. In each case, the inferences are to first-order normative propositions.

From means and ends to norms. For stoics, means/end reasoning is the underlying form of all practical reasoning. It is implicit even in apparently noninstrumental inferences from desires or categorical commitments, for example, because those inferences depend on assumptions about their connection to eudaimonia, human happiness, or flourishing. And there is no *practical* reasoning about that end, as opposed to a philosophical defense of it. It is an axiom of the system. However, it would not be instructive, in a normative logic, to represent all inferences simply in terms of means/end relationships. That would obscure many important distinctions. Here we will treat means/end inferences on a par with those about desires, commitments, appropriateness, and so forth.

Such means/end inferences at a given ordinal level take several forms, depending on the possibilities for action. One is what we may call the rule of the best means: If we can identify some course of action or trait c as a practically possible means to achieving one or more of the goals we are pursuing, and it is the best of the practical possibilities, then *nothing-else-considered*, we ought to do c. (This also covers the case in which c is the only available means.) Translating this into something closer to our notation, we may say that if e is an Endeavor for agent s, and g is a Goal of e, and c is a course of conduct or state of being that is a practically possible Means by which s can achieve g, and there is no other Means by which s can achieve g that is equal to or superordinate to c, then s ought to Undertake to do or be c in e. Note that we do not allow the construction of a normative requirement from these facts. If the goal involved is an optional one, a requirement to pursue it does not follow merely from the fact that there is a best way, or even only one way, to do so. Thus:

The Best Means

$\{eEs \; \& \; gGe \; \& \; \Diamond_p(cMsg) \; \& \; [\sim(\exists x)\,(xMsg) \; \& \; (x \geq c)]\} \;/\therefore\; O_1(sUce)$

That leaves the cases in which there are several routes to the same goal, none superior to the others. In such cases, though we need to avoid the indecision of Buridan's ass, the choice is arbitrary. So we will resolve such cases with an inference that the agent ought to make an arbitrary choice between the means. Thus the rule of multiple means is this: if e is an Endeavor for agent s, and g is a Goal of e, and c is a practically possible Means by which s can achieve g, and b is another (coordinate) Means by which s can achieve g, then (again, nothing-else-considered), s ought to make an Arbitrary choice between c and b.

Multiple Means

$\{eEs \; \& \; gGe \; \& \; \Diamond_p(cMsg) \; \& \; [(bMsg) \; \& \; (b <> c)]\} \;/\therefore\; O_1(sAcb)$

Inferences to the conclusion that we ought not to do c may of course arise from our other endeavors, or from considerations of desire, commitment, and so forth. Such conflicts must be resolved with inferences to self-consistent superordinate normative propositions.

From desires to norms. In some endeavors the desires of the participants are allowed to trump all other considerations; the mere desire to do (or be) c counts as a sufficient reason for doing or being c, nothing-else-considered. Improvised games come to mind as an example—games in which the shifting whims of the players are allowed to overturn any of the rules, so that what begins as (say) a backyard game of croquet can mutate first into a test of love and then into an indefinite range of games that are not croquet. In other endeavors, desires are subordinate to certain considerations (e.g., efficiency), but are otherwise defined as sufficient reasons for action. And it may be that in still other endeavors, a desire to do c never counts as sufficient reason for doing it—or even counts as sufficient reason for *not* doing it.

We may represent these situations together in the following rule of inference: If e is an Endeavor for agent s, and d is a Desire of s to do or be c in e, and d is a Sufficient reason in e for s to Undertake c, then (nothing-else-considered) s ought to Undertake to do or be c in e. In our notation, this is

Desires

$(eEs \; \& \; dDsc \; \& \; dSesc) \;/\therefore\; O_1(sUce)$

Again, of course, desires can conflict, or conflict with other sorts of considerations.

From commitments to norms. A given endeavor, practice, or institution may define participants as categorically committed to various courses of action merely from the fact of their being participants in the endeavor. Such commitments are categorical in the sense that within the endeavor they are not conditioned on anything but participation—not on the desires or goals of individual participants, or the consequences of the required acts, for example. Such commitments are not optional within the endeavor. If e is an Endeavor for agent s, and c is defined as a Commitment for s in e, then (nothing-else-considered) s is required to Undertake to do or be c in e. Thus:

Commitments

(eEs & cCse) $/\therefore$ $R_1(sUce)$

From standards to norms. Many endeavors have standards of good form and appropriateness that fall short of the requiredness of categorical commitments but are nonetheless important practical considerations. Such endeavors have an etiquette as well as a set of goals, an aesthetic as well as a set of commitments, a conception of what is fitting as well as a conception of what is effective. When we disapprove of an admittedly licit and effective practice as ugly, uncouth, or tacky—or commend a failure as classy—we appeal to such standards. They are not typically employed, however, to identify a particular course of action or way of being that must or ought to be pursued. Rather they are employed to assess conduct or character in terms of some threshold of objectionability. Such appeals may be represented in a rule of inference about things we ought *not* to do or be—a rule of this general form: if e is an Endeavor for agent s, and c is defined as Standard or fitting conduct or character for s in e, then (nothing-else-considered) s ought not to Undertake to do or be anything other than c in e. Thus:

Appropriateness

(eEs & cSse) $/\therefore$ $\sim O_1(sU\sim ce)$

From ideals to norms. Appeals to standards of excellence, or to ideals for conduct and character, may be represented straightforwardly. They are not requirements, but they do identify a specific standard of conduct or character as something we ought to achieve. Thus if e is an Endeavor for agent s, and c is Ideal conduct or character for s in e, then (nothing-else-considered) s ought to Undertake to do or be c in e.

Ideals

(eEs & cIse) $/\therefore$ $O_1(sUce)$

From transactions to norms. Many endeavors define ways in which participants can create commitments, standards, and ideals for themselves within the endeavor. Obligations are sometimes distinguished from duties in this way by saying that while both are requirements, duties are imposed by the structure of the endeavor and obligations arise from voluntary transactions, such as contracts, within it. Whether a commitment, standard, or ideal is structural or transactional is sometimes normatively important in a given endeavor in a way that can be represented as a fact about its ordinal status. The nontransactional duty not to murder, for example, may make murder-for-hire contracts void, while certain ordinary duties of care (say, not to hit a baseball into a crowd) may be voided by the voluntary assumption of risk in coming to an organized baseball game. So we must have a way of representing the difference between these sources of commitments. Let us say that if e is an Endeavor for agent s, and t is a Transaction in e that Generates commitment c for s, then s is *transactionally* required to Undertake to do or be c in e. We will represent the transactional source of the norm with the subscript $_t$. (Normative operators without $_t$ will be understood as nontransactional or "structural.")

Transactional Commitments

(eEs & cCse & tTe & tGcs) $/\therefore$ R_{t1}(sUce)

For standards, or fittingness: if e is an Endeavor for agent s, and t is a Transaction in e that Generates a Standard of fittingness c for s, then *transactionally*, s ought not to Undertake to do or be anything other than c in e.

Transactional Standards

(eEs & cSse tTe & tGcs) $/\therefore$ $\sim O_{t1}$(sU$\sim$ce)

And for ideals: if e is an Endeavor for agent s, and t is a Transaction in e that Generates an Ideal c for s, then *transactionally* s ought to Undertake to do or be c in e.

Transactional Ideals

(eEs & cIse & tTe & tGcs) $/\therefore$ O_{t1}(sUce)

From amendments to norms. Practical reasoning about changing the nature of a given endeavor also needs special attention. Some endeavors have explicit or implicit rules for transforming themselves—for making changes in their own goals, commitments, standards, ideals, transactional rules, the definition of a participant, and so forth. Let us call

such changes amendments. We can represent such reasoning as follows:
If e is a given Endeavor, f is a given Factor or element of e, g is a licit
amenDment to f in e, then g Replaces f in e.

Amendments

(eEs & fFe & gDfe) /∴ R_{t1}(gRfe)

(2) Ranking Same-Level, Same-Endeavor Norms

Conflicts between norms constructed from different endeavors must be
settled by the rules in section (5) below. Here we deal with conflicts that
occur within a given endeavor at the same ordinal level. Because $R >
O > I$ here, the rules for resolving some of those conflicts are straight-
forward.

Requirements and oughts. If an agent s is required to do c in e but
(from other considerations within the endeavor) ought to do b, and undertaking both is logically or theoretically or practically impossible, then
the requirement dominates the ought.

Requirements over Oughts

R_n(sUce) & O_n(sUbe)

~◇(sUce & sUbe)

/∴ R_n(sUce) > O_n(sUbe)

Requirements and indifference. If an agent s is required to do c in e but
(from other considerations within the endeavor) b is a matter of indifference, and undertaking both is logically or theoretically or practically impossible, then the requirement dominates the indifference.

Requirements over Indifference

R_n(sUce) & I_n(sUbe)

~◇(sUce & sUbe)

/∴ R_n(sUce) > I_n(sUbe)

Oughts and indifference. If an agent s ought to do c in e but (from other
considerations within the endeavor) b is a matter of indifference, and
undertaking both is logically or theoretically or practically impossible,
then the ought dominates the indifference.

Oughts over Indifference

O_n(sUce) & I_n(sUbe)

$\sim\Diamond$(sUce & sUbe)

/∴ O_n(sUce) > I_n(sUbe)

Conflicting norms of the same type. Within an endeavor at ordinal level n, there may be conflicts between requirements, between oughts, or between judgments about indifference in cases where it is logically or theoretically or practically impossible to carry out all the norms. The norms in such conflicts may or may not be coordinate. Coordinate conflicting requirements or oughts are replaced by a judgment of indifference together with a requirement to choose. Coordinate conflicting indifferences generate a requirement to choose. (Such open propositions generate a determinate result at ordinal level n + 1. See the heading "(3) Escalation" below.)

Coordinate Conflicting Requirements

R_n(sUce) & R_n(sUbe)

R_n(sUce) < > R_n(sUbe)

$\sim\Diamond$(sUce & sUbe)

/∴ I_n(sUce) & I_n(sUbe) & R_n[(sUce) ⩔ (sUbe)]

Coordinate Conflicting Oughts

O_n(sUce) & O_n(sUbe)

O_n(sUce) < > O_n(sUbe)

$\sim\Diamond$(sUce & sUbe)

/∴ I_n(sUce) & I_n(sUbe) & R_n[(sUce) ⩔ (sUbe)]

Coordinate Conflicting Indifference

I_n(sUce) & I_n(sUbe)

I_n(sUce) < > I_n(sUbe)

$\sim\Diamond$(sUce & sUbe)

/∴ R_n[(sUce) ⩔ (sUbe)]

If the norms are not coordinate, the superordination relation simply falls through into the conclusion. (For the sake of economy, only half of each rule has been written out. In each case, of course, the conclusion changes in an obvious way if the ordinal relationship of the conflicting norms is reversed.)

Superordinate Conflicting Requirements

$R_n(sUce)$ & $R_n(sUbe)$

$R_n(sUce) > R_n(sUbe)$

$\sim\Diamond(sUce$ & $sUbe)$

$/\therefore R_n(sUce) > R_n(sUbe)$

Superordinate Conflicting Oughts

$O_n(sUce)$ & $O_n(sUbe)$

$O_n(sUce) > O_n(sUbe)$

$\sim\Diamond(sUce$ & $sUbe)$

$/\therefore O_n(sUce) > O_n(sUbe)$

(3) Escalation

When normative propositions from different endeavors conflict at level n, we will represent the resolution of the conflict in terms of rules for generating normative propositions at level n + 1. We will do the same for forced choices—requirements at level n to choose between conflicting courses of conduct or states of being, either within or across endeavors. Let us call these the rules of escalation.

Escalation from endogenous rankings. The order $R > O > I$ does not hold across endeavors. A requirement generated by a party game, for example, does not typically dominate an ought generated by a rescue effort. Indeed, in practice a judgment of indifference from an enterprise that is taken seriously may trump a requirement from one that is not. Our logic would misrepresent such facts if it formulated dominance rules that were applicable to all conflicts across endeavors merely from the meanings of the operators considered alone. We must instead take care to represent the ordinal relationships between the endeavors.

Sometimes these ordinal relationships come from the endeavors themselves, in the sense that each one is defined as having (or lacking) certain priorities. Let us say that such priorities are *endogenous* when they arise in this way. (Idle chat, for example, is typically defined as interruptible for almost any reason. Its ordinal claims for itself are minimal.) If the various endogenous rankings for conflicting normative propositions at level n are identical and determinate, we may resolve the conflict at n + 1, as follows.

For example, if one endeavor defines its requirements as superordinate to those of another, and the other agrees (i.e., defines its requirements as subordinate), then the rankings are identical and determinate. The rule of inference is this: If both e and f are Endeavors for agent s, and s is required at level n to Undertake both c in e and b in f, but although undertaking both is logically or theoretically or practically impossible, each endeavor Defines c as superordinate to b, then s ought, at level n + 1, to Undertake c in e. Note that this rule yields only an ought at n + 1. The fact that these endeavors agree that one of the requirements has priority over the other would be overstated if we escalated to a requirement at n + 1.

Superordination for Coincident Endogenous Rankings

for conflicting requirements

eEs & $R_n(sUce)$

fEs & $R_n(sUbf)$

$\sim\Diamond(sUce$ & $sUbf)$

$R_n(sUce) > R_n(sUbf)$

$/\therefore O_{n+1}(sUce)$

for conflicts between oughts, requirements and oughts, etc.

The rule applies, *mutatis mutandis*, for any ordering > or < of any norms (R, O, I) governing sUce and sUbf.

When the various endogenous rankings agree that neither of the conflicting norms at level n dominates the other, they in effect agree that the choice between the norms is arbitrary. We will represent this by deriving norms of indifference at n + 1, coupled with a requirement to choose.

Equivalence for Coincident Endogenous Rankings

for conflicting requirements

eEs & $R_n(sUce)$

fEs & $R_n(sUbf)$

$\sim\Diamond(sUce$ & $sUbf)$

$R_n(sUce) <> R_n(sUbf)$

$/\therefore I_{n+1}(sUce) \& I_{n+1}(sUbf) \& R_{n+1}[(sUce) \veebar (sUbf)]$

for conflicts between oughts, requirements and oughts, etc.

The rule applies, *mutatis mutandis*, for any ordering $<>$ of any norms (R, O, I) governing sUce and sUbf.

When endogenous rankings are absent, or are not identical, or are indeterminate (i.e., $\leq$ or $\geq$), conflicts must be resolved with the rules for exogenous rankings. See below.

Forced choice under indifference. Within or across endeavors, we sometimes face a requirement to choose between coordinate, thus indifferent, options. If various acts or states of being are matters of indifference at some normative level n, but it is required that we choose one or the other, then we will say that we ought, at level n + 1, to make an arbitrary choice between the two. (It is clear that the requirement to choose can be resolved with an ought, and since it does not matter which of the two oughts we adopt, it seems implausible to represent the resolution as a requirement to do the option we choose.) Thus if it is a matter of indifference at level n whether agent s Undertakes c in e, b in e, or b in f, but s is required to choose exactly one, then s ought at n + 1 to make an Arbitrary choice between c and b.

Forced Choice under Indifference

within an endeavor

$I_n(sUce) \& I_n(sUbe)$

$\sim\Diamond(sUce \& sUbe)$

$R_n[(sUce) \veebar (sUbe)]$

$/\therefore O_{n+1}(sAcb)$

across endeavors

$I_n(sUce) \& I_n(sUbf)$

$\sim\Diamond(sUce \& sUbf)$

$R_n[(sUce) \veebar (sUbf)]$

$/\therefore O_{n+1}(sAcb)$

Escalation from exogenous rankings. Each of us engages in a multitude of endeavors. We define some of these as embedded in more comprehensive endeavors. For example, a game of Go Fish with a younger sister may be embedded in a baby-sitting operation for several siblings that controls when and how the game is played, and the baby-sitting may itself be controlled by more general filial obligations derived from family life. In such cases, when norms at level n conflict, those from the more comprehensive endeavor are elevated to level n + 1. Thus, for example, if both e and f are Endeavors for agent s, and s is required at level n to Undertake both c in e and b in f, but although undertaking both is logically or theoretically or practically impossible, endeavor e is defined as more Comprehensive than f for s, then s is required, at level n + 1, to Undertake c in e. Note that this rule preserves the normative operator from e, to represent the fact that e is the more comprehensive and controlling of the two endeavors for agent s. However, it leaves the less comprehensive norm intact at level n to represent the fact that the norm from f has not been altered but merely overridden in this case.

Comprehensiveness

for requirements

eEs & $R_n(sUce)$

fEs & $R_n(sUbf)$

$\sim\diamond(sUce$ & $sUbf)$

eCfs

$/\therefore R_{n+1}(sUce)$

for other norms

The rule applies, *mutatis mutandis*, for any combination of norms. Whatever the norm from the more comprehensive and controlling of the endeavors at n, it escalates to n + 1 as a norm of the same type.

Exogenous rankings also arise from the fact that some of our endeavors are designed to assess or evaluate others. Judicial review, for example, assesses the constitutionality of statutes passed by legislatures. Peer review procedures in various professions assess the job performance of individuals. And within our own lives we regularly monitor and assess our own activities—in terms of their prudence, consequences for others, conformity to law, morality, religious doctrine, and so forth. When we adopt one endeavor as an assessment mechanism for other (target) endeavors, we use it to construct norms that are about those of its targets, and superordinate to them. We will represent that situation here by saying that when the norms of an assessment (or critical endeavor) conflict at level n with those of its target endeavor, the target's norms are rejected, and the norms from the assessment (critique) are elevated to level n + 1.

Thus, for example, if both e and f are Endeavors for agent s, and s is required at level n to Undertake both c in e and b in f, but although undertaking both is logically or theoretically or practically impossible, endeavor e is defined as an exogenous aSsessment of f for s, then s is required, at level n + 1, to Undertake c in e.

Exogenous Assessment

for conflicting requirements

eEs & R_n(sUce)

fEs & R_n(sUbf)

$\sim\diamondsuit$(sUce & sUbf)

eSfs

$/\therefore R_{n+1}$(sUce)

for other norms

The rule applies, *mutatis mutandis*, for any combination of norms. Whatever conflicting norm emerges from the assessment endeavor at n escalates to n + 1 as a norm of the same type.

(4) Transcendence

By definitional convention in this logic, normative propositions representing practical reasoning all-things-considered are written (or may be rewritten) with unsubscripted normative operators, and are interpreted as representing moral norms. Thus if endeavor e for s is an aSsessment, and e for s is Practical reasoning all-things-considered, and these things generate a normative proposition via the rule of exogenous assessment, then that normative proposition is unsubscripted.

Transcendent Assessment

for requirements

eEs & ePs & R_n(sUce)

fEs & R_n(sUbf)

$\sim\diamondsuit$(sUce & sUbf)

eSfs

$/\therefore$ **R**(sUce)

The same holds for applications of the rule of comprehensiveness. Thus:

Transcendent Comprehensiveness

for requirements

eEs & ePs & $\mathbf{R_n}$(sUce)

fEs & $\mathbf{R_n}$(sUbf)

$\sim\Diamond$(sUce & sUbf)

eCfs

$/\therefore$ **R**(sUce)

for other norms

The rule applies, *mutatis mutandis,* for any combination of normative propositions. Whatever the proposition from practical reasoning all-things-considered, it escalates to an unsubscripted one of the same type.

Forced moral choice. Conflicts among unsubscripted, coordinate normative propositions may force an arbitrary choice. When this happens, the requirement of an arbitrary choice has effectively become the more encompassing norm. We will resolve this state of affairs in a series of rules. For example, if it is impossible for s to do both c and b, in the same or different endeavors, and if both c and b are unsubscripted requirements for s, and there is an unsubscripted requirement that s do one or the other, then the forced-choice requirement generates a moral requirement to make an Arbitrary choice between the two.

Conflicting Moral Requirements

$\sim\Diamond$(sUce & sUbf)

R(sUce) & **R**(sUbf)

RsUce < > **R**sUbf

R(sUce $\veebar$ sUbf)

$/\therefore$ **R**(sAcb)

If c and b are unsubscripted oughts that are jointly impossible to undertake, and a choice between them is forced, we get a moral requirement to make an Arbitrary choice between the two.

Conflicting Moral Oughts

$\sim\Diamond$(sUce & sUbf)

O(sUce) & O(sUbf)

OsUce < > OsUbf

R(sUce $\veebar$ sUbf)

/∴ R(sAcb)

If c and b are unsubscripted indifferences, and a choice is forced, we also get a moral requirement to make an Arbitrary choice.

Conflicting Moral Indifference

$\sim\Diamond$(sUce & (sUbf)

I(sUce) & I(sUbf)

IsUce < > IsUbf

R(sUce $\veebar$ sUbf)

/∴ R(sAcb)

If it is a matter of indifference whether or not s Undertakes c in e, but a choice between undertaking c or $\sim$c is forced, then a modified version of the rule of conflicting moral indifference applies. By definitional equivalence, I(sUce) may be written as I$\sim$(sUce), so we use the conjunction of them to represent the forced choice, which then generates a moral requirement for s to make an Arbitrary choice between c and $\sim$c.

Closure for Moral Indifference

$\sim\Diamond$[(sUce & $\sim$(sUce)]

IsUce & I$\sim$(sUce)

R(sUce $\veebar$ $\sim$sUce)

/∴ R(sAc$\sim$c)

Axioms of Stoic Normative Logic

Stoics add the following postulates specific to their ethical doctrines, which are given a metaethical defense in other chapters.

IX. **Axiom of Encompassment.** The exercise of our agency through practical intelligence, including practical reasoning all-things-considered, is the most comprehensive of our endeavors. That is, in every case, if endeavor x for agent s is the exercise of Agency through practical intelligence all-things-considered and endeavor y for s is not, then x is more Comprehensive than y for s.

$\vdash$ (x) (y) [(xEs & yEs & xAs & y~As) ⊃ xCys]

X. **Axiom of Finality.** There is no assessment endeavor exogenous to the exercise of practical reasoning all-things-considered. That is, in every case, if endeavor x for agent s is pracTical reasoning all-things-considered and endeavor y for s is not, then y is not an aSsessment mechanism for x for s.

$\vdash$ (x) (y) [(xEs & yEs & xTs & y~Ts) ⊃ y~Sys]

XI. **Axiom of Moral Priority.** Unsubscripted norms are superordinate to subscripted ones. To state this in a compact way without quantifying over normative operators, we will use a schema in which N stands for any normative operator, and P stands for a wff of any form. The schema asserts that NP is superordinate to N_nP.

$\vdash NP > N_nP$

XII. **Axiom of Moral Rank.** The order $R > O > I$ holds for unsubscripted (i.e., moral) normative propositions.

$\vdash RP > OP > IP$

XIII. **Axiom of Closure.** If no normative proposition at any level can be constructed for a given course of conduct or state of being (that is, if a situation is normatively open), the relevant proposition is closed with an unsubscripted ought-not. That is, if it is not the case that either a subscripted or unsubscripted normative operator N governs c for s in e, then s ought not to Undertake c in e.

$\vdash \sim[N(sUce) \vee N_n(sUce)] \supset O\sim(sUce)$

XIV. **Axiom of Futility**. If any norm represented by an atomic normative proposition, as opposed to a conjunction of them, is logically, theoretically, or practically impossible to carry out, it yields an unsubscripted prohibition. That is, if any normative operator N governs c for s in e, and it is logically or theoretically or practically impossible for s to Undertake c in e, then s is required not to Undertake c in e, and that requirement dominates the original norm.

$$\vdash [N(sUce) \;\&\; \sim\!\Diamond(sUce)] \supset \mathbf{R}\!\sim\!(sUce) \;\&\; [\mathbf{R}\!\sim\!(sUce) > N(sUce)]$$

Immediate Inferences

From stronger to weaker. Requirements and prohibitions at the same ordinal rank are equivalent in normative force or strength. Propositions about what ought to be done are weaker. (Indifference is a special case. In an obvious sense it is the weakest of the three, but it has some special powers that make a straightforward ranking problematic. See the inferences below.) Thus within a given ordinal level the following immediate inferences may be made *a fortiori*. That is, if we have proved the stronger, we may immediately conclude that we have thereby also proved its weaker counterparts. Stating the premise first, followed by "therefore" $(/\!\therefore)$ and the conclusion, we have

$$\mathbf{R}_n w \;/\!\therefore\; \mathbf{O}_n w$$

$$\mathbf{I}_n w \;/\!\therefore\; \sim\!\mathbf{O}_n w \;\&\; \sim\!\mathbf{R}_n w$$

From opposites. Two normative propositions at a given ordinal level are logical opposites if each member of the pair is a denial of the other. Aristotelian logic distinguishes two kinds of opposites: contradictories, which can be neither jointly true nor jointly false; and contraries, which cannot be jointly true, but which can be jointly false. Here we make the same distinction with respect to jointly sound or unsound pairs. (Inconsistent sets of atomic normative propositions form open, rather than sound or unsound, compounds.)

Contradictories
Rp and ~Rp cannot be either jointly sound or jointly unsound, so from Rp we may immediately infer ~(~Rp), and from ~Rp we may infer ~~(~Rp). The same is true of Op and ~Op, Ip and ~Ip. These are not very interesting contradictories, since double negation is provable as a theorem in this system, and ~(~Rp) becomes Rp, etc. Slightly more inter-

esting is the fact that Ip is the "complete" contradictory of both Rp and Op—that is, it contradicts R~p as well as Rp, and O~p as well as Op. So the following *reversible* immediate inferences are available:

$I_n w$ /∴ $\sim(R_n w)$, and vice versa

$I_n w$ /∴ $\sim(R_n \sim w)$, ...

$I_n w$ /∴ $\sim(O_n w)$, . . .

$I_n w$ /∴ $\sim(O_n \sim w)$, . . .

$R_n w$ /∴ $\sim(I_n w)$, . . .

$R_n \sim w$ /∴ $\sim(I_n w)$, . . .

$O_n w$ /∴ $\sim(I_n w)$, . . .

$O_n \sim w$ /∴ $\sim(I_n w)$, . . .

(Note that Rp and R~p, Op and O~p, are contraries rather than contradictories. See below. Recall that Ip and I~p are definitionally equivalent.)

Contraries

As is evident from the above, some pairs of normative propositions are contraries. That is, each denies the other, and while it remains logically possible for them both to be unsound, it is not logically possible for them both to be sound. Rp and R~p conflict in this way, because although it is logically impossible to prove that p is *both* required and forbidden, it might be that p is neither required nor forbidden, but rather something we merely ought (or ought not) to do—or perhaps even a matter of indifference. The same logical contrariety holds between Rp and ~Op, R~p and Op, and Op and O~p, because each inconsistent pair might be jointly false. Thus we have these *nonreversible* immediate inferences:

$R_n w$ /∴ $\sim(R_n \sim w)$

$R_n w$ /∴ $\sim(O_n \sim w)$

And:

$R_n \sim w$ /∴ $\sim(R_n w)$

$R_n \sim w$ /∴ $\sim(O_n w)$

And:

$O_n w \: / \therefore \: \sim(O_n \sim w)$

$O_n \sim w \: / \therefore \: \sim(O_n w)$

(Recall again that $I_n w$ and $I_n \sim w$ are definitional equivalents, and thus not contraries.)

Commentary

For careful, lucid, and detailed accounts of the contributions of the ancient stoics to the development of logic, with copious reference to the fragmentary texts, see Benson Mates, *Stoic Logic*, and William Kneale and Martha Kneale, *The Development of Logic*. For the texts themselves, with the usual illuminating commentary, see sections 31–38 of Long and Sedley, eds., *The Hellenistic Philosophers*. Note especially the discussions of the stoics' long misunderstood invention of propositional logic, their debates about conditionals (material and strict implication), their debates about necessity, and their statement of the conditionalization principle (that an argument is valid if we get a logical truth when we form a conditional whose antecedent is the conjunction of the argument's premises and whose consequent is the argument's conclusion). The Kneales' book also puts stoic logic into historical context.

This Normative Logic in Relation to Others

Vocabulary and notation. The normative operators used here are not the ones standardly found in deontic logic. There are some logicians who have proposed something like them. But most writers use prohibition, obligation, and permission rather than requirement, ought, and indifference. This is not a mere notational difference, and its significance will be discussed more fully below in the section on the "modal approach" to deontic logic. One wrinkle that deserves special mention now, however, is that here as in standard accounts the normative operators operate upon descriptive sentences—propositions—rather than upon verbs or verb phrases that identify actions or activity. This is indicated by the way the operators are read: R is read as "it is required that _____" where the blank is filled by a proposition. It is not read as "s is required to _____" where the blank is filled with a verb phrase. Some formidable logicians treat this distinction as an important one, and claim standard deontic logic runs into difficulties here. See Wright, "On the Logic of Norms and Actions," 9ff.; Castañeda, "The Paradoxes of Deontic Logic: The Simplest Solution to All of Them in One Fell Swoop," 40–41. The examples designed to exhibit the difficulties, however, do not seem to embarrass the logic outlined here, largely due to our severe constraints on the construction of normative propositions. See the section below on construction.

Quantification and generality. While it is clear that normative operators can range over quantifiers unproblematically, logicians are quite cautious about the reverse. See Wright, "On the Logic of Norms and Actions," 32–33. To be on the safe side, we do not allow any quantifiers to range over deontic operators. We use quantifiers in the descriptive components of normative propositions to define the range of agents or acts or circumstances covered by the norms involved.

The modal approach. At least as early as the fourteenth century, logicians noted similarities between the "alethetic" modalities (impossibility, necessity, and possibility) and the normative concepts of prohibition, obligation, and permission. See Knuuttila, "The Emergence of Deontic Logic in the Fourteenth Century."

Following out these similarities has been the standard approach to deontic logic in the latter half of the twentieth century, though the putative paradoxes of this strategy and its difficulties in representing the full complexity of moral life (particularly moral conflicts) have led to many refinements. Some of these, such as the attempt to anchor deontic logic in temporal concepts in Thomason, "Deontic Logic as Founded in Tense Logic," we do not pursue here. Others, notably the use of hierarchies in resolving conflicts in Alchourrón and Makinson, "Heirarchies of Regulation and their Logic," we do pursue. But the greatest apparent difference between our normative logic and the standard modal approach is in the normative concepts we employ.

The standard modal approach maps obligation onto necessity and prohibition onto impossibility, leaving the alethic remainder of possibility to correspond to permission. We, on the other hand, do this:

1. We think of the normative notion of requirement as incompletely analogous to *two* alethic ones—necessity and impossibilty. "It is required that p" represents the affirmative notions of duty and obligation, and its interpretation corresponds in a limited way to necesssity. "It is required that not-p" represents the idea of prohibition, or of duty or obligation *not* to do something, and corresponds, again in a very limited way, to impossibility. The limitations of this interpretation are severe, however. As noted in the presentation of modal axioms, we do not accept their deontic analogs, and to refuse to extend those alethic truisms into the deontic realm is to limit the analogy at a very fundamental level. Moreover, we involve the notion of correctness in one disjunct of the interpretation of requirement: It is unclear how that would be interpreted in modal terms.

2. We employ an "ought" operator interpreted solely in terms of "advisability," and it does not seem to correspond to any combination of modal ones, or to any logical operation upon them. While falling short of stating obligations or duties, ought-statements represent conclusions about what it is right to do or be—conclusions constructed from the ends, values, ideals, and standards of our endeavors. So conceived, ought is a normative notion that falls immovably between requirement on the one side and the absence of a conclusive norm on the other.

3. The absence of a conclusive norm, which we call indifference, is equivalent to the joint denial of requirement and mere correctness. "It is indifferent that p" means p is neither required nor prohibited, and neither advisable nor inadvisable. In one sense this merely renames the standard deontic operator of permission, since it is natural to say, for example, that if it is a matter of normative indifference whether we do b or c, then both are permitted, and vice versa. But the ordinary concept of permission has some complexity that makes its use as a normative "remainder" inconvenient. In particular, the notion of permission (as in *having* permission) seems go beyond the mere joint denial of requirement and recommendation. So we do not try to equate indifference to permission. Indifference, however, does not map very well onto the modal notion of possibility. For one thing, necessity is typically understood to entail possibility: If $\Box p$, then $\Diamond p$. While there is a similar relation between what is affirmatively required and what is *a fortiori* permitted, there is obviously no such relation between requirement and indifference.

4. We take permission out of the realm of normative operators altogether, and instead make its various forms into nonnormative predicates that represent the choice set available to an agent in the logical space defined by her possibilities and requirements. This avoids the controversies introduced by attempts to make a permission operator interdefinable with prohibition and obligation. See Wright, "On the Logic of Norms and Actions," 6. Recall that one of the attractive features of the modal approach is supposed to be that the elegant interdefinability of modal operators is mirrored in deontic ones. Thus just as we need only one basic alethic modality plus negation to construct the others, and it does not matter which one we choose, so it has seemed to some that we need only one basic deontic modality. For example, on the alethic side if possibility is taken as the basic notion, then impossibility is its negation ($\sim\diamondsuit p$), and necessity is the impossibility of not-p ($\sim\diamondsuit \sim p$). Some have thought that an analogous thing holds for Permission to do p: Forbiddenness (prohibition) is simply its negation ($\sim Pp$), and Obligation is just the prohibition of not doing p ($\sim P \sim p$). The problem is that in this scheme, when forbiddenness is treated as basic, permission is defined as its negation ($\sim Pp$)—that is, simply as the absence of a prohibition. And that seems incapable of adequately representing the ordinary and juridical notions *being permitted* (having license) to do something.

These and other disanalogies with alethic modalities (Wright, "On the Logic of Norms and Actions," 7ff.) make us wary of any version of the standard modal approach, though the startling suggestion in Schotch and Jennings, "Non-Kripkean Deontic Logic," that alethic logic might be a special case of deontic logic is intriguing. In any case, given our interpretations of the ought and requirement operators, it appears that we cannot simply borrow the semantics of alethic modal logic for this normative one in any straightforward way. We are encouraged, moreover, in thinking that this will not be fatal to our project by some related (and more rigorous) attempts to provide alternative semantics for deontic logic. Though these efforts are typically directed to making room for notions of good, better, and best rather than precisely the norms we want to use, they often include something like our notions of indifference and ought, and sometimes employ possible world semantics. For various aspects of such work, see Feldman, *Doing the Best We Can: An Essay in Informal Deontic Logic*; Hansson, "Preference-Based Deontic Logic"; and Goble, "A Logic of Good, Should, and Would," Parts I and II.

The paradoxes of standard deontic logic. The modal approach, while elegant in intent, has been a decidedly mixed blessing for deontic logic. In particular, two features of the standard logic that developed from von Wright's 1951 paper "Deontic Logic" generate counterintuitive or "paradoxical" results. One is an unrestricted rule of well formedness that allows deontic operators to be affixed willy-nilly to any proposition that is well-formed in the propositional or predicate calculus. Thus if anything p is a wff, so is Fp, Op, or Pp (it is Forbidden, Obligatory, or Permitted that p). The other troublesome feature is the variety of ways that one can derive, delete, and distribute modal operators, even in the weakest systems of modal logic, that cause problems when extended to deontic contexts. As noted in the text of the Appendix, we certainly cannot accept the normative version of $\Box p \supset p$, which every system of modal logic contains. Similarly, the derivation of alethic propositions in $(p \supset q) \supset (\Box p \supset \Box q)$, leads to paradoxes of "derived obligation" when O (or **R**) is substituted for $\Box$. (We surely do not want to say that just because q is a material consequence of p, a requirement that q is a material consequence of a requirement that p. Rather, we want to be able to hold that in some cases q is only an unfortunate, unintended consequence of a requirement that p.) More problems arise in the use of some distributive equivalences drawn from alethic modal logic, where these biconditionals for

Possibility: $\Diamond(p \vee q) \equiv \Diamond p \vee \Diamond q$

Impossibility: $\Box\sim(p \vee q) \equiv \Box\sim p \;\&\; \Box\sim q$

Necessity: $\Box(p \;\&\; q) \equiv \Box p \;\&\; \Box q$

are unproblematic. The corresponding deontic rules for

Permissibility: $P(p \vee q) \equiv Pp \vee Pq$

Forbiddeness: $F(p \vee q) \equiv Fp \;\&\; Fq$

Obligation: $O(p \;\&\; q) \equiv Op \;\&\; Oq$

are decidedly problematic, however. Even the weaker $(\Box p \;\&\; \Box q) \supset \Box(p \;\&\; q)$ leads to problems. See Schotch and Jennings, "Non-Kripkean Deontic Logic."

Well-formed Formulas

In the logic outlined in the Appendix, the normative propositions that enter into inferences are understood to be constructed in accord with the rules given in the section "Normative Constructs." To leave no doubt in the matter, we make such construction a rule of well-formedness. Recall that, in the Appendix, rule 4 for wffs is

> 4. If anything w is a wff, and if Rw, Ow, or Iw is a construct as defined in the section "Normative Constructs" below, then Rw, Ow, or Iw is a wff, provided no quantifiers in it range over $\Box$, $\Diamond$, **R**, **O**, or **I**.

The so-called "standard paradoxes of deontic logic" thus do not arise here. For example in the propositional calculus, given p, we can infer $(p \vee q)$, but there is nothing embarrassing about that for normative propositions in this logic, since Rq cannot be a substitution instance of q in $p \supset (p \vee q)$ unless it is a normative construct. This blocks some of the well-known paradoxes of derived obligation. Further, since we do not expect our normative logic to mirror an alethic one, we need not be lumbered with the paradoxes that arise from its specifically modal axioms and theorems. We simply decline to import problematic modal elements into our normative logic. We do not doubt that some vexing technical problems will emerge to surprise us. Such things have plagued standard deontic logic for decades. See, for example, recent discussions of James Forrester's "paradox of gentle murder," which seems to follow from three ordinary-sounding premises: that (1) Jones ought not to murder Smith, but that (2) if Jones does so, he ought to do it gently (swiftly, painlessly), and regrettably (3) Jones does so. It then follows, from (2) and (3), that (4) Jones ought to murder Smith gently. But that obviously conflicts with (1). (Readers who want to pursue the puzzle in the context of standard deontic logic will find it helpful to consult Forrester, "Gentle Murder, or the Adverbial Samaritan"; Sinnott-Armstrong, "A Solution to Forrester's Paradox of Gentle Murder"; and Goble, "Murder Most Gentle: The Paradox Deepens.") Our approach to all such puzzles is to resolve them with minor changes in the formalism where possible, but in any case to resolve them, even if that means imposing restrictions on something as fundamental as the rule of detachment.

Does this mean that the normative logic outlined in this appendix will be too weak to interest logicians? Perhaps. See, for example, Almeida, "Deontic Logic and the Possibility of Moral Conflict," for arguments against weakened versions of deontic logic. But a more pressing concern at the moment is the question of whether rule 4 for wffs may be too strict (in addition to being too ugly). In the discussion of heteronomous norms (Chapter 5), we say that although such norms are "outside the normative logic" of our agency because they are not constructed from facts about our endeavors, we nonetheless must acknowledge them as facts about our psychology. This suggests that our logic should be able to represent them in well-formed formulas. Perhaps the wiser course, then, would be to drop rule 4, and *rewrite* rule 3 as follows:

3. If anything w is a wff, then $\sim w$, $\Box w$, $\Diamond w$, $\mathbf{R}w$, $\mathbf{O}w$, or $\mathbf{I}w$ is a wff, provided no quantifiers in it range over $\Box$, $\Diamond$, $\mathbf{R}$, $\mathbf{O}$, or $\mathbf{I}$.

The embarrassments of the standard paradoxes would still be minimal, since only constructs can be used in the inferences defined as sound in the system.

Construction

The logic offered here is far from pure. In particular, its insistence that well-formed normative propositions (or at least those that are usable in sound inferences) be constructed from facts about the endeavors of individual agents is a restriction that logicians may find vexing. It seems to impoverish the logic by making it incapable of representing much everyday normative language. What are we to do with social norms, conventions, laws, signs that say "No smoking," and so on? Chapter 5 has more to say about this, but in brief, for philosophical reasons we insist on tethering all normative propositions to the purposive behavior of individual agents. So conventions are understood as facts about general norms that are shared by individuals. The "No Smoking" sign in the doctor's office is her norm for everyone who enters, and it comes from some endeavor she is pursuing (say, the health of her patients, or her own comfort, or conforming to the expectations of others). People who work in the office may share the norm—either because they share the doctor's endeavor or because they are pursuing another endeavor (keeping their jobs) that entails accepting it. It is true that this restatement of the meaning of a "No Smoking" sign takes us quite far from its meaning in ordinary speech or thought, where attention to metaphysical detail is often absent. And it is true that we want logic generally to be able to represent ordinary language so that it can represent philosophical arguments about the metaphysical assumptions in the ways we ordinarily speak and think. Standard assertoric and alethic logic seem capable of that, however. What we offer here is a normative

logic for ethics in the stoic tradition. Readers who insist that an adequate normative logic must be completely "neutral" between competing moral theories face
severe difficulties. See Sayre-McCord, "Deontic Logic and the Priority of Moral
Theory."

Bivalence

The stoics of antiquity were committed to bivalence. Readers may wonder how
well the appendix honors that tradition. Normative propositions are interpreted
as three-valued, here, in order to represent the "openness" that results from our
inability to construct coherent sets of normative propositions at a given level n.
Our view is that this is harmless as long as the rules and axioms force closure at
n + 1 or better, but even so, we are sensitive to the pull of bivalence. James Cargile
has reminded us in correspondence that there may be a way to interpret conflicting normative propositions perspectivally so as to be able to state and resolve
conflicts with the resources of standard bivalent logic. The idea, drawn from work
on the paradoxes of standard deontic logic, would be to represent norms in more
detailed propositional forms, always distinguishing them temporally (or perhaps
in terms of the specific aspects of the endeavors from which they are drawn). See
Voorbraak, "The Logic of Actual Obligation: An Alternative Approach to Deontic Logic," for discussion of some of this work. We are not confident that this
could be done in all cases (though it surely works for many), but we would like to
see it pursued, so long as it does nothing to damage our ability to represent in the
logic the contradictory motivational tugs of our ordinary practical experience. A
related matter raised by Cargile illustrates our worry. He asks, about the meaning
of "Nothing-else-considered, s ought to Undertake c in e": "Does this mean 'If s
does not consider anything else, then he ought etc.,' or is it rather 'If s does not
consider anything else then it will appear to s that he ought etc.'?" The answer is,
we think, that it means both, and more. Nothing ontological is at stake here. The
idea is simply to represent, in a perspicuous way, the norms operating in s's endeavors. If s is baby-sitting, and playing a game with the child, two connected
endeavors are being pursued simultaneously—endeavors that, described separately, may yield conflicting motivated norms for a given situation, such as an
opportunity to take advantage of the child's inexpert play. The rules of the game
may be silent on this (or may require cutthroat play), while the baby-sitting enterprise requires something else, which for the baby-sitter may or may not dominate
the playing of the game. So we say that playing the game per se, nothing-else-
considered, requires c, but playing it as a baby-sitter with an inexpert child may
require ~c. We want to be able to represent the opposing motivations clearly
present in some such situations.

The array of rules and axioms for propositional, predicate, and modal logic
used here is a mixture drawn from several sources. Whitehead and Russell, in
Principia Mathematica, originally proposed five axioms for the propositional calculus, but Bernays (Hilbert and Ackermann, *Principles of Mathematical Logic*,
28) showed that the fifth, namely $p \vee (q \vee r) \supset q \vee (p \vee r)$, was unnecessary.
Hilbert and Ackermann's classic presentation of propositional and predicate logic
gives two axioms for the predicate calculus, and two rules governing the use of
quantifiers. See Hilbert and Ackermann, *Principles of Mathematical Logic*, 68–

70. This makes certain things about the system nicely transparent, but it also makes it necessary to complicate the rule of substitution greatly. We have therefore followed Feys's more streamlined presentation in his *Modal Logics*, which makes use of some elegant simplifications introduced by Quine. See, for example, Quine, *Methods of Logic*, 89–94.

Acknowledgments

A number of people read and thought carefully about early versions of this chapter, and saved me from some egregious errors. My colleague Steven Harris identified a crucial use-mention error as well as errors in the use of quantifiers in the axioms. James Cargile and Mitchell Green each caught errors that infected all the rules of inference having to do with conflicting normative propositions, as well as the Axiom of Futility. Mitchell Green corrected my naïveté on several other matters, and gave me valuable bibliographic advice. In particular, he encouraged me to read, rather than merely continue to stare at, several books that rested on my logic shelf. And he pressed me to explain the semantics of the normative operators used here in relation to modal ones. My thanks to all these people for taking an interest in this project.

Bibliography

Alchourrón, Carlos E, and David Makinson. "Heirarchies of Regulation and Their Logic." In *New Studies in Deontic Logic*, edited by Risto Hilpinen, 125–48. Dordrecht: Reidel, 1981.

Algra, Keimpe. "The Early Stoics on the Immobility and Coherence of the Cosmos." *Phronesis* (1988).

Allport, Gordon W. *Becoming: Basic Considerations for a Psychology of Personality*. New Haven: Yale University Press, 1943.

———. *Pattern and Growth in Personality*. New York: Holt, Rinehart, and Winston, 1961.

———. *The Person in Psychology*. Boston: Beacon Press, 1968.

Almeida, Michael J. "Deontic Logic and the Possibility of Moral Conflict." *Erkenntnis* 33 (July 1990): 57–71.

Annas, Julia. "The Good Life and the Good Lives of Others." *Social Philosophy and Policy* 9 (Summer 1992): 133–48.

———. *The Morality of Happiness*. New York: Oxford University Press, 1993.

———. "Reply to Cooper." *Philosophy and Phenomenological Research* 55 (1995): 587–610.

———. "Schofield's 'The Stoic Idea of the City.'" *Polis* 11 (1992): 95–101.

Anscombe, G.E.M. "On Brute Fact." *Analysis* 18 (1958): 69–72.

Arnim, Hans von. *Stoicorum Veterum Fragmenta*. 4 vols. Dubuque, Iowa, 1967 [1903–1924].

Baron, Marcia. *Kantian Ethics Almost without Apology*. Ithaca: Cornell University Press, 1995.

Becker, Lawrence C. "Community, Dominion, and Membership." *Southern Journal of Philosophy* 30 (1992): 17–44.

———. "The Finality of Moral Judgments." *Philosophical Review* 82 (1973): 364–71.

———. "Good Lives: Prolegomena." *Social Philosophy and Policy* 9 (1992): 15–37.

———. *Reciprocity*. London and Boston: Routledge, 1986.

———. "Trust as Noncognitive Security About Motives." *Ethics* 107 (1996): 43–61.

Blundell, Mary Whitlock. "Parental Nature and Stoic Oikeiosis." *Ancient Philosophy* (fall 1990): 221–42.

Botros, Sophie. "Freedom, Causality, Fatalism and Early Stoic Philosophy." *Phronesis* 30 (1985): 274–304.

Brown, Roger. *Social Psychology*. New York: Free Press, 1965; 1986.

Brunschwig, Jacques. "The Cradle Argument in Epicureanism and Stoicism." In *The Norms of Nature: Studies in Hellenistic Ethics*, edited by Malcolm Schofield and Gisela Striker, 113–44. Cambridge: Cambridge University Press, 1986.

Brunschwig, Jacques. *Papers in Hellenistic Philosophy.* Translated by Janet Lloyd. New York: Cambridge University Press, 1994.

Campbell, Keith. "Self-Mastery and Stoic Ethics." *Philosophy* 60 (1985): 327–40.

Cargile, James. "Some Comments on Fatalism." *American Philosophical Quarterly* 46, no. 182 (January 1996): 1–11.

Castañeda, Hector-Neri. "The Paradoxes of Deontic Logic: The Simplest Solution to All of Them in One Fell Swoop." In *New Studies in Deontic Logic,* edited by Risto Hilpinen, 37–86. Dordrecht: Reidel, 1981.

———. *Thinking and Doing: The Philosophical Foundations of Institutions.* Dordrecht: Reidel, 1975.

Chaplin, James P., and T. S. Krawiec. *Systems and Theories of Psychology.* 4th ed. New York: Holt, Rinehart, and Winston, 1979.

Cicero, Marcus Tullius. *De Fato.* Edited by T. E. Page. The Loeb Classical Library. Cambridge, Mass., and London: Harvard University Press and William Heinemann Ltd., 1933 [c. 44 B.C.].

———. *De Finibus.* Edited by T. E. Page and translated by H. Rackham. The Loeb Classical Library. Cambridge, Mass., and London: Harvard University Press and William Heinemann Ltd., 1951 [c. 45 B.C.].

———. *De Natura Deorum.* Edited by T. E. Page and translated by H. Rackham. The Loeb Classical Library. Cambridge, Mass. and London: Harvard University Press and William Heinemann Ltd., 1933 [c. 45 B.C.].

———. *De Officiis.* Edited by T. E. Page and translated by Walter Miller. The Loeb Classical Library. Cambridge, Mass., and London: Harvard University Press and William Heinemann Ltd., 1928 [c. 44 B.C.].

———. *Tusculan Disputations.* Edited by T. E. Page and translated by J. E. King. The Loeb Classical Library, 2d. Cambridge, Mass., and London: Harvard University Press and William Heinemann Ltd., 1945 [c. 45 B.C.].

Cooper, John. "Eudaimonism, the Appeal to Nature, and 'Moral Duty' in Stoicism." In *Duty, Interest, and Practical Reason,* edited by Jennifer Whiting and Stephen Engstrom. New York: Cambridge University Press. Forthcoming.

———. "Posidonius on Emotions." In *The Emotions in Hellenistic Philosophy,* edited by Troels Engberg-Pedersen and Juha Sihvola. Dordrecht: Kluwer Academic Publishers. Forthcoming.

Crivelli, Paolo. "Indefinite Propositions and Anaphora in Stoic Logic." *Phronesis* 39 (1994): 187–206.

Darley, John M., and C. Daniel Batson. " 'From Jerusalem to Jericho': A Study of Situational and Dispositional Variables in Helping Behavior." *Journal of Personality and Social Psychology* 27 (1973): 100–108.

Dickinson, Emily. *The Complete Poems of Emily Dickinson.* Edited by Thomas H. Johnson. Boston: Little, Brown, 1960.

Diogenes Laertius. *Lives of the Eminent Philosophers.* Edited by T. E. Page and translated by R. D. Hicks. The Loeb Classical Library. Cambridge, Mass., and London: Harvard University Press and William Heinemann Ltd., 1931 [2d century C.E.].

Engberg-Pedersen, Troels. "Discovering the Good: Oikeiosis and Kathekonta in Stoic Ethics." In *The Norms of Nature: Studies in Hellenistic Ethics,* edited by

Malcolm Schofield and Gisela Striker, 145–83. Cambridge: Cambridge University Press, 1986.

————. "Stoic Philosophy and the Concept of Person." In *The Person and the Human Mind: Issues in Ancient and Modern Philosophy*, 109–35. New York: Clarendon/Oxford Press, 1989.

————. *The Stoic Theory of Oikeiosis*. Denmark: Aarhus University Press, 1990.

Engstrom, Stephen, and Jennifer Whiting, eds. *Aristotle, Kant, and the Stoics: Rethinking Happiness and Duty*. New York: Cambridge University Press, 1996.

Epictetus. *The Discourses as Reported by Arrian, the Manual, and Fragments*. Edited by T. E. Page and translated by W. A. Oldfather. The Loeb Classical Library. Cambridge, Mass., and London: Harvard University Press and William Heinemann Ltd., 1961 [c. 100 C.E.].

Feldman, Fred. *Doing the Best We Can: An Essay in Informal Deontic Logic*. Dordrecht: Reidel, 1986.

Feys, Robert. *Modal Logics*. Edited by Joseph Doff. Collection de Logique Mathématique, Série B, Vol. 4. Louvain and Paris: E. Nauwelaerts and Gauthier-Villars, 1965.

Flanagan, Owen. *Varieties of Moral Personality*. Cambridge: Harvard University Press, 1991.

Flavell, John H. *Cognitive Development*. 2d ed. Englewood Cliffs, N.J.: Prentice-Hall, 1985.

————. *The Developmental Psychology of Jean Piaget*. New York: D. Van Nostrand Company, 1963.

Foot, Philippa. "Morality as a System of Hypothetical Imperatives." *Philosophical Review* 81 (1972): 305–16.

Forrester, James. "Gentle Murder, or the Adverbial Samaritan." *Journal of Philosophy* 81, no. 4 (1984): 193–97.

Fortenbaugh, William W., ed. *On Stoic and Peripatetic Ethics*. New Brunswick, N.J.: Transaction Books, 1983.

Frankfurt, Harry G. "Freedom of the Will and the Concept of a Person." *Journal of Philosophy* 68 (1971): 5–20.

Frede, Michael. *Essays in Ancient Philosophy*. Minneapolis: University of Minnesota Press, 1987.

————. "The Stoic Doctrines of the Affections of the Soul." In *The Norms of Nature: Studies in Hellenistic Ethics*, edited by Gisela Striker and Malcolm Schofield, 93–110. Cambridge: Cambridge University Press, 1986.

Frede, Michael, and Gisela Striker, eds. *Rationality in Greek Thought*. Oxford: Clarendon Press, 1996.

Frohlich, Norman, and Joe A. Oppenheimer. *Choosing Justice*. Berkeley: University of California Press, 1992.

Galen. *On the Doctrines of Hippocrates and Plato*. Translated by Phillip De Lacey. Berlin: Akademie-Verlag, 1984.

Gill, Christopher. "The Human Being as an Ethical Norm." In *The Person and the Human Mind: Issues in Ancient and Modern Philosophy*, edited by Christopher Gill, 137–61. New York: Clarendon/Oxford University Press, 1989.

Goble, Lou. "A Logic of Good, Should, and Would: Part I." *Journal of Philosophical Logic* 19 (May 1990): 169–99.

———. "A Logic of Good, Should, and Would: Part II." *Journal of Philosophical Logic* 19 (August 1990): 253–76.

———. "Murder Most Gentle: The Paradox Deepens." *Philosophical Studies* 64 (1991): 217–27.

Gosling, Justin. "The Stoics and 'Akrasia.'" *Apeiron* 20 (1987): 179–202.

Gould, Carol C. *Rethinking Democracy.* Cambridge: Cambridge University Press, 1988.

Griffin, James. *Well-Being.* Oxford: Clarendon Press, 1986.

Hansson, Sven Ove. "Preference-Based Deontic Logic." *Journal of Philosophical Logic* 19 (1990): 75–93.

Harris, George W. *Dignity and Vulnerability.* Berkeley: University of California Press, 1997.

Herman, Barbara. "Agency, Attachment, and Difference." *Ethics* 101 (1991): 775–97.

———. *The Practice of Moral Judgment.* Cambridge: Harvard University Press, 1993.

Hilbert, David, and Wilhelm Ackermann. *Principles of Mathematical Logic.* 2d ed. Translated by Lewis M. Hammond, George G. Leckie, and F. Steinhardt. New York: Chelsea Publishing Company, 1950 [1938].

Hilpinen, Risto. *Deontic Logic: Introductory and Systematic Readings.* Edited by Risto Hilpinen. Dordrecht: Reidel, 1971.

———. *New Studies in Deontic Logic.* Edited by Risto Hilpinen. Dordrecht: Reidel, 1981.

Huby, Pamela. "The First Discovery of the Free-Will Problem." *Philosophy* 42 (1967): 353–62.

Hughes, G. E., and M. J. Cresswell. *An Introduction to Modal Logic.* London: Methuen and Co., 1968.

Ierodiakonou, Katerina. "The Stoic Division of Philosophy." *Phronesis* 38, no. 1 (1993): 57–74.

Inwood, Brad. "Comments on H. Gorgemanns' 'Oikeiosis in Arius Didymus.'" In *On Stoic and Peripatetic Ethics*, edited by W. W. Fortenbaugh, 190–202. New Brunswick, N.J.: Transaction Books, 1983.

———. *Ethics and Human Action in Early Stoicism.* Oxford: Clarendon Press, 1985.

———. "Goal and Target in Stoicism." *Journal of Philosophy* 83 (1986): 547–56.

———. "Seneca and Psychological Dualism." In *Passions & Perceptions*, edited by Jacques Brunswchwig and Martha Nussbaum, 150–83. New York: Cambridge University Press, 1993.

Irwin, T. H. "Stoic and Aristotelian Conceptions of Happiness." In *The Norms of Nature: Studies in Hellenistic Ethics*, edited by Gisela Striker and Malcolm Schofield, 205–44. Cambridge: Cambridge University Press, 1986.

———. "Virtue, Praise and Success: Stoic Responses to Aristotle." *Monist* 73 (1) (January 1990): 59–79.

Kahneman, D., and A. Tversky, eds. *Judgment under Uncertainty: Heuristics and Biases.* New York: Cambridge University Press, 1982.

Kekes, John. *The Morality of Pluralism*. Princeton: Princeton University Press, 1993.

Kidd, I. G. "Posidonius on Emotions." In *Problems in Stoicism*, edited by A. A. Long, 200–215. London: Athelone Press, University of London, 1971.

———. "Stoic Intermediates and the End for Man." In *Problems in Stoicism*, edited by A. A. Long, 150–72. London: Athelone Press, University of London, 1971.

Kimpel, Ben. *Stoic Moral Philosophies: Their Counsel for Today*. New York: Philosophical Library, 1985.

Kneale, William, and Martha Kneale. *The Development of Logic*. Oxford: Oxford University Press, 1964.

Knuuttila, Simo. "The Emergence of Deontic Logic in the Fourteenth Century." In *New Studies in Deontic Logic*, edited by Risto Hilpinen, 225–48. Dordrecht: Reidel, 1981.

Kohlberg, Lawrence, *Essays on Moral Development*. Volume 1: *The Philosophy of Moral Development*. Volume 2: *The Psychology of Moral Development*. San Francisco: Harper & Row, 1981.

Korsgaard, Christine M. "Skepticism About Practical Reason." *Journal of Philosophy* 83 (1986): 1–25.

Lesses, Glenn. "Austere Friends: The Stoics and Friendship." *Apeiron* 26, no. 1 (March 1993): 57–75.

Long, A. A. "Arius Didymus and the Exposition of Stoic Ethics." In *On Stoic and Peripatetic Ethics: The Work of Arius Didymus*, edited by William W. Fortenbaugh, 41–66. New Brunswick, N.J.: Transaction Books, 1983.

———. "Freedom and Determinism in the Stoic Theory of Human Action." In *Problems in Stoicism*, edited by A. A. Long, 173–99. London: Athelone Press, University of London, 1971.

———. *Hellenistic Philosophy: Stoics, Epicureans, Skeptics*. London: Duckworth, 1974.

———. "The Logical Basis of Stoic Ethics." *Proceedings of the Aristotelian Society* 71 (1970–71): 85–104.

———. "Representation and the Self in Stoicism." In *Psychology (Companions to Ancient Thought: 2)*, edited by Stephen Evenson, 102–20. New York: Cambridge University Press, 1991.

———. "Soul and Body in Stoicism." *Phronesis* 27 (1982): 34–57.

———. "The Stoic Concept of Evil." *Philosophical Quarterly* 18 (1968): 329–43.

———. "Stoic Eudaimonism." *Proceedings of the Boston Colloquium in Ancient Philosophy* 4 (1988): 77–101.

———. "The Stoic Legacy on Naturalism, Rationality and the Moral Good." Unpublished manuscript.

———.*Stoic Studies*. New York: Cambridge University Press, 1996.

Long, A. A., ed. *Problems in Stoicism*. London: Athelone Press, University of London, 1971.

Long, A. A., and D. N. Sedley, eds. *The Hellenistic Philosophers*. New York: Cambridge University Press, 1987.

Malinowski, Grzegorz. *Many-Valued Logics*. Oxford: Clarendon Press, 1993.

Mates, Benson. *Stoic Logic*. Berkeley: University of California Press, 1953.

McDowell, John. "Virtue and Reason." *Monist* 62 (1979): 331–50.

Meyer, Michael J. "Stoics, Rights, and Autonomy." *American Philosophical Quarterly* 24 (July 1987): 267–71.

Milgram, Stanley. *Obedience to Authority*. New York: Harper & Row, 1974.

Mitsis, Phillip. "Seneca on Reason, Rules and Moral Development." In *Passions & Perceptions*, edited by Jacques Brunswchwig and Martha Nussbaum, 258–312. New York: Cambridge University Press, 1993.

Mueller, Ian. "The Completeness of Stoic Propositional Logic." *Notre Dame Journal of Formal Logic* 20 (January 1979): 201–15.

Nagel, Thomas. *Mortal Questions*. Cambridge: Cambridge University Press, 1979.

———. *The Possibility of Altruism*. Oxford: Clarendon Press, 1970.

———. *The View from Nowhere*. New York: Oxford University Press, 1986.

Nisbett, Richard E., and Lee Ross. *Human Inference: Strategies and Shortcomings of Social Judgment*. Englewood Cliffs, N.J.: Prentice-Hall, 1980.

North, Helen. *Sophrosyne: Self-Knowledge and Self-Restraint in Greek Literature*. Ithaca: Cornell University Press, 1966.

Nozick, Robert. *Anarchy, State and Utopia*. New York: Basic Books, 1974.

Nussbaum, Martha C. "Pity and Mercy: Nietzsche's Stoicism." In *Nietzsche, Genealogy, Morality*, edited by Richard L. Schacht. Berkeley: University of California Press, 1994.

———. "Poetry and the Passions: Two Stoic Views." In *Passions & Perceptions*, edited by Jacques Brunswchwig and Martha Nussbaum, 97–149. New York: Cambridge University Press, 1993.

———. *The Therapy of Desire*. Princeton: Princeton University Press, 1994.

Pembroke, S. G. "Oikeiosis." In *Problems in Stoicism*, edited by A. A. Long, 112–49. London: Athelone Press, University of London, 1971.

Quine, Willard Van Orman. *Methods of Logic*. New York: Henry Holt & Company, 1955.

Rachels, James, and William Ruddick. "Lives and Liberty." In *The Inner Citadel: Essays on Individual Autonomy*, edited by John Christman, 221–33. New York: Oxford University Press, 1989.

Rawls, John. *A Theory of Justice*. Cambridge, Mass.: Belnap Press of Harvard University Press, 1971.

Rorty, Amélie. *Explaining Emotions*. Berkeley: University of California Press, 1980.

———. "The Two Faces of Stoicism: Rousseau and Freud." *Journal of the History of Philosophy*. forthcoming.

Ross, Lee, and Richard E. Nisbett. *The Person and the Situation*. New York: McGraw-Hill, 1992.

Sandbach, F. H. *The Stoics*. 2d ed. Indianapolis, Ind.: Hackett, 1994.

Saunders, Jason Lewis. *Justus Lipsius: The Philosophy of Renaissance Stoicism*. New York: Liberal Arts Press, 1955.

Sayre-McCord, Geoffrey. "Deontic Logic and the Priority of Moral Theory." *Nous* 20 (June 1986): 179–97.

Schofield, Malcolm. "Ariston of Chois and the Unity of Virtue." *Ancient Philosophy* 4 (spring 1984): 83–96.

———. "Two Stoic Approaches to Justice." In *Justice and Generosity*, edited by

A. Laks and M. Schofield, 191–212. New York: Cambridge University Press, 1995.

Schofield, Malcolm, and Gisela Striker, eds. *The Norms of Nature: Studies in Hellenistic Ethics*. Cambridge: Cambridge University Press, 1986.

Schotch, Peter K., and Raymond E. Jennings. "Non-Kripkean Deontic Logic." In *New Studies in Deontic Logic*, edited by Risto Hilpinen, 149–64. Dordrecht: Reidel, 1981.

Searle, John. "How to Derive Ought from Is." *Philosophical Review* 73 (1964): 43–58.

———. "The Mystery of Consciousness: Part I." *New York Review of Books*, November 2, 1995, 60–66.

———. "The Mystery of Consciousness: Part II." *New York Review of Books*, November 16, 1995, 54–61.

———. *The Rediscovery of the Mind*. Cambridge, Mass.: A Bradford Book, MIT Press, 1992.

Sedley, David. "Chrysippus on Psychophysical Causality." In *Passions & Perceptions*, edited by Jacques Brunswchwig and Martha Nussbaum, 313–31. New York: Cambridge University Press, 1993.

Seidler, Michael J. "Kant and the Stoics on Suicide." *Journal of the History of Ideas* 44 (July 1983): 429–54.

Sharples, R. W. "Aristotelian and Stoic Conceptions of Necessity in the 'De Fato' of Alexander of Aphrodisias." *Phronesis* 20 (1975): 247–74.

Sinnott-Armstrong, Walter. "A Solution to Forrester's Paradox of Gentle Murder." *Journal of Philosophy* 82 (March 1985): 162–68.

Statman, Daniel, ed. *Moral Luck*. Albany: State University of New York Press, 1993.

Striker, Gisela. "Antipater, or the Art of Living." In *The Norms of Nature: Studies in Hellenistic Ethics*, edited by Malcolm Schofield and Gisela Striker, 185–205. Cambridge: Cambridge University Press, 1986.

———. "Ataraxia: Happiness as Tranquility." *Monist* 73 (January 1990): 97–110.

———. "Following Nature: A Study in Stoic Ethics." *Oxford Studies in Ancient Philosophy* 9 (1991): 1–73.

———. "The Role of Oikeiosis in Stoic Ethics." *Oxford Studies in Ancient Philosophy* 1 (1983): 145–67.

Taylor, Richard. *Metaphysics*. Englewood Cliffs, N.J.: Prentice-Hall, 1974.

Thomason, Richard. "Deontic Logic as Founded in Tense Logic." In *New Studies in Deontic Logic*, edited by Risto Hilpinen, 165–76. Dordrecht: Reidel, 1981.

Voorbraak, Frans. "The Logic of Actual Obligation: An Alternative Approach to Deontic Logic." *Philosophical Studies* 55 (1989): 173–94.

Watson, Gerard. "The Natural Law and Stoicism." In *Problems in Stoicism*, edited by A. A. Long, 216–38. London: Athelone Press, University of London, 1971.

White, Nicholas P. "The Basis of Stoic Ethics." *Harvard Studies in Classical Philology* 83 (1979): 144–78.

———. "Comments on Long's 'Arius Didymus and the Exposition of Stoic Ethics.'" In *On Stoic and Peripatetic Ethics: The Work of Arius Didymus*, edited by William W. Fortenbaugh, 67–74. New Brunswick, N.J.: Transaction Books, 1983.

White, Nicholas P. "The Role of Physics in Stoic Ethics." *Southern Journal of Philosophy* 23, Supplement (1985): 57–74.

———. "Stoic Values." *Monist* 73 (1) (January 1990): 42–58.

Whitehead, Alfred North, and Bertrand Russell. *Principia Mathematica* [1910]. Cambridge: Cambridge University Press, 1935.

Williams, Bernard. *Ethics and the Limits of Philosophy*. Cambridge, Mass.: Harvard University Press, 1985.

———. *Moral Luck*. Oxford: Oxford University Press, 1981.

Wright, Georg Henrik von. "Deontic Logic." *Mind* 60 (1951): 1–15.

———. "Is There a Logic of Norms?" *Ratio Juris* 4 (1991): 265–83.

———. "On the Logic of Norms and Actions." In *New Studies in Deontic Logic*, edited by Risto Hilpinen, 3–36. Dordrecht: Reidel, 1981.

———. *Practical Reason*. Ithaca: Cornell University Press, 1983.

Index

accordance with nature, 72 ff. *See also* living: in accord with nature
achievement, 18
Ackermann, Wilhelm, 190
action: causal structure of, 78; formal features of, 84
adaptability, 107
adding to virtue, 140
adversarial endeavors, 98
adversity, 109
advisability, 36–37, 161, 186 ff.
aeronautical analogy, 142–145
aesthetic criteria, 21
aesthetics, 41, 91
aesthetic value, 30
affect(s), 13, 14, 47, 89, 91, 95, 103, 110, 128–132
affection, 71; for onself, 72
affective disposition, 70
affective responses, 96
affective value, 15, 16
Agamemnon, 130
agency, 54 ff.; as assent, 92 ff.; autonomous, 59–68; as balance of control and stability, 142 ff.; boot sector of, 143, 144; constitutive elements of, 60, 84 ff.; constructed and perfected, 103–111; constructed elements of, 93–111; defeat of, 147–148; as deterministic, 61; formal accounts of, 83–84; full-fledged, 92 ff.; imperfect, 119; not rationality, 117–118; powers, 82 ff.; proper, 103, 106, 108 ff.; received elements of, 84–93; recursive hegemonic nature of, 83; as robust, 63, 95; as self-constructed, 94; as self-transformative, 61, 62; as single faculty, 130 ff.; structure of, 82–102; stunted development of, 156
agent(s): constitutive facts about, 17; energy, 88–89, 104; as integrated in environments, 156; normatively integrated, 52; normatively isolated, 52; particularity of, 5, 6; as purposive, 81; types of, 115–118
aggression, 62, 92
aggressors, 16

aims, 13, 81. *See also* ends; goals; purposes
akrasia, 15, 125, 126 *See also* weak agency; weakness of will
Alchourron, Carlos E., 186
alethic modalities, 36, 38, 161 ff.
alethic modal notions, 161 ff.
alienation, 70
alien norms, 58 ff.
Allport, Gordon, 123
all-things-considered, 10, 11, 12, 14, 19, 20, 24, 39, 42, 43, 51, 54, 55, 63, 76, 77, 106, 120, 136, 146, 160 ff.
Almeida, Michael J., 189
altruism, 10, 74
ambitious men, 155
amendments, 171; rule of, 172
Amherst College, Trustees of, ix
amplitude of emotion, 97
analogies, examples and devices used in arguments, 97; aeronautical analogy, 142–145; angry soldier, 132; archer analogy, 73, 113, 114, 121, 133; babysitting example, 177, 190; boot sector of agency, 143, 144; Calvin, John (parody), 68; circles of affection (Hierocles), 74; drowning analogy, 119; favorite jeans example, 99; game playing analogy, 39, 167, 177, 190 ff.; gravitational force, 144 ff.; happiness in a palace, 109; health, analogies to, 103–111, 124–126; hospital story, 147; Lazy Argument, 79; Master Argument, 79, 80; medical analogies, 124–126, 133; navigation, 161; oasis analogy, 130, 135; paradox of gentle murder, 188–189; perfect kiss, 157; pilgrim example, 146–147; skinned knee, 97; slave(ry), 19, 43, 48; Spartan boys, 154; stone, man hardened to by argument, 118; stone, teaching a, 118; suicide, 44, 48, 135; suttee (women in India), 154; teaching table manners example, 95; torture examples, 146–148, 154; velociraptors, 118; vice correlated to psychopathology, 103–104; "we stoics" conceit, of this book, 3–4, *and throughout*; "Wild Nights," 131

androgynous sages, 110
anger, 16, 131–132
anhedonia, 104
Annas, Julia, ix, 22, 24, 26, 28, 31, 69, 74, 75, 122, 127, 134, 137, 150, 158
anthropology, 48
Antipater of Tarsus, 24
anti-semitism, 91
anxiety, 47, 62, 144
apatheia, 128
appropriate action (act(s)), 25, 57, 70, 73, 76, 120, 121, 126, 127, 133, 134 ff.
appropriateness, 15, 40; rule of, 170
appropriation, 56, 60, 70, 71 ff.
archer analogy, 73, 113, 114, 121, 133
argos logos, 79
argument for virtue, representation in the calculus, 117
Aristo, 27
Aristotelian ethical theory, 156
Aristotelian Principle, 105, 123
Aristotelians, 75, 150 ff.
Aristotle, 24, 25, 35, 127–132, 137, 151; formal conditions for highest good, 127–128
Arius Didymus, 23
arousal, 86
Arrian, 22
asocial dispositions, 104
assent, 66, 72
assessment, 41, 50. *See also* reformative assessment
assessment endeavor, 177
attachment, 70, 99–100, 109; to oneself, 56
attachments, 12, 13, 16, 91–92, 95, 101, 102, 110, 141
Atwood, Trevor, 31
Augustus, 23
autism, 143
autonomous agency, 59–68
autonomous ends, 60 ff.
autonomy, 77–80; of ethics, 8
axiomatic system, 159 ff.
axioms of modal logic, 165
axioms of propositional logic, 164
axioms of quantificational logic, 165
Axioms of Stoic Normative Logic, 16–18; defined informally; 42, formally, 181–182
—Closure, 181
—Encompassment, 42, 51, 106, 117, 181

—Finality, 42, 51, 106, 117, 181
—Futility, 42, 44–46, 99, 118, 182, 191
—Moral Priority, 42, 181
—Moral Rank, 181
Ayer, A.J., 78

babysitting example, 177, 190
Bacon, Francis, 6
Bannister, Roger, 45
Baron, Marcia, 136
Barry, Brian, 35
basic definitions, rules, and axioms, of the calculus, 163–167
basic tenors of personality, 92, 98, 102, 103, 104 ff., 143
beauty, 20, 47
Becker, Charlotte B., ix, 76
Becker, Lawrence C., 30, 31, 76, 80, 158, 168
behavioral dispositions, 95, 102, 109 ff.
behavioral norms, 36
belief, 14
beneficence, 10, 97, 117, 118; impartial, 76; radiating, 76
benefits, 96
benevolence, 13, 30, 92, 96–97, 97, 103, 110, 112, 117, 121, 143
Bentham, Jeremy, 6
Bernays, Paul, 190
best means, rule of, 40, 169
biological organisms, 81
biology, 6
bivalence, 36, 64, 65, 162, 190
bodies, 27, 28, 29, 84–85
body image, 87, 102
Botros, Sophie, ix, 78
boundaries, 12, 16, 17, 85 ff.
boundary-keeping, 86, 102
boundary making, 102
brain damage, 143
Brown, Roger, 76, 124
Brunschwig, Jacques, 70
brute fact, 160
"bull of Phalaris," 154
Buridan's ass, 40, 50

Calcidius, 26
calculus of normative logic, 35, 150–191; definitions, rules, axioms, 163–167; in relation to other logics, 185–188
Calvin, John (parody), 68
cardinal virtues, 112

care, 103, 105, 121
Cargile, James, 80, 190, 191
Castañeda, H.-N., 185
categorical commitments. *See* commitments
categorical fatalism, 64 ff.
categorical imperatives, 39
Cato, 71 ff.
causality, 11
causation, 64; Humean account, 78
Chaplin, James P., 123
character, 5, 9, 12, 13, 30, 102; flaw, 109; integrated and stable, 124; stable, 110
child development, 85 ff.
childhood, 97, 101, 144
child(ren), 48, 58, 70, 72, 74, 95, 96, 99, 100, 113, 118, 125, 132, 138
choice, 63, 65, 73, 78, 83, 93 ff.
Christianity, 3
chronology, 23–24
Chrysippus, 3, 22, 24, 27, 69, 78, 79, 80, 114, 124, 125, 129 ff.
Cicero, ix, 23, 24, 25, 27, 56, 71, 74, 75, 76, 79, 122, 133, 150, 152–155
circles of affection, 74
civility, 112
Cleanthes of Assos, 24
Closure, Axiom of, 181
closure, rule of, 41
closure for moral indifference, rule of, 180
cognition, 89, 91
cognitive development, 57; recursive, 87; stage-theories of, 86–87
cognitive dissonance, 87
cognitive functions, 89
cognitive psychology, 71
coherence, 45, 101, 102
coherentist interpretation of moral truth, 4
College of William & Mary, ix, 30, 31
commanding-faculty, 27
commensurability, 15, 120–122
commitments, 6, 10, 12, 13, 14, 40, 58, 109, 110; categorical, 16, 19, 20, 39, 41, 91 ff.; conditional, 17; rule of, 170
commonsense, 3
community, 152
community of ideal agents, 110
compassion, 112
compatabilism, 78
competitive endeavors, 98
completed life, 139

complete good, 127–128
completeness, 166, 166–167
comprehensive activity, 39
comprehensive and controlling endeavor, 82, 113, 116, 117, 121 ff.
comprehensive and controlling norms, 50
comprehensive integration, 155–156
comprehensiveness, 41; rule of, 177
compulsions, 89
conation, 89, 91
conative powers, 62
conceit, of this book, 3–4
concept formation, 69
concepts, 28
conceptual schemas, 87
conditional constructs, 39
conditionalized fatalism, 64 ff.
conditional norms, 145
conditioning, 103; classical and operant, 100
confidence, 56
conflicting attachments, 101
conflicting goals, 101
conflicting moral indifference, rule of, 180
conflicting moral oughts, rule of, 180
conflicting moral requirements, rule of, 179
conflicting norms, 38, 45, 173
conflicting requirements, 101
conflicts, 38, 41, 50–52, 101, 114, 115–118, 159 ff.
conflicts and priorities, 49
conformity, 44, 73
connectedness, 87, 155–156
conscientiousness, 112
consciousness, 11, 28, 29, 30, 84, 87–88, 102, 103 ff., 137
consistency, 35, 45, 75, 87, 102, 159, 166–167 ff.
consistent action, 101
consistent and coherent life, 25
constitutive motive, 53, 54
constitutive powers, 62, 63
constructed elements of agency, 93–111
constructed traits, 94 ff.
constructivism, 4
contemplative life, 21, 156
contingent truth, 9
contract, 3
contractarians, 83
contradiction, 45

contradictories, 182–183
contraries, 182, 183–184
control in character, 142 ff.
controlled life, 142–146
control of one's situation, 19
conventions, 12, 15, 18
conviviality, 104, 112
Cooper, John, 26, 77, 80, 128
cooperation, 10, 14, 18, 104
cooperative ventures, 144
coordinate conflicting indifference, rule of, 173
coordinate conflicting oughts, rule of, 173
coordinate conflicting requirements, rule of, 173
coordinate norms, 173 ff.
coordination, 18, 110, 124
Cornelius, Casey, 31
cosmic history, 139
cosmic plan, human role in, 22
cosmic significance, 140
cosmic *telos*, 6, 11, 25–27, 31, 74, 133
cosmologists, 23
cosmology, 6, 11, 26
cosmopolitanism, 43
cosmos: as god, 77; as rational being, 26, 77
counterirritants, 97
"count no man happy . . . ," 141
courage, 98–99, 112, 114, 117, 121, 143
courtesy, 49
cradle argument, 23, 70–76, 83, 134, 137
craft analogy, 133
criminal conduct, 104
criterial goods, 30
critical endeavors, 101
curiosity, 56, 89, 104, 143

Darwall, Stephen, 80, 137
Darwin, Charles, 6
death, 44, 81, 120, 139, 141
definitional equivalence, 165–166
definitional replacement, 164
degradation, 16
De Lacey, Phillip, ix
deliberation, 6, 63, 65, 82–94, 100, 104, 106, 112, 114, 119
deliberative field, 13
deliberative powers, 120
deliberative processes, 101
deontic logic, 161, 186–187; modal ap-

proach, 185–187; standard paradoxes, 187–188
depression, 104
depth of attachments, 99–100
Descartes, Rene, 6
descriptive bases, 162
desire(s), 14, 39, 40, 65, 78, 83, 114, 150; rule of, 169; second order, 79
destiny, 78
detachment, 18, 44, 104, 109; capacity for, 156; rule in logic, 164
determinism, 11, 61, 63, 77–80 ff.
developmental project of agency, 139
developmental psychology, 23, 56, 76, 123–124
developmental story, 71 ff.
development as agents, 141
development of agency, 121
development of virtue, 81–114
Devereux, Daniel, 80
deviant logics, 45
Dickinson, Emily, 131
dictatorial endeavor, 49
dignity, 16, 76; of virtue, 122
Diogenes of Babylon, 24, 69
Diogenes Laertius, 22, 23, 24, 26, 27, 71, 128, 133
Diogenes of Sinope, 24
disabilities, 104
discount rate, 51
disease, 104, 125
disintegration, 16
dispositional fact, 15
dispositional powers, 120
dispositional states, 113
dispositions, 56 ff., 90, 93 ff.; emotional, 16; stable, 142
dissemination of attachments, 99–100
dogmatism, 4
domesticating animals, 118
dominance, 38
drink, 140
drowning analogy, 119
dualism, 29; emergent property, 28; mind-body, 84; substance, 28
duration of emotion, 97
duties, 3, 19, 108; natural, 4; prima facie, 10
Du Vair, Guillaume, 24

effective agency as comprehensive and controlling, 106

effective means, 14
effects, 14
efficiency, 49
egoism, 5, 10, 24, 96
Egyptians, 154
Einstein, Albert, 38
Einsteinian physics, 163
elementary argument forms, 101
embeddedness, 139
embedded norms, 50
embodiment, 85
emergent processes, 87
emergent properties, 47
emotion(s), 44, 47, 102, 103, 110, 128,
    128–132, 145
emotionality, 97–98, 104
emotional release, 144–146
emotional response, 16
emotion as determinant, 98
empathy, 104
empirical hypotheses, 63
empirical knowledge, 8, 11
empirical truth, 9
encapsulated attachments, 100
encompassing project, 52
Encompassment, Axiom of, 42, 51, 106,
    117, 181
endeavor(s), 36 ff., 52–59, 81–90, 101–
    118, 167 ff.; comprehensive and control-
    ling, 42, 50, 82, 113, 116, 117, 121 ff.;
    dictatorial, 49; heteronomous, 59–68;
    incoherent, 45; integration of, 49 ff.;
    isolated, 50; tyrannical, 49. *See also*
    projects
endogenous rankings, 174 ff.
endowments, 5, 54 ff., 84–93, 139, 143,
    145
ends, 81; autonomous, 60 ff.; heterono-
    mous, 60 ff.
endurance, 98–99, 112, 154
Engberg-Pedersen, T., 26, 70, 71, 74, 134
Epictetus, 22, 23, 24, 44, 118, 157
Epicureanism, 21
Epicureans, 56
Epicurus, 24, 117, 148, 153, 154
epistemic norms, 50, 51
epistemologists, 101
equivalence for coincident endogenous
    rankings, rule of, 175
error-correction, 54
error(s), 57, 87; excluded a priori, 46
escalation, of normative propositions, 41

escalation rules, 42; in the calculus, 174–
    178
ethical arguments from human nature,
    12
ethical doctrines, stoic, 4
ethical reasoning: as all-things-considered,
    10; as most inclusive, 10
ethical theory, 3, 74; comprehensive, 7
ethical truth, 8, 9
ethics, 8–14; as about particulars, 13–14;
    foundations of, 8, 9; general purpose
    of, 9; unique purpose of, 9, 10
ethnic cleansing, 99
ethnic conflict, 91
ethnic group, 74
etiquette, 10, 41, 49, 80
eudaimonia, 21, 39, 133, 138, 140, 168
eudaimonism, 3, 6, 20, 24–25, 25, 26
eudaimonism, stoic: ancient doctrine, 150–
    155; Long and Sedley on, 150–152
eupatheia, 128
events, simple and complex, 79–80
evils, 153
evolutionary biology, 13
evolutionary change, 11
exalted virtue, 119–122, 126
examples. *See* analogies, examples, and de-
    vices in arguments
excellence, 15, 20, 21, 25, 30, 170
excellence-of-its-kind, 6, 47
excessive emotions, 128 ff.
exercise of agency, 82 ff.
exogenous assessment, rule of, 178
exogenous rankings, rule of, 176 ff.
expediency, 25
experience, breadth of, 139
experimental method, 9
expert routines, 106
expression of emotion, 97
external goods, 127–128
externalism, 76–77
extirpation of the passions, 131–132
extrinsic good, 29

facts about the world, 9, 12, 25, 27, 28–
    30, 35–36, 77
fact-value distinction, 3
failure, 18, 98
fallibility, 132
false beliefs, 48, 87, 129, 130–131, 154
falsehood, 57
fame, 109, 122, 140, 155

familial love, 74
family, 153
fatalism, 64, 78–80 ff.
fate, 27, 77–80
favorite jeans example, 99
favoritism, 48
fear, 68
fearlessness, 98
feelings, 97
Feldman, Fred, 187
Feys, Robert, 165, 191
fidelity, 48, 112
final end, 20, 29, 114; of rational
    activity, 8
Finality, Axiom of, 42, 51, 106, 117,
    181
first order constructs, 39–41, 167–172
fit agents, 138 ff.
fitness, 70, 105–107, 120, 125; preferred
    to health, 105
fittingness, 15, 41, 96, 112
Flanagan, Owen, 30, 76, 123, 124, 125
Flavell, John H., 71, 123
flourishing, 5, 6, 20, 39, 168
following nature, 25
following the facts, 39, 43–80, 118
"follow nature," 5, 6, 8, 39, 43, 168
food, 140
Foot, Philippa, 80
forbiddenness, 187
forced choice(s), 38, 41, 176 ff.
forced choice under indifference,
    rule of, 176
forced moral choice, 179–180
formal logic, 35
Forrester, James, 188, 189
fortitude, 155
fortune, 108, 109, 122, 153
Fowler, Mark, 31
fragility (of goodness), 109
frame of reference, 139
Frankfurt, Harry, 79
Frede, Michael, 125, 128, 129
free act, 65
freedom, 59–68; human, 11
free life, 67–68
free will, 78
"fresh" distress, 130
Freudian tradition, 111
friends, 140
friendship(s), 29, 121, 153
futility, 136

Futility, Axiom of, 42, 44–46, 99, 118,
    182, 191
future events, 27

Galen, ix, 22, 24, 29, 69, 124, 128 ff.
Galileo's paradox, 140
game, rules of the, 39
game playing analogy, 167, 177, 190 ff.
generalization, 5, 54, 89, 94, 100–101,
    108, 111, 112 ff.; stimulus and re-
    sponse, 86
generalization (rule), 164
generalizations, 13, 93
generosity, 112
genetic endowments, 62
genius, 44
genocide, 48, 99
genotypes, 60
gentle murder, paradox of, 188–189
"getting it right," 77, 113, 134
Gill, Christopher, 70
global context, 140
global optimization, 116
glory, 155
goal directed activity, 86
goals, 14, 46, 76, 81, 101
Goble, Lou, 187, 189
Gocer, Asli, 137
God, 68
god, 27
good, 57
good fortune, 148
good life, 5, 6, 7, 18, 20, 21, 29–30, 68,
    138
good-of-its-kind, 15
goods, 29–30
good times, 140–141
Gosling, Justin, 125
Gould, Carol, 137
gravity analogy, 144
Greek ethics, 150
Green, Mitchell, 191
grief, 145
Griffin, James, 30, 77
guidelines, 40
guilt, 16, 68

habituation, 98, 130
hallucinations, 135
handbook, 7
Hansen, Robert, 158
Hansson, Sven Ove, 187

happiness, 5, 6, 8, 10, 20–21, 39, 67, 100,
    113, 127–132, 133, 138–157, 150, 168
    ff.; as all or nothing, 151; as complete,
    151; narrow vs. stoic meanings of, 138
hard determinism, 78
hard doctrines, 113, 119
harmonization of reason, desire, will, 30
harmony, 25
harmony with nature, 73 ff. *See also* living:
    in harmony with nature
harms, 96
Harris, George, 16, 137
Harris, Steven, 191
hate, 121
Hattauer, Abbie, 31
Hayes, Darlene, 31
health, 72, 120, 125, 144; analogy to,
    124–126; preferred to ill health, 70,
    104 ff.
healthy agents (-agency), 76, 117–118,
    134, 138 ff., 148; analogy to physical
    health, 103–111; as robust, 120
hegemonikon, 136
Hellenistic ethics, 70
Hellenistic period, 22
Hellenistic philosophy, 5, 24, 150
Hellenists, 4, 23
Herman, Barbara, 13
heroism, 44
Herzog, Werner, 77
heteronomous endeavors, 59–68
heteronomous ends, 60 ff.
heteronomous norms, 58 ff.
heteronomy, converted to autonomy,
    60–61
Hierocles, ix, 22, 24, 70, 74, 75
highest good, 127
Hilbert, David, 190
Hindu sages, 154
history, 9
Hobbes, Thomas, 6
holy wars, 99
homeostatic devices, 16
homeostatic systems, 103 ff.
homologia, 73
homologuemenos, 151
honesty, 112
honor, 16
horizontal integration, 49, 52, 101, 102 ff.
hormai, 135, 136
hospital analogy, 147
hospitality, 49

human beings, 122; natural role of, 5; nor-
    mally formed, 12
human development, 69
human diversity, 12, 13
human freedom, 11
human history, 11
humanity and anger, 132
human life as purposive, 150
human nature, 9, 12, 13, 26, 27, 150; as
    central to stoicism, 69
human personality, 96
human race, 74
human traits, 12
Hume, David, 6, 8, 35, 112

ideal agency, 119, 120, 134, 138; as virtu-
    oso agency, 107, 107–111; virtue as,
    112–114
ideals, 40, 46, 58; rule of, 170
identity through time, 11
Ierodiakonou, Katarina, 27
ignorance, 57
ill health, 104 ff.
imagination, 92, 108, 111
imitation, 97
immediate inferences, 182–184
immortality, 81
immortals, 27
impartial beneficence, 76
impartial spectator, 10
imperatives, 37, 162
impossibilities, 44–46
impossibility, 11, 12, 36, 161, 186 ff.
impulse control, 95–96
impulses, 84, 135–136 ff. *See also* primal
    impulses
impulsiveness, 104
inclusiveness, 38
indeterminacy, 64 ff.
indeterminism, 11
indifference, 10, 14, 16, 20, 36, 133, 156,
    186 ff.; defined, 162; meaning of, 37; of
    the universe, 11
individual, situated, 14
individuals and norms, 46–47
indolence, 154
induction, 65
infancy, 54, 89, 139, 141
infants, 56, 62, 70, 72, 83, 85, 95, 118
inferences, 54
"inferior" agents, 124–125
infinity, 140

information processing, 54, 55, 84 ff.
injury, 104, 105
institutional fact, 160
institutions, 9, 18, 46; defined, 18–19
instrumental good(s), 29, 30
instrumental reasoning, 55
instrumental value, 113
integrated endeavors, 138 ff.
integration of endeavors and norms, 49 ff.,
    55, 87, 101, 104, 119, 131; horizontal,
    49, 52, 101, 102 ff.; optimal, 113; verti-
    cal, 49, 52, 101, 102 ff.; vertical and
    horizontal, 115–118
integrity, 16, 30, 101–102
integrity project, 102
intellect, 27
intellectual dispositions, 107
intellectualism, 6
intelligence, 73, 153
intention, 83
internalism, 76–77
internal motive force, 14 ff.
internal relation(s), 91, 137
interpersonal integration, 51–52
intimate relationships, 111
intrinsic good(s), 30, 73
intrinsic worth, 29; of human beings, 4
intuitionism, 4, 9, 48, 69
intuitionists, 83
Inwood, Brad, 24, 79, 128, 130, 133, 156
irony, 4
irrationality, 91
Irwin, T. H., 25, 127
isolated endeavors, 50
is/ought problem, 6, 8, 14, 35
iterative (-ed) processes, 13, 55, 66, 71, 79,
    89, 92

Jennings, Raymond E., 187, 188
Johnson, Thomas H., ix
Jones, David, 28, 137
joy, 47, 68, 128, 140, 148–149, 152, 153
judicial review, 50, 177
justice, 3, 20, 114, 117, 118, 153, 155; nar-
    row and wide senses, 112; theories of,
    112

Kahneman, D., 124
Kant, Immanuel, 6, 8, 112, 122, 134, 135,
    136, 152
Kantian interpretation of stoic doctrine,
    134 ff., 151

Kantians, 83
Kantian theories, 48
katalepseis, 72
kathekon, 73
Kekes, John, 30
Kidd, I. G., 28, 29, 128, 133
Kimpel, B., 23
King, J. E., ix
kingdom of ends, 118
Kneale, Martha, 79, 185
Kneale, William, 79, 185
knowledge, theoretical and practical, 108
Knuuttila, Simo, 185
Kohl, Marvin, 158
Kohlberg, Lawrence, 38, 123, 163
Korsgaard, Christine, 76
Krawiec, T. S., 123

language acquisition, 55, 62, 86, 93, 100,
    124
language acquisition device, 86, 92
Lazy Argument, 79
learned helplessness, 86
learning, 13
Ledger, George, 137
legality, 16
legal requirements, 161
legal system, 18, 133
leisure, 153
lemma of stoic practical reasoning, 19
libertines, 146
liberty, metaphysical, 67–68
life: complete, 138–142; normative ele-
    ments of, 55; on the rack, 146–148; ra-
    tional plan for, 81, 141–142, 157; with-
    out liberty, 68
life-plan, 81
life-prospects, 51
linguistic representation, 62
Lipsius, Justus, 24
Lipson, Steve, 31
living: in accord with nature, 126; in ac-
    cordance with reason, 151; according to
    nature, 155; in agreement with nature,
    25; "comformably to nature," 25; in
    harmony with nature, 155; well, 5,
    150
local context, 140
local optimization, 115–116
Locke, John, 6
logic, 8, 8–14, 27–28
logical operations, 92

logical positivism, 69
logical remainder, 37, 162
logical truth, 64
logic circuits, subconscious, 55
logicians, 4, 101
logos, 26, 151
Long, A. A., ix, 22, 23, 24, 25, 26, 27, 28, 29, 31, 70, 71, 77, 79, 128, 132, 133, 150, 185
loss, 136
love, 99, 105, 109, 121; familial, 74; natural tendency to, 75
loyalty, 99
luck, 127
lust, 145
luxury, 154
lying, 48

MacIntyre, Alastair, 77
Makinson, David, 186
malevolence, 144
Marcus Aurelius, 22, 23, 24; as "the emperor," 109
Marshall, John, 80, 137, 158
Marx, Karl, 6
Master Argument, 79, 80
matched motives, 53
material conditionals, 64
materialism, 28, 84–85, 87, 103
material liberty, 67
Mates, Benson, 185
matter, 26, 27
Matthews, J. Rosser, 31
maturation; normal human, 57; stages of, 57; transformations from, 86–87
mature agency, 88, 138 ff.
maximization rule, 51
McClelland, Stephanie, 31
meaningful activity, 30
meaningful necessity, 30
means/end reasoning, 39, 168 ff.
means/end relationships, 40
Medea, 125
medical analogies, 124–126, 133
medicine, 3, 5
memories, 102
memory, 87, 92
men as sages, 110–111
mental faculties, 129 ff.
metaethics, 69
metaphysical categories, 28
metaphysical liberty, 67–68

metaphysics, 11
Middle Ages, 3
Milgram, Stanley, 123
Mill, John Stuart, 112
mind, 27, 28, 29, 152 ff.
mind/body problem, 87
minimization-of-loss rule, 51
mirroring responses, 86
misery, 18, 148
misogynists, 111
modal approach to deontic logic, 185–187
modality (rule), 164
modal logic, 161, 186–187 ff.
modal operators, 38, 159 ff.
moderation, 112, 131, 132
modernity, 21
modern moral philosophy, 82–83
modulating endeavors, 138 ff.
modus vivendi, peaceful, 110
Moore, G. E., 78
moral action, 79
moral argument, 71, 80
moral deliberation; and errors of fact, 46
moral development, 70, 123; theory of, 163
moral duty, 25
moral education, norms for, 144
moral geometry, 9
moral goodness, 75, 150
moral judgments, 10, 35, 36
moral law, 121
moral life, 151, 152; as intrinsically desirable, 151
moral norms, a priori, 48
moral philosophy, 3
moral point of view, 10, 160
Moral Priority, Axiom of, 42, 181
Moral Rank, Axiom of, 181
moral reasoning, 63; representation of, 159–191
moral theories, 76
moral theory, 56; of life, 55
moral training, 3, 5, 13, 14–19, 22, 120; emotional price of, 109; manuals, 131
moral truth, 4
Moral Worth, 4, 73
mortality, 81
motherhood, 111
motivated abstraction, 55
motivated moral theory, 54–58
motivated norms, 52–59, 70, 76

motivation, 134
motivational assumption, 105
motives, matched, 53
multiple means, rule of, 169
murder, 48
music, 140
Musonius Rufus, 24
mutual love, 30

Nagel, Thomas, 28, 134
narcissism, 102
narrative art, 9
narratives, 94, 141–142, 157. *See also*
    plans and narratives
National Endowment for the Humanities
    (NEH), ix, 30, 31
natural deduction, 159
natural development, 69
naturalism, 6, 25, 69–70, 103, 134; an-
    cient Greek, 69–70
naturalistic arguments, 13
naturalistic ethical theory, 5, 27, 84
natural life, 69
natural rights theory, 48
nature, 5; as a rational being, 69; as a teleo-
    logical system, 5
navigation analogy, 161
Nazi death camps, 132
necessary connection, 64
necessary goods, 30
necessity, 11, 12, 15, 16, 17, 27, 36, 38,
    64, 161, 186 ff.
negative liberty, 67–68
neostoicism, 3, 23
neural nets, 87
neurological processes, 29
neurological structures, 84
neurological system, 28
neurophysiology, 63
neuroscience, 86, 87, 102
Newton, Isaac, 6
Nisbett, Richard E., 124
nobility, 44
non-agency goods, 140, 141; pleasures,
    140, 141; processes, 91 ff.
noncognitivism, 4, 9
non-ethical judgments, 12
non-maturational development, 89 ff.
nonnaturalism, 3
normal form, 159–160
normative constructs, 39, 167–180, 189–
    190

normative inferences, 159 ff.
normative logic, 35–42, 45, 54, 55, 58, 60,
    63; a calculus for, 159–191
normative operators, 36, 37, 49, 159–191
normative propositions, 6, 13, 14, 19, 20,
    36–42, 43, 115–118, 159–191 ff.; all-
    things-considered, 5; a posteriori, 46–
    52; a priori, 82; constructing, 12, 53 ff.;
    ordinal relationships among, 41–42;
    overriding, 12; superordinate, 41, 45; un-
    subscripted, 54
normative remainder, 186
norm-construction, 53, 54
norm-generating, 51
norm-making, 46, 47
norms, 12, 13, 29–30, 36–42, 43, 115–
    118, 156 ff.; abstract, 58; alien, 58 ff.;
    autonomous, 59 ff.; distinct from norma-
    tive propositions, 36; heteronomous,
    58 ff.; and individuals, 46–47; internal
    to projects, 77; and interpretation in the
    calculus, 159–163; and moral training,
    14–19; orphan, 58 ff.; overriding, 10;
    ranking, 172–180
nothing, 27
nothing-else-considered, 16, 19, 40, 41,
    46, 48, 82, 115–118, 190
Nozick, Robert, 30
nullity, 161
Nussbaum, Martha, 22, 23, 109, 125, 131

oasis analogy, 130, 135
objective point of view, 134, 135
objectivity, 71
object recognition, 92
obligation(s), 36, 68, 161 ff.; institutional,
    19; transactional, 40
obsessions, 89
Oedipus, 79
oikeiosis, 23, 56–58, 70–76, 117, 123 ff.;
    translation of, 70–71
Old Academy, 154
open normative proposition, 162
operators, 49
opportunity, 108, 109
oppression, 44
optimal integration, 121, 133
optimism, 56, 62, 92, 143
optimization norm, 116
optimization problems, 115
optimization project, 120
optimization rule, 51

optimized endcavors, 138 ff.
ordinal operators, 49
ordinal rank, of normative propositions, 41
ordinal relations, 15; between norms, 101
ordinary experience, 148
ordinary goods, 126–127
ordinary morality, 104
ordinary pleasures, 140
orphan norms, 58 ff.
orthos logos, 79
ought, 36, 133, 186 ff.; definition of, 161; meaning of, 36
oughts, 115–118, 118, 172
oughts over indifference, rule of, 173
overlapping elements, 52
ownership, 70

pain, 72, 89, 96, 98, 146, 153–155; avoidance, 56; fear of, 154
Panaetius (of Rhodes), 24, 25, 27, 151
paradoxes, 45
paradox of gentle murder, 188–189
parents, 74, 96, 99, 100, 126
Parker, Paulette, 80
partial virtue, 120
particular agents, 134
particularism, 28–29, 48–50
passion, 44, 109, 114, 128–132, 145, 155; comforting, 132
passionate acts, 125
passivity, 44
pathe, 136
pathological agents, 108
patience, 155
patterned responses, 95
peace, 99, 121
Pembroke, S. G., 70
perceptions, 72
perfection, 17
perfection of agency, 20, 21, 129, 133
perfect kiss story, 157
Peripatetics, 127, 152, 154
permission, 36, 161, 186, 187 ff.
perseverance, 98–99, 112, 143
person, concept of, 71
personality structure, 99–100
personal relationships, 99
personal space, 86
pessimism, 56, 92, 104, 144
phantasiai, 135, 136
phantasmata, 135

philosophy, 5; divisions of, 27
phronesis, 112
physics, 6, 25, 27, 28, 64
physiological development, 54
physiological possibilities, 139
Piaget, Jean, 71, 87, 123
pilgrim example, 146–147
plans and narratives, 141–142, 157
Plato, 23, 128, 151 ff.
playfulness, 56
pleasure, 47, 72, 89, 96, 113, 121, 148, 153; harmless, 145
pleasure seeking, 56
pluralism, 4, 29–30
Plutarch, 24
Posidonius, 22, 24, 25, 27, 114, 125, 128–132, 132
positive liberty, 67–68
possibilities, 17; logical, theoretical, practical, 160; types defined, 38
possibility, 11, 12, 36, 38, 64, 161, 186 ff.
Potkay, Adam, 31
poverty, 121
power, 127; self-transformative, 13
practical intelligence, 30, 42, 112, 119, 140, 145, 146
practical possibilities, 142, 143
practical rationality, 101, 134, 135
practical reason, 6, 14, 19, 20, 50–51, 118; all-things-considered, 5
practical reasoning, 12, 15, 16, 39, 42, 45, 51, 54, 55, 60, 63, 88, 94, 95, 106, 115–118, 160
predestination, 68
predicate logic, 159 ff.
preferences, 12, 13, 15, 16, 19, 65, 156; intransitive, 106
preferred indifferents, 29, 126, 154
prescriptions, universalizable, 10
prescriptive language, 38
pride, 68
primal affection, 76
primal agency (agents), 93, 94, 101, 103, 108, 113, 121, 141 ff.
primal agent energy, 98
primal curiosity, 86
primal dispositions, 143
primal impulses, 56–95 ff.
primal impulse to self-preservation, 151
primal traits, 144
primary impulse, 72
Princeton University Press, 137

principled action, 76, 112
Principle of Minimal Psychological Real-
    ism, 124
principles, a priori, 3
principles of choice, 57
priorities, 38, 48, 50, 160 ff.; and conflicts,
    49
priority problems, 10
privacy, 16
prohibition(s), 19, 36, 58, 161, 186 ff.
projects, 12, 13, 17, 18, 102; comprehen-
    sive, 17; disabling, 17; dominance of,
    17; enabling, 17; indelible, 17; inescapa-
    ble, 17
promises, 10
proof in the calculus, 166
propatheiai, 136
propensities to act, 85 ff.
property ownership, 70
proportionality, 96, 112
propositional attitudes, 129
propositional logic, 162 ff.
propositional representation, 92 ff., 100;
    of norms, 53 ff. *See also* representation
propriety, 49
proprium, 86, 123
prudence, 10, 28, 153
psychodynamic processes, 62
psychodynamics, childhood, 111
psychological development, 74, 83, 117
psychological egoism, 56
psychological health, 142, 143
psychological processes, 9
psychological realism, principle of mini-
    mal, 124
psychological tenors, 62
psychological theory, 70, 83, 143
psychology, 63, 76, 88, 105, 123–124; of
    development, 141
psychopathology, correlated to vice,
    103–104
psychotherapy, 3, 4, 50
punishment, 97
pure practical reason, 48, 117, 134
pure reason, 134
purpose, life empty of, 148
purposes, 65
purposiveness, 17, 46
Pyrrho of Elis, 24

quantification and generality, 185
quantifiers, 160 ff.

quietism, 44
Quine, W. V. O., 165, 191

Rachels, James, 137, 158
racism, 91
Rackham, H., 71
radiating beneficence, 76
rage, 16, 131–132
ranking norms, 172–180
rational activity, final end of, 8
rational agency, 13, 122; infinite worth of,
    76; possible forms of, 85
rational agent(s), 117–118; unifying aim
    of, 21
rational being, 28
rational beings, the good of all, 152
rational choice, 13, 83
rational consistency, 151
rational contractor, 10
rationalism, 134
rationalists, 122
rationality, 6, 13, 71, 77, 100–101, 102,
    110, 112, 135–136
rational life plan, 81, 141–142, 157
Rawls, John, 105, 112, 123
reason, 26, 27, 73, 75, 122, 125, 128,
    129, 134, 153 ff.; controlling role of,
    20; for action, 14 ff.
reasoning as hard wired, 92
rebellion, 19, 44
received elements of agency, 84–93
reciprocal sociality, 86
reciprocating responses, 86
reciprocity, 18, 96, 97, 103, 104, 110, 143
rectitude, 30
recursive operations, 13
reductivism, 12, 69
reformative assessment, 50, 52, 55
regret, lack of, 114
reinforcement, 97
relatives, 74
relativism, 4
release and recapture, 144–146
religion, 3, 8
Renaissance, Italian, 3
repetition, 98
representation(s), 55, 92; linguistic, 62
representational powers, 70
reproductive instinct, 75
requirement, 17, 36, 186 ff.; definition of,
    161–162; meaning of, 37; as a necessary
    condition, 161

requirements, 16, 19, 46, 58, 101, 115–118, 118; over indifference, rule of, 172; over oughts, rule of, 172
resentment, 16
responsibility, 60, 66–67, 78
responsive activity, 86
retaliation, 16
retrospective assessment, 106
revenge, 16
rights, 3, 19
risk aversion, 51, 62
Robertson, John, 76
robustness of connectedness, 155–156
Rogers, Carl, 123
romanticism, 44
romantics, 122
Rorty, Amelie, ix, 22, 135, 158
Ross, Lee, 124
routines, 89–90
Ruddick, William, 137, 158
rule-governed endeavors, 94 ff.
rule making, 100
rules defining institutions, 18–19
rules of conduct, 57
rules of inference, 159 ff.; standard, 164
rules of inference, in the calculus: amendments, 172; appropriateness, 170; the best means, 168–169; closure, 41; closure for moral indifference, 180; commitments, 170; comprehensiveness, 177; conflicting moral indifference, 180; conflicting moral oughts, 180; conflicting moral requirements, 179; coordinate conflicting indifference, 173; coordinate conflicting oughts, 173; coordinate conflicting requirements, 173; desires, 169; equivalence for coincident endogenous rankings, 175; exogenous assessment, 178; exogenous rankings, 176 ff.; forced choice under indifference, 176; ideals, 170; multiple means, 169; oughts over indifference, 173; requirements over indifference, 172; requirements over oughts, 172; superordinate conflicting oughts, 174; superordinate conflicting requirements, 174; superordination for coincident endogenous rankings, 175; transactional commitments, 171; transactional ideals, 171; transactional standards, 171; transcendence, 51; transcendent assessment, 178–179; transcendent comprehensiveness, 179

rules of the game, 39
Russell, Bertrand, 190

sadism, 48
sage, 5, 8, 25, 70, 74, 79, 109, 124; life of a, Cicero's description, 152–155
sagehood, 125; as developmental achievement, 111
sages, 5, 8, 21, 25, 30, 70, 74, 79, 108, 109, 110, 114, 124, 126, 134, 138–157; as androgynous, 110; as embodied humans, 135–136; in fortunate circumstances, 148–149; as men, 110; as most passionate about virtue, 132; and passion, 128 ff.; as women, 110–111
Salazkina, Maria I., ix
salience, 63, 90–91, 93, 109
Sandbach, F., 24, 75, 128
satisfaction, 56, 139; of desires, 150 ff.
Sayre-McCord, G., 190
Schlick, M., 78
Schotch, Peter, 187, 188
science, 3, 8, 8–14, 9, 29, 72, 76, 83
scientific consensus, 6
scientific theory, 11
Searle, John, 28, 80, 87, 137, 160
security, 143
Sedley, D. N., ix, 22, 26, 27, 28, 29, 70, 71, 79, 128, 132, 133, 150, 185
Seidler, Michael J., 135
self-command, 30
self-concept, 101–102, 104
self-consciousness, 30, 72
self-deception, 102
self-destruction, 131
self-esteem, 30, 92
self-fulfillment, 151
self-interest, 5, 10, 13, 70, 73, 112; narrow and wide, 56–57
self-love, 72
self-mastery, 6
self/other boundary, 86, 101–102
self-preservation, 56, 73, 75, 151
self-protectiveness, 104
self-sufficiency, 109
self-transformative power, 13
self-transformative processes, 66
semantic interpretation, 36 ff.
Seneca, 22, 24, 131, 132, 151
sentiment, 3
sentimental education, 97
sequencing endeavors, 51, 138 ff.

sex, 140
sexism, 91
Sextus Empiricus, 24, 26
sexual differences, 111
sexual experience, 111
sexuality, 30
shame, 16, 68
sheltered lives, 108
sickness of soul, 129–130
similar cases treated similarly, 112
Sinnott-Armstrong, Walter, 189
situated individual, 14
skinned knee example, 97
slave(ry), 19, 43, 48
sleep, 145
sociability, 56
social environment(s), 96, 108, 110
social facts, 46
social justice, 76
social learning, 92–103, 111 ff.
social life, 52, 98
social relationships, 144
social roles, 18, 19
social structures, 111
social systems, non-teleological, 47
Socrates, 23, 79, 148
soft determinism, 78–79
soldier(s), 4, 132
sophia, 112
sophrosyne, 112
soul, 125, 129–130, 152 ff.; greatness of, 155; tripartite, 130
sound-normative proposition, 162
Spartan boys, 154
speech, 75
speech acts, 37, 162
spontaneity, 155
spontaneous affect, 97 ff.
stability: negative and positive, 142 ff.; in character, 142 ff.
Stalin, Josef, 114
standards, 17, 18, 41, 46, 58, 170
stimulus response behavior, 86
Stoa, 22 ff.; dates of, 23
Stobaeus, Ioannes, 23
stochastic craft, 133
Stocker, Michael, 76
stoic-approved emotions, 128
stoic doctrines, reconstruction of, 22
stoic ethics, a new agenda for, 5–7
stoicism: bibliography, 24; hard doctrines of, 81

stoic lives, diversity of, 21, 30
stoic logic, 185
stoics: versus Aristotle, 127–132; versus stoics, 128–132
stoic texts, 7
stoic tradition, 6
stone: man hardened to, 118; teaching a, 118
strength: of attachments, 99–100; of character, 109
Striker, Gisela, 24, 25, 26, 27, 70, 71, 74, 132, 133, 150
structural linguistics, 86
subconscious processes, 87 ff.
subconscious salience, 90–91
subjective point of view, 134
subjectivist ethical theory, 134
subjectivity, 11, 28, 71
subliminal learning, 98
subordinating endeavors, 138 ff.
substance, 26, 27
substance dualism, 28, 85, 87
substitution, 164
substrate, 28
suffering, 47, 150
suffering of sages, 146–148, 147
suicide, 44, 48, 135
suitability, 71
summation, 15
superordinate conflicting oughts, rule of, 174
superordinate conflicting requirements, rule of, 174
superordination for coincident endogenous rankings, rule of, 175
superstitions, 154
supervenience, 129
supreme good, 25
supreme principle, 5
supreme value, 113
surprise, 138, 139
survival trait, 145
suspicion, 144
suttee (women in India), 154
symbolic representation, 92
sympathetic responses, 86

task accomplishment, 56
Taylor, Richard, 80
teaching table manners example, 95
technology, 12
teleological explanation, 8

teleological system, 43
teleological universe, 11
teleology, 26, 151
telos, 6, 11, 14, 18, 25–27
temperament, 92
temperance, 112, 114, 117, 155
theologians, 122
theology, 3, 26, 48, 77
things up to us, 100
things within our control, 100
Thomason, Richard, 186
three-valued normative propositions, 162
tolerance, 52
torture, 152, 153–155; examples, 146–148
tragedians, 109
tragedy, 44
trait(s), 13, 18, 92, 103, 117; fixed, 143–
    144; malleable, 143–144; stable, 102;
    transformability, 143
tranquility, 114, 152
transactional commitments, rule of, 171
transactional ideals, rule of, 171
transactional obligations, 40
transactional standards, rule of, 171
transactions, 171
transcendence in normative logic, 42
transcendent assessment, 117; rule of,
    178–179
transcendent comprehensiveness, rule of,
    179
trust, 16, 56, 62, 92, 104, 143
truth, criteria for, 101
truth functional operators, 159 ff.
Tversky, A., 124
two-valued logic, 162
tyrannical endeavor, 49, 115

ultimate aim, 116
understanding, 30
unified activity, 101
unity, 124; of virtues, 113–114
universalizability, 82
universalizable rules, 97
universalization, 117
universalized imperative, 152
universalized propositions, 118
universal moral norms, 44
universals, 28
universe, 122, 152; as a rational being, 3;
    as teleological, 11, 43
unsound normative propositions, 162
utilitarianism, 155–156

utilitarians, 83
utilitarian theories, 48
utility, 3; maximizing expected, 83
utopians, 52

valuables, 15
value, 47, 73, 133; concept of, 91; of
    human life, 135; of a life, 20; of virtue,
    120–122
value judgments, 14 ff.
values, 12, 13, 14, 29–30, 79 ff.
velociraptors, 118
versatility, 105
vertical integration, 49, 52, 101, 102 ff.
vicarious experience, 96–97
vice correlated to psychopathology, 103–
    104
vices, 121
victims, 16
violation, 16
virtue, 5, 6, 7, 20–21, 24, 25, 29–30, 38,
    44, 57, 67, 81–137; as an activity, 113,
    133–135; as all or nothing, 81, 119–
    120, 151; argument for versus develop-
    ment of, 114, 134; as complete, 151; de-
    velopment of, 26, 81–114; dignity of,
    122; as the final end, 8, 29, 70, 81, 113,
    120, 133–135, 138 ff.; as the final end,
    ancient doctrine, 150–155; as incommen-
    surably good, 121–122; independent in-
    terest in, 57 ff.; as necessary for happi-
    ness, 138 ff., 150–155; as not a matter
    of degrees, 81; as one thing, 81; as the
    only good, 30, 81, 119, 133–135; as per-
    fection of agency, 70, 81–118; as perfec-
    tion of agency, argument for, 114–118,
    134; as sufficient for happiness, 81,
    127–132, 138 ff; as sufficient for happi-
    ness, Cicero's defense of, 152–155; as
    uniquely and unconditionally good,
    120–121; as within our power, 155
virtues, 3; unity of, 6
virtuosic exercise of agency, as final end,
    113
virtuosity, 70, 105–107, 117, 125, 141; de-
    fined, 106; including versatility, 107; pre-
    ferred to fitness, 105, 107
virtuoso agents, 122, 138 ff.
virtuous activity, 100
vocation, 60
void, the, 26, 28
von Arnim, Hans, 150

Voorbraak, Frans, 190
vulnerability, 144

war, 99, 121, 144
watchfulness, 128
way of life, 102; coherent, 81
weak agency, 62–63, 119, 125–126. See
    also *akrasia*
weakness of soul, 129–130
weakness of will, 13, 62, 63. See also
    akrasia
wealth, 108, 122, 127, 140
welfare of others, 118
welfarism, 21
well-being, 10
well-formed formulas, 163, 188–189 ff.;
    definition of, 163–164
"we stoics" conceit, of this book, 3–4 *and
    throughout*
White, Nicholas P., ix, 23, 25, 29, 70, 126
Whitehead, A.N., 190

whole life, 20, 21, 24, 51, 75, 113, 139,
    148, 151
whole lives, 112, 138
Wiesel, Elie, 132
wildness, 145–146
"Wild Nights," 131
Williams, Bernard, 77, 134
"willing suspension of disbelief," 145
will to fail, 116
wisdom, 108, 114, 117; two senses of, 112
wishing, 128
Wisnewski, Jeremy, 31
women as sages, 110–111
world-historical ambitions, 139
worldly goods, 156
worldly life, 108
world-order, 27
Wright, G. H., 185, 187

Zeno (of Citium), 3, 23, 24, 25, 69, 122,
    151

About the Author

Lawrence C. Becker is William R. Kenan, Jr., Professor in the Humanities and Professor of Philosophy at the College of William and Mary. He is the author of several books, including *Reciprocity* and *Property Rights: Philosophic Foundations*. He is the coeditor, with Charlotte B. Becker, of the *Encyclopedia of Ethics*.